THE THRESHOLD

THE THRESHOLD

Trials at the Crossroads of Eternity

The Collected Works of St Ignatius (Brianchaninov)—Volume 3

BY BISHOP IGNATIUS (BRIANCHANINOV)

Translated from the Russian by Nicholas Kotar

HOLY TRINITY PUBLICATIONS
The Printshop of St Job of Pochaev
Holy Trinity Monastery
Jordanville, New York
2023

Printed with the blessing of His Grace,
Bishop Luke of Syracuse
and Abbot of Holy Trinity Monastery

The Threshold: Trials at the Crossroads of Eternity
© 2023 Holy Trinity Monastery

PRINTSHOP OF
SAINT JOB OF POCHAEV

An imprint of

HOLY TRINITY PUBLICATIONS
Holy Trinity Monastery
Jordanville, New York 13361-0036
www.holytrinitypublications.com

ISBN: 978-0-88465-493-3 (paperback)
ISBN: 978-0-88465-502-2 (ePub)

Library of Congress Control Number: 2023934893

Cover Art: "The Ninth Wave" by Hovhannes Aivazovsky, oil on canvas, 1850.
Image Source: Google Art Project, en.wikipedia.org.

New Testament Scripture passages taken from the New King James Version.
Copyright © 1982 by Thomas Nelson, Inc. Used by permission.
Psalms taken from A Psalter for Prayer, trans. David James
(Jordanville, N.Y.: Holy Trinity Publications, 2019).
Old Testament and Apocryphal passages taken from the Orthodox Study Bible.
Copyright © 2008 by Thomas Nelson, Inc. Used by permission.

This book was made possible
in part by an anonymous donation
in honor of St Timothy of Prusa.

Contents

Foreword

With this volume we continue our publication of the first complete English translation of the Collected Works of St Ignatius (Brianchaninov). You have in your hand what is the third volume in the Russian original, which we have entitled *The Threshold: Trials at the Crossroads of Eternity.*

A threshold is both an entrance and the foundation underpinning it. It is also the place where we begin to encounter the reality that is being crossed over into. St Ignatius examines the mystical boundaries that constitute for the Christian a threshold: on the one hand between life and death; and on the other, between the visible, physical realm and the invisible—but no less real—spiritual realm. He explicates the nature of the soul and the essence of incorporeal beings as he instructs the monks in his care on the profound mystery of Christianity that can transform humanity from a carnal to a spiritual state. He teaches the necessity to act on this knowledge in order to move from earthly life into eternal life—to cross the threshold into their home—prepared by God—in the kingdom of heaven.

Throughout this work St Ignatius weaves together the Scripture (especially the Psalms) with the wisdom of many Christian saints of the first millennium, in particular St Basil the Great, St Isaac the Syrian, St John of Damascus, and St John of the Ladder. May this volume aid the reader in the battle against "principalities, against powers, against the rulers of the darkness of this age, against spiritual hosts of wickedness in the heavenly places" (Eph 6:12) as is needful for the salvation of his/her soul.

Holy Trinity Monastery
Pascha 2023

CHAPTER I

Homily on the Physical and Spiritual Vision of Spirits

Introduction

As I begin this examination concerning a remarkable vision of created spirits, which is necessarily limited by my own human imperfection, I feel it necessary to set out a teaching concerning man's extreme blindness, which is a natural consequence of his fall. Most people have no idea of this blindness; they do not even suspect it exists! Most people have no comprehension of spirits, or they have only a theoretical, mostly superficial, wholly indistinct understanding, which is almost the same thing as complete ignorance.

In contemporary society, especially among the educated, many doubt the existence of spirits completely, many reject it outright. They doubt it and they reject it even when they believe in the existence of their own soul,[1] believe it to be immortal and existing after death, admitting it to be a spirit. What a strange combination of two completely contradictory ideas! If souls exist after their separation from bodies, that is the same thing as saying that spirits exist. If the souls of villains do not die in the same way as the souls of virtuous people, this means that both good and evil spirits exist. They exist! Their existence becomes completely clear and obvious for anyone who has carefully and correctly examined Christianity. Those who reject the existence of spirits are in effect rejecting Christianity. For this purpose the Son of God was manifested, that "He might destroy the works of the devil. . . . that through death He might destroy him who had the power of death, that is the devil" (1 John 3:8, Heb 2:14). If there are no fallen spirits, then the incarnation of God has neither a reason nor a goal.

The existence of spirits remains an obscure subject to anyone who has not studied Christianity or has studied it superficially, while the Lord Jesus Christ Himself commanded that we study Christianity both through His preaching and through the fulfillment of the commandments of the Gospel (see Matt 28:19-20). The Lord commanded that we study Christianity both theoretically and practically; He connected both forms of study intimately, commanding that practical study always follow theory. Without the latter, the former has no purpose before God! Without the former, the latter can bring us no benefit (see Matt 7:21-23). The latter is proof of the sincerity of the former and is crowned with a gift of divine grace (see John 14:21-24). The theory can be compared with the foundation, the practical study to the structure on top of the foundation. The building cannot be raised until the foundation is laid, and the laying down of the foundation will remain a pointless labor if no building will be raised on top of it. The results of scientific inquiry and the techniques of science itself are incomprehensible to people who have not studied the sciences. As for the science of sciences, the science that has descended from the heavens, given to man by God, the science that completely transforms humanity from a carnal to a spiritual state, that is, the science of Christianity, all the more so does the knowledge and technique of this science remain incomprehensible for those who do not study its laws, according to the techniques established by God Himself. How foolish is the demand of some people that the exalted and profound mysteries of Christianity be revealed to them without any extensive study of it! Do you wish to know the mysteries of Christianity? Study them!

Even a purely intellectual and literal study of books alone is not only very beneficial, but necessary to give exact and thorough knowledge of Christianity, according to the tradition of the Orthodox Church. For eighteen centuries many have attacked Christianity with the aim of dethroning it, and now especially there are many countless false teachings. And so now, more than ever before, there is an urgent need for a thorough preaching and examination of Christianity. But theoretical knowledge requires that active, practical knowledge accompany it. "The law of freedom ... is understood through the practice of the commandments."[2] A Christian scholar must study the Kingdom of Heaven not only through listening to teachings about it, but also by acting on them (see Matt 13:52). Without this, scholarly study remains a human thing, only leading to the expansion of our fallen nature. We see much proof of this in the tragic reality of the priesthood of Israel living at the time of Christ. If study by the letter alone is left to itself, it will inevitably lead to self-conceit and pride, thereby isolating a man from God. Appearing on the surface to be knowledge of God, such study in essence can become complete ignorance of, or even rejection of, God. While appearing to preach the faith, one may be actually drowning in faithlessness! The mysteries that are revealed to unlearned Christians very often remain dark for scholars who are satisfied with only a bookish study of theology, as though it were only one among many merely human sciences.[3] Unfortunately, this is exactly the character of theology in the heterodox West, both in Papist and Protestant countries. Because of their lack of experiential knowledge of Christianity, in our own time it is very difficult to find the correct, authoritative teaching concerning the unseen realm, though such knowledge is so necessary for every monk who desires to labor spiritually in the realm of the spirits, to which we belong with our soul, and with whom we must share both eternal blessedness and eternal suffering (see Matt 22:30, 25:41).

The degrees of spiritual vision are twofold. There is physical vision of spirits, when we see them with our physical, bodily eyes, and there is spiritual vision of spirits, when we see them with our spiritual eyes, with our mind and heart, purified by the grace of God. In the usual state of fallenness in which all mankind abides, we see spirits neither physically nor spiritually; we are, in effect, blind to both. For the blind, various colors and objects of the physical world are as though nonexistent; the same is true for those who have become blind by the fall. They do not see the spiritual world, and so, spirits are as though nonexistent. Lack of vision, however, in no way means nonexistence.

Alas, Alas! I interrupt my words with the Scriptures: "Israel will come into the land ... which was entirely a desert. Many are gathered together against the land of Israel ... to plunder them and take spoils" (Ezek 38: 8,12). St Isaac the Theban, a hermit of Egypt said, "How can I fail to weep? Where will we go now? Our fathers have died. Before we did not have enough money to rent the boats in which we rode [on the Nile] to visit our elders.

Now we are orphaned, and therefore I weep."[4] "Save me, Lord, for there is not one godly man left, for truth is minished from among the children of men. They have talked of vanities everyone with his neighbor; they do but flatter with their lips, and dissemble in their double heart" (Ps 11:1-3).

If Isaac the Theban, during his own time of monastic flourishing, wept at the diminishment of elders, then how difficult is it for a monk of our time, who sincerely wishes to be saved, to find counsel, which is so necessary in his difficult labor? "But evil men and impostors will grow worse and worse, deceiving and being deceived" (2 Tim 3:13), the apostle predicted, speaking of the last days of the world. This prophecy is becoming true before our very eyes. I have often talked with my fellow brothers in private conversations in their cells, and now I find it necessary to write these same things down on paper. I who am enslaved to sin shouldn't dare to instruct the brethren. Instead, in profound silence and solitude it would be better for me to weep over my pitiful spiritual condition. But I am forced to speak and write for edification, lest my neighbors and those who love me in the Lord be abandoned with no instruction. St Pœmen the Great said, "It is better to eat impure bread and be nourished than to be left with no bread at all."[5] And so, seeing myself and the necessity of my surrounding circumstances, I write this instruction concerning the vision of spirits, admitting that a correct understanding of the vision of spirits is essential and necessary for monks, who will soon enter the field of battle not "against flesh and blood, but against principalities, against powers, against the rulers of the darkness of this age, against spiritual hosts of wickedness in the heavenly places" (Eph 6:12). This knowledge is essential. The spirits of wickedness battle against man with such cunning that the thoughts and desires that they bring to our souls seem as though they are our own, not given to us by evil spirits who act and try to hide at the same time.[6] In order to battle with the enemy, we have to see him. If we cannot see the spirits, battle against them is pointless; all that is possible in that case is enthrallment with them and slavish submission to them. Having called to my aid the grace of God, I will first speak of physical vision of spirits, of its danger and of how it is not necessary for our salvation. Then I will speak of the spiritual vision of spirits, both of its necessity for us and its benefit.

Concerning Physical Vision of Spirits

Before the fall of man, his body was immortal, lacking any infirmities or weakness or heaviness. It did not tend toward sinful or carnal sensations, which now have become essential to it.[7] The body's sensations were incomparably more refined, its activity was incomparably broader and entirely free. Enveloped in such a body, with such organs of sensation, man was capable of seeing spirits physically, because he belonged to that host through his soul. Man was capable of companionship with the spirits, as well as the kind of vision of God and communion with Him that is natural to holy spirits (see Gen 2–3). The holy body of man was not an obstacle to such communion; it did not separate man from the world of the spirits. Man, enveloped in such a body, was capable of living in paradise, in which only the righteous are now allowed to abide, and only in their souls, to which paradise they will also ascend with their bodies after the general resurrection. Then these bodies will abandon the weakness they assumed after the fall, leaving it in their graves. Then they will become spiritual, even spirits, as St Macarius the Great expressed it.[8] They will reveal in themselves those qualities that [Adam] was given at creation. Then mankind once again will enter the ranks of holy spirits and be able to communicate with them openly. The model of that body, which is simultaneously body and spirit, we see in the resurrected body of our Lord Jesus Christ.

The fall changed both the soul and body of man. Technically speaking, the fall was also their death. The visible passing that we call death, in essence, is nothing more than the separation of the body and soul, both of which have already died by deviating from the true life, that is, God. We are born already stricken with eternal death! We do not feel that we are dead, in the same way as all corpses do not feel that they have deceased! The sicknesses of our bodies, the subjection of the body to influences of various substances from the material world, its weakness—these are the consequences of the fall.

Because of the fall, our body became the same kind of matter as the bodies of animals; it lives the life of the animals, the life of its own fallen nature. It has become a prison and tomb for the soul. Yes, these expressions I have used are very harsh! But they still do not adequately reflect the depth of the fall of our body from its primal state of exalted spirituality to a fallen state of carnality. We need purification through deep repentance, we need to feel at least in a small part the freedom and exaltedness of the spiritual state, in order to come to know the true calamity of our body, its moribund state that occurred as a result of alienation from God. In this state of deadness, because of the extremes of weakness and crudity, the sensations of our bodies are incapable of communion with spirits. We cannot see them, hear them, or sense them in any way. We are like axes that are so dull we can no longer cut anything. The holy spirits turned away from companionship with mankind, since we have become unworthy of it; the fallen spirits who seduced us into their own fallen state have intermingled with us and, the better to keep us enslaved, those dark spirits try to make both their presence and their chains invisible to us. If they do reveal themselves to us, they do it to strengthen their hold over us. All of us who are enslaved to sin must know that communication with the holy angels is unnatural to us by reason of our separation from them after the fall. For the same reason, it is natural to us to commune with the rejected spirits, since we belong to their ranks in our soul. This means that any spirits that appear to people visually, while those people remain enslaved to sin, are demons, and never the holy angels.

"A defiled soul," says St Isaac the Syrian, "does not enter the pure kingdom and does not unite with the souls of the righteous."[9] The holy angels only appear to holy people who have reestablished communion with God through a holy life. Even though the demons, who do appear to men, more often than not put on an aspect of bright angels, all the better to fool us; and even though they sometimes try to convince us that they are the souls of humans, not demons[10]; and even though sometimes they even predict the future and reveal secrets—still, we must never trust them. For them, truth is intermixed with lies, and if they do speak truth, it is only to more effectively delude us. "Satan himself transforms himself into an angel of light .... his ministers also transform themselves into ministers of righteousness" (2 Cor 11:14–15).

St John Chrysostom, in his second homily concerning the rich man and Lazarus, tells of the following events during his own time:

> What then if the demons say, "I am the spirit of such and such a monk"
> Neither because of this do I credit the notion, since evil spirits say so

to deceive those who listen to them. For this reason St Paul stopped their mouth, even when speaking the truth, in order that they might not, on this pretext, at another time mingle falsehood with the truth, and still be deemed worthy of credit. For when they said, "These men are the servants of the most high God, which show unto us the way of salvation," (Acts 16:17); being grieved in spirit, he rebuked the sorceress, and commanded the spirits to go out. What evil was there in saying, "These men are the servants of the most high God"? Be that as it may, since many of the more weak-minded cannot always know how to decide aright concerning things spoken by demons, he at once put a stop to any credence in them. "If," he implied, "thou art one of those in dishonor, thou hast no liberty of speaking: be silent, and open not thy mouth; it is not thy office to preach; this is the privilege of the apostles. Why dost thou arrogate to thyself that which is not thine? Be silent! thou art fallen from honor." The same thing also Christ did, when the evil spirits said to Him, "We know Thee who Thou art," (Mark 1:24; Luke 4:24). He rebuked them with great severity, teaching us never to listen to spirits, not even when they say what is true. Having learnt this, therefore, let us not trust at all in an evil spirit, even though he speak the truth; let us avoid him and turn away. Sound doctrine and saving truth are to be learned with accuracy, not from evil spirits, but from the Holy Scripture.[11]

Later in the same homily, Chrysostom says that the souls of both the righteous and the sinners immediately after death are taken away from this world into another, one to receive crowns, the other punishments. The soul of the poor Lazarus immediately after death ascended with the angels to the bosom of Abraham, while the soul of the rich man was cast down into hellfire. In his twenty-eighth homily on the Gospel of Matthew, Chrysostom also says that in his own time some possessed people said, "I am the soul of this or that person." Chrysostom explains that this is not correct: "But this too is a kind of stage-play, and devilish deceit. For it is not the spirit of the dead that cries out, but the evil spirit that feigns these things in order to deceive the hearers."[12]

The demons do not know the future, which is known only to the One God and those reasoning creatures to whom God has revealed the future.

However, just as intelligent and experienced people can foresee or guess coming events based on context, so the cunning and extremely experienced evil spirits can sometimes assume with accuracy the events of the future.[13] Often they make mistakes; very often they simply lie and confuse and delude those to whom they prophesy. Sometimes they will prophesy an event that has already been pre-ordained in the world of the spirits, but has not yet come to pass in the human world. This is how, before Job was stricken with his afflictions, the counsel of God decided to allow them to happen, a fact well known to the fallen spirits who were present (see Job 1). The same is true when the counsel of God, which is known to both the holy heavenly powers and the rejected angels, decreed that a wicked spirit would bring to pass the defeat of King Ahab of Israel, even before that king began his campaign (see 3 Kgdms 22:19–23). Thus also a demon prophesied to St John, Archbishop of Novgorod, that he would be stricken with a temptation, and subsequently the devil did tempt him.[14]

There have been situations when holy angels appeared to sinful people, but this happened by a special dispensation from God: an exceedingly rare event. Thus, for example, a holy angel appeared to the false prophet and magician Balaam, even though he communed with the evil spirits (see Numbers 22). Such extreme cases, which are allowed by a special providence of God, in no way change the general rule for everyone.[15] The general rule is that we must never trust spirits when they appear to us in visible form, we should not speak to them, not even pay any attention to them, because we must acknowledge that this vision is a great and very dangerous temptation. During this temptation, we must strive with our minds and hearts to God with prayer for deliverance from this temptation. The desire to actually see spirits, a curiosity to know something from them and about them, is a sign of great foolishness and complete ignorance of the moral and active traditions of the Orthodox Church. Knowledge of spirits is acquired in a completely different fashion than an inexperience and careless seeker might imagine. Open communication with spirits, for the inexperienced, is a terrible calamity, or may become the source of terrible calamities.

The divinely inspired scribe of Genesis wrote that after the fall of the first people, having pronounced His judgment over them, even before they were cast out of paradise, "God made garments of skin, and clothed them" (Gen 3:21). As the Holy Fathers explain this passage, the tunics of skin represent the crude flesh of fallen humanity; having lost its original subtlety and spirituality, this body acquired its present weakness.[16] Though the original reason for this change was the fall, the change was directed by the almighty Creator, according to His unutterable mercy to us, for the purposes of our eternal benefit. Among other beneficial consequences of this new state in which our bodies are now found, we must indicate that through this new weakness we became incapable of seeing the spirits with our physical vision, even though we have fallen into their domain.

Let us explain this in more detail. We received, after our fall, as it were, a natural attraction to evil. This attraction has become normal for our fallen nature; it is a similar attraction that the demons feel for evil: "although the mind of man is diligently involved with evil things from his youth" (Gen 8:21). However, within us good is mixed in with the evil; we incline toward evil, but sometimes we abandon that inclination and turn to the good. The demons, on the contrary, always and completely strive toward evil. If we found ourselves able to communicate with the demons through our physical senses, then they would have very quickly (and permanently) corrupted us by constantly suggesting evil, by openly and constantly cooperating with our evil, and by infecting us through the example of their constantly sinful activity, so hateful to God. They would have been able to do this very easily, since fallen man naturally turns to evil, since man finds himself in subjection to the demons, having willingly submitted himself to them. In the shortest possible time, mankind, having become experienced totally in evil, would have become demonized completely. Repentance and rising up from the fallen state would have become impossible for us.

The wisdom and goodness of God placed a barrier between the people who were cast out of Eden and the spirits who were cast out to earth from heaven. This barrier is the crude, physical human body. In the same way, civil authorities in human societies separate criminals from the rest of mankind by erecting prison walls, lest they continue to willfully harm that society by corrupting other people.[17] The fallen spirits act on people by bringing to them various sinful thoughts and sensations, but thankfully very few people ever reach the level of physical vision of the demons.

Considering the severity of the fallen state, the way the body serves the soul can be compared favorably with the act of swaddling for a newborn baby. A baby's development is aided by swaddling; without it, the softness of the baby's members could lead to deformity in development. In a similar way, the soul, swaddled by the body, closed off and separated from the world of the spirit, slowly finds its proper form through a study of the law of God or, which is the same thing, a study of Christianity, and eventually it acquires the ability to tell the difference between good and evil (see Heb 5:14). Then the soul is given spiritual vision of spirits and, if this corresponds to the goals of God Who leads it, eventually it receives physical vision of the spirits as well, since the delusion and seduction of the spirits is for it much less dangerous than before, while experience and new knowledge are beneficial. After the body's separation from the soul, we once again join the ranks and the communion of spirits. From this it becomes obvious that, to better enter the world of spirits, it is necessary to come to know the law of God in good time, that for this education a certain amount of time is allotted, determined for every person by God for his personal wandering on this earth. This wandering is what we call earthly life.

People become capable of seeing spirits after a certain change of their sensory apparatus, which occurs in an unnoticeable and indescribable manner. All that they notice is that suddenly they see things that before they could never see and that other people do not see, and that they hear things that before they never did. For those who have experienced such a sensory change, it seems quite natural and simple, even though they cannot explain it to themselves or others. For those who have yet to experience it, this process is strange and incomprehensible. Everyone knows that people are capable of falling asleep. But what sort of phenomenon is sleep, and how, unnoticeably to our own selves, do we pass from a state of wakefulness to a state of sleepiness and forgetfulness—this remains a mystery. This transformation of the senses, through which a person enters physical communication with the creatures of the invisible world, is called in the Scriptures "the opening of the senses." Here are some examples: "Then God opened Balaam's eyes, and he saw the Angel of the Lord standing in the way with His drawn sword in his hand; and he bowed his head and worshiped" (Num 22:31). When surrounded by enemies, Prophet Elisha prayed to God to calm Gehazi, his frightened servant: "'Lord, open the eyes of the servant and let him see.' And the Lord opened the eyes of the young man, and he was now able to see, and beheld, the mountain full of horses and chariots of fire round about Elisha. Then the Syrians marched toward him, and Elisha prayed to the Lord and said, 'Strike these people with blindness.' And He struck them with blindness according to the word of Elisha" (4 Kgdms 6:17–20). When the two disciples walked with the Lord on the road from Jerusalem to Emmaus, "their eyes were restrained, so that they did not know Him." But when they came to the inn, then, as soon as He broke the bread, "their eyes were opened and they knew Him" (Luke 24:16, 31).

From these examples in the Scriptures, it becomes clear that the physical senses serve like doors of gates to the internal cell where the soul resides, and that these gates can open and shut by God's command. Through His wisdom and kindness, these gates remain constantly shut in fallen people, lest our sworn enemies, the fallen spirits, break in and destroy us. This protection is all the more necessary considering that we, after the fall, exist in the realm of the fallen spirits, being constantly surrounded by them and in bondage to them. Not having any ability to break through to us, they try to make themselves known to us from outside, by offering various sinful thoughts and images, by which they try to seduce our easily swayed souls into communion with them.

It is impermissible for man to remove this protection of God's, to try to forcefully open these senses and enter open communion with the spirits, in direct rejection of God's will. However, this does happen. Evidently, it is possible to use external means to enter communion with the spirits, but only with the fallen ones. It is not natural for the holy angels to take part in any action that does not accord with God's will, in any deed that is not pleasing to God. What is the attraction to such open communion with spirits? Frivolous people, who do not know practical Christianity, are sometimes distracted by curiosity, ignorance, or lack of faith, not knowing that once they have begun such communion with the demons, they are opening the door to terrifying harm. People who have abandoned themselves to their sins and who have rejected God, however, begin this communion for the most corrupt reasons and goals.

That which occurs by God's providence is always filled with the greatest wisdom and goodness, occurring by essential need for our essential benefit, not for the appeasement of our curiosity or some other trivial reason, unworthy of God. For this reason, the usual way of things is very rarely broken. It is very rare for a person to experience physical vision of spirits. It pleases God that His servant remained constantly in the greatest state of reverence before Him, in exclusive obedience to Him, in completely faithfulness to His holy will. Any violation of such an interaction with God is not pleasing to Him, and it places on us the stamp of God's wrath.[18] Those who frivolously try to break this natural order of things, established by God, and to force entry willfully into that which God has hidden from us, are branded tempters of God and are cast out from before His face into the outer darkness, in which the Light of God does not shine.

We will offer several examples that will clearly show with what salvific care God allows some to have physical vision of spirits, and how He does this only for our spiritual benefit in rare cases. There was a publican in Africa named Peter.[19] This Peter was an extremely cruel man who had given alms to the poor only a single time in his entire life, and even then, not because he felt pity, but anger. When Peter was carrying a large amount of bread loaves, a poor man started to ask him for alms without stopping. Peter, angered by the man and having no ability to strike him with anything nearby, threw a bread loaf at him. Two days after this occurred, Peter fell ill; the sickness grew steadily worse; he was already, it seemed, at death's door. At this moment, his eyes were opened. He saw before him a set of scales. On one side of the scales stood dark demons, on the other the holy angels. The demons, having gathered all the evil deeds that Peter had committed during his life, put them on the scales. The light-bearing angels, finding not a single good deed to place on the other side of the scales, stood in despair and confusion, saying to one another: "We have nothing!" But one of them said, "That's true, we have nothing here except the single loaf of bread that Christ gave Peter two days ago, and even that unwillingly." They placed the bread on the scales, and it immediately began to outweigh all the evil deeds. Then the angels said to the publican, "Go, you pitiful Peter, add to this loaf of bread, lest the dark demons seize you and cast you into eternal flames." Peter got better and became incredibly merciful to his poor brethren, eventually spending his extensive holdings on them. Then he freed all his slaves, and, having moved to Jerusalem, sold himself into slavery to one of the pious inhabitants of the holy city, so that by humility he might be even more assimilated to God, to Whom he had already been assimilated through almsgiving. Peter eventually was found worthy of great spiritual gifts.[20]

In the Russian Orthodox monastery, the Kiev Caves Lavra, there was a monk named Arethas. He had significant personal wealth, and he kept it hidden in his cell, being extremely stingy not only to the poor, but to himself as well. At night, he was robbed. Arethas fell into despair, almost going so far as to commit suicide. He began to search for his stolen riches everywhere, subjecting many to unpleasant treatment. His fellow monks asked him to stop this searching and to lay his sorrow at the feet of the Lord (see Ps 54:23 LXX), but he did not even want to listen, often answering cruelly and harshly. A few days later, Arethas became very sick and was close to death. The brotherhood gathered to his bed; he lay unmoving, as though already dead, saying nothing. Suddenly, he began to cry out in a loud voice: "Lord, have mercy! Lord, forgive me! Lord, I have sinned! The riches are Yours! I don't care about them anymore."

He immediately got better, and this is what he said to the brethren about the reason for his outburst: "I saw that the angels and an army of demons came to me. They began to argue over me concerning my riches. The demons said that I never praised God for the riches, but only complained, and so I should be given to them. But the angels said to me, 'You miserable person! If only you had given God thanks for your riches being stolen, then immediately it would have counted for you as almsgiving, just as it did with Job. Whenever anyone gives alms, this is great in the eyes of God, because the person acts from his own good will; however, those who accept the forceful loss of their goods with gratitude transform a temptation of the devil into a good act. The devil, thinking to cast the person into blasphemy against God, arranges such a robbery; but a person who thanks God and leaves everything to His will does the same as a willing almsgiver.' So when I heard the angels say this, I exclaimed, 'Lord, forgive me! Lord, I have sinned!' Immediately, the demons disappeared, and the holy angels rejoiced and, having counted the lost riches as almsgiving, they left me."

After this vision, Arethas changed in his manner of thinking and living, and became an extremely virtuous ascetic, becoming rich in God. He was counted worthy of a blessed end, and his sanctity was proven through the incorruption of his relics, which lie in the caves with the relics of many other saints, into whose ranks Arethas was rightly added by the Holy Church.[21]

In the same Kiev Caves Lavra lived a blind elder named Theophilus, who constantly labored in repentance. Because of his constant compunction, he had the gift of abundant tears, which is admitted to be a true sign of a holy soul who has already transferred his thoughts to eternity, even during earthly life.[22] However, Theophilus used to weep over a vessel, collecting his vast volume of tears. This occurred as a result of arrogance so subtle even he did not notice it, though it was so very harmful for an ascetic like him, who must never assess his own labors, leaving their worth to be determined exclusively by God (see Phil 3:12–14). Three days before his death, Theophilus's eyes were opened, as was predicted for him by his elder, St Mark. Having understood that his had come to pass into eternity, Theophilus doubled his tears, and he begged God to accept the tears he had shed, having in mind the vessel of tears he had gathered.

Suddenly, an angel appeared before him, holding a vessel of fragrant liquid. The angel said, "Theophilus! It is good that you prayed and wept; however, in vain do you hope on those tears that you gathered in a vessel. Here is another vessel, much larger than yours, which is also filled your tears, but the ones that you shed during intense prayer, wiping them away with your sleeve or hand or letting them fall into the ground or your clothing. I have gathered every single one of those tears, by the command of my Lord and Creator, and now I am sent to declare to you the joy of your passing to the one Who said, 'Blessed are they who mourn, for they shall be comforted'" (Matt 5:4).

These examples clearly indicate the general character of appearances of spirits, when they are permitted by God's providence. Spirits only appear, by God's permission, in times of extreme need, for the purpose of saving or correcting a person. They appear in such a manner that their appearance will not have any negative repercussions. Peter and Arethas were taken out of the abyss of sin through fear inspired by seeing the demons argue with the angels, while Theophilus, whose only sin was found not in his manner of life, but his way of thinking, was instructed toward humble-mindedness and at the same time told of his coming blessedness. He could not possibly have puffed himself up because of the appearance of the angel promising blessedness, because he also came to know of his sin, and because his salvation was announced to him in advance not as a reward for labors, but as a mercy of God. Only the most perfect Christians, primarily from among the monastics who have been found worthy of having their spiritual eyes opened, have seen the world of the spirits. However, even in the flourishing of Christianity, there were very few such people in the world, as St Macarius the Great said.[23]

A quality of all visions sent by God, according to St John of the Ladder, is that they bring to the soul humility and compunction, filling it with fear of God and an acknowledgment of one's own sinfulness and worthlessness. On the contrary, visions that we forcefully inspire within ourselves, against the will of God, lead us into arrogance, conceit, and a joy that is nothing other than the satisfaction of our vanity and self-will.[24] In such cases demons, most often in the form of angels, try to seduce the person through praise, to satisfy his curiosity and vanity; then, they find it very easy to cast the person into self-delusion, thereby harming him in the worst possible way, whether visibly or not. The thought that there is some wisdom to be found in the physical vision of spirits is simply false. Any physical vision of spirits that lacks spiritual vision gives no knowledge of spirits. It only gives a superficial intimation, and very often this knowledge is false, leading easily to the person being infected with vanity and self-conceit. Only true Christians reach the level of true spiritual vision of spirits, while even people living the most corrupt kind of life can see spirits physically. What sort of people can see spirits physically, being in a state of a physical communication with them? Magicians who have rejected God and have come to worship Satan as their god. The apostle Paul said to such a sorcerer, "O full of all deceit and all fraud, you son of the devil, you enemy of all righteousness, will you not cease perverting the straight ways of the Lord?" (Acts 13:10).

If we read the lives of saints, we will understand as much as we need about magicians. People who have abandoned themselves to their

passions, and who have come to magicians to better satisfy those passions, can, through the magician's aid, begin physical association with
the fallen spirits, a state that can only be reached through open rejection of Christ.[25] These are people who have been emptied by drunkenness and a dissolute life; ascetics who have fallen to pride and arrogance.
Very few are naturally capable of this vision; it is very rare that spirits
appear to people, and then only because of some unusual event in life. In
such cases, the person who sees spirits is not guilty of any evil act; however, he must use all of his strength to come out of this situation, for it is
extremely dangerous. In our own time, many allow themselves some form
of converse with the fallen angels through "magnetism,"[26] and in these
cases the demons usually appear as bright angels, seducing and deluding people with various interesting stories in which they intermix truth
with lies, and the results of such encounters are always extreme spiritual
and even mental distress. Such magnetism is simply another version of
dark magic. Although there is no open denial of God during this process,
this rejection is implicit, since in our time the devil very often hides his
traps, taking care more to act toward the destruction of the essential,
not the superficial. Paying no attention to God's commands, not both-
ering to find out whether what he does is pleasing to God or according
to His will, such a frivolous seeker of the mystical blindly abandons himself to the power of magnetism, and without any prior preparation, he
suddenly comes into contact with demons, allowing them control over
himself, acting under their direction and according to their instructions.
What is this if not apostasy?

It is true that God has allowed holy spirits occasionally to appear
to people who live sinful lives, even to pagans. These people received
no benefit from seeing holy angels; moreover, such visions were not
arranged for their sake, and so in no way reflected their own worthiness.
The Scriptures tell of a time when the patriarch Jacob left Mesopotamia
secretly, escaping from his father-in-law Laban, a pagan. Laban planned
to pursue his son-in-law, but then "God had come to Laban the Syrian
in a dream by night, and said to him, 'Be careful that you do not speak
evil things to Jacob at any time'" (Gen 31:24). (Here we must understand
that "God" is actually an angel, a messenger bearing the name of the One

Who sent him.) God appeared to Laban, a pagan, not for Laban's sake, but to save Jacob. The idol-worshiper remained an idol-worshiper, in spite of the fact that he saw God face to face and spoke to Him. Having seen the true God, the pagan did not cease to worship his idols as gods; he continued to say of them, "Why did you steal my gods?" (Gen 31:30).

Here is another example. The pagan false prophet and magician Balaam saw, with his physical eyes, an angel standing before him on the road, and he spoke to him. By the inspiration of this angel, he spoke a true prophecy, a divinely inspired prophecy concerning the nation of Israel, but this did not bring him any benefit. He remained in his iniquity, and he dared act against the will of God and so was convicted to death together with the other enemies of God (Num 22:23–24, 31).

Saul, the king of Israel, who never openly rejected God but often acted against God's commands, which was counted for him as apostasy (see 1 Kgdms 15:22–23), completed his iniquity by consulting a witch. He knew that sorcery was a heavy sin, for he had already convicted all magicians in Israel to death; however, having become enamored of his sinful life-style, he decided to act against God's will. Desiring to know what the result of a battle against the Philistines would be, Saul asked the witch to call from Hades the soul of the dead prophet Samuel, to speak together with him. The witch did as she was asked. Having appeared to her summons from the prison of the underworld, the prophet predicted Saul's defeat and death in the battle. However, instead of repenting at this message, Saul despaired. The appearance of the prophet and the foreknowledge he received brought him terrible harm instead of good (see 1 Kgdms 28 LXX).[27] In a different event, an army of Syrian pagans that invaded the land of Israel was suddenly faced with an army of angels and fled in terror (see 4 Kgdms 7:6 LXX). The holy angels and the departed souls of the saints have in similar manner often stopped thieves and barbarians from attacking the residences of God's saints.[28]

And so, let those who have physically seen spirits, even angels, not think highly of themselves. Such vision, in and of itself, in no way proves the worth of those who had the visions. Not only sinful people, but even irrational animals can be given physical vision of spirits (e.g., Balaam's ass, see Num 22:23).

The Holy Fathers preferred spiritual vision to physical vision of spirits. The great instructor of monks, St Isaac the Syrian, said, "He who has been found worthy of seeing himself is greater than one who has seen angels. For the latter sees with physical eyes, but the former sees with the eyes of the soul."[29] The holy monks who were found worthy of extensive spiritual vision also had extensive spiritual discernment and other exalted gifts of the Holy Spirit. The reverse is also true: those venerable fathers who were given, for their simplicity and purity, physical vision of spirits, were still lacking in those exalted gifts of the Spirit we have already mentioned. St Daniel of Sketis told of a certain elder of extremely strict life who lived in lower Egypt, who said in his ignorance, "Melchizedek, the King of Salem,[30] is the Son of God." This was then passed to St Cyril of Alexandria. It must also be noted that this elder was so holy that he performed miracles and God directly answered his questions. Cyril invited the elder to his home, and acted very wisely with him. He said to the elder, "Abba! Pray for me. One thought tells me that Melchizedek is the Son of God, while another thought tells me that no, he is but a man and a high priest of God. I am of two minds! Therefore, I have invited you. Please pray to God and ask Him to tell you the answer in a vision." The elder, trusting in his manner of life, said, "Give me three days. I will ask God about this, and I will tell you who Melchizedek is."

Three days later, the elder returned to the patriarch, and said, "Melchizedek is a man." The patriarch asked, "How did you come to know this, father?" The elder answered, "God showed me all the patriarchs, from Adam to Melchizedek. Then an angel said to me, here is Melchizedek. Be assured that this is so." Having returned to his cell, the elder himself began to tell everyone that Melchizedek was a man, not the Son of God. St Cyril rejoiced at the salvation of his brother, who, in spite of such great holiness that he performed miracles, received revelations from God directly, communicated with angels and the souls of dead saints, was still in danger of perdition from a blasphemous thought, not even knowing his spiritual danger.[31]

A similar thing happened with a certain holy priest who lived in the first centuries of Christianity. Because of his purity and lack of malice, he was constantly found worthy of seeing an angel concelebrating the liturgy with him. A certain wandering deacon visited this priest. The priest offered the deacon to serve the liturgy with him. When they began to serve, the deacon told the priest that some of the words he was speaking during the liturgy contained heretical blasphemy. The priest was astounded at this rebuke. He turned to his angel, who was standing next to him as always, and asked him, "Is what the deacon says true?" The angel answered, "Yes." The priest rebuked the angel: "Why did you never tell me this, though you have stood next to me so long?" The angel answered, "It is pleasing to God that men be instructed by other men." In spite of the fact that he constantly communicated with angels, the priest still remained in disastrous spiritual error.

The physical vision of spirits always brings more or less harm to people who lack spiritual vision. Here on earth, images of truth are always intermingled with images of falsehood[32] since this is a country in which good is intermingled with evil, a country of exile for both fallen humanity and fallen spirits. Into this country, the God-Man descended for the salvation of mankind; into this country, even before the Incarnation, holy angels sometimes descended to visit people, as fallen creatures who had received the promise of future salvation. In this country, after the Incarnation of God the Word, the holy angels continue to descend to help people work out their own salvation. However, in this country some people continue to willfully remain in their fallen state, and this country also houses the fallen angels who have become confirmed in their fallen state, in their enmity toward God. Such people who have become besotted with their own fallen state, their own sinfulness, use all possible means to attract all other people to their way of life. And the fallen angels do this likewise, straining all their efforts toward this aim, being better destroyers of people than murderers. The iniquity of humanity is evident in the intermixing of good with evil; however, the iniquity of the fallen spirits is found in the total victory of evil, the total absence of good. Thus the abilities of the fallen spirits to seduce people are far greater than the abilities of sinful people, who are limited in all their efforts (both good and evil) by the heaviness and crudity of their own bodies.

The demons freely and quickly fly across the entire cosmos, and they also freely perform deeds that are impossible for any person (see Job 1:67).

Human beings, whether they will it or not, must be satisfied with a limited experience of evil during their short earthly life; their evil intentions themselves are destroyed in the hour when they leave the earthly life, being called to God's judgment in eternity. On the contrary, the demons are fated to remain on earth from the moment of their final fall (see Gen 3:14) to the end of the world. Anyone can easily imagine what expertise they have acquired in evildoing over the course of such a long period of time, considering their natural abilities and their constant evil intentions, which are in no way diluted by any good intentions or interests. Even if they pretend to have good intentions, they do so only with the goal of more completely succeeding in their evil intentions. They are completely incapable of good intentions.

And so, whoever sees spirits with his physical eyes can easily be deluded, to his own harm and eventual perdition. If he, upon seeing the spirits, shows any trust to them or tends to believe them, he will inevitably be fooled, seduced, stamped with delusion (which is incomprehensible to those who lack this stamp), a stamp of horrible damage in the spirit, which often results in the loss of any ability to improve or even be saved. This has occurred with many, with very many. It occurred not only with pagans, whose priests were for the most part in open communion with demons; it occurred not only with many Christians who did not know the mysteries of Christianity or who for some reason began to communicate with spirits; it occurred even with many ascetics and monks who did not strive to acquire spiritual vision of spirits and who instead saw them with their physical eyes.

Only Christian asceticism provides the correct, lawful entry to the world of spirits. All other means are unlawful, and must be rejected as unnecessary and harmful. God Himself leads a true ascetic of Christ to proper vision. When God leads, then all phantoms of truth dissipate, in which truth and falsehood are intermixed; only then does God give the ascetic, first of all, spiritual vision of spirits, while also carefully and exactly revealing to him the qualities of these spirits. Only after this do some ascetics receive physical vision of spirits, which adds to their knowledge of the spiritual world, introduced by spiritual vision. Evil spirits are limited in their ability to act upon the ascetic of Christ by the power and wisdom of God Who leads that ascetic. Although they are consumed by especial hatred for such a servant of God, they can cause him no evil, no matter how much they may wish to. Any attacks that they are allowed to perpetrate on him only add to his victories.[33]

An extremely detailed and important teaching concerning the spirits of evil can be found in an instruction of Anthony the Great to his disciples. St Anthony took this teaching from the experience of his own holy efforts, from the abundant grace of his spiritual state; furthermore, this teaching is confirmed by the Scriptures. Anthony spoke of both spiritual and physical vision of spirits. He acquired both to an extremely high degree. Because of his self-denial, because of his profoundly silent life, his "citizenship is in heaven" (Phil 3:20), to which the Holy Spirit raised him, Anthony was like a spirit already, though he was still in the body.[34] He was constantly either speaking to angels or battling demons.[35] His instruction is meant for hermits, monks who had already reached great spiritual heights. The physical vision of spirits is the domain of the hermit; monks who live in monasteries undergo a more subtle warfare, the demons offering them sinful thoughts, images, senses, but only very rarely appearing physically. Anthony the Great, who had taught Paul the Simple the monastic life, built a hermit's cell for him at a large distance from his own, and he led the holy disciple into it, saying to him, "Behold! Through the grace of Christ that gave you help, you have learned the monastic life. From this moment, remain alone, so that you may learn how to battle the demons."[36]

Here, then, are excerpts from that instruction of St Anthony (from his life, written by St Athanasius the Great):

It is written, "keep our heart with all diligence" (Proverbs 4:23). "For we do not wrestle against flesh and blood, but against principalities, against powers, against the rulers of the darkness of this age, against spiritual hosts of wickedness in the heavenly places" (Ephesians 6:12). Great is their number in the air around us, and they are not far from us. Now there are great distinctions among them; and concerning their nature and distinctions much could be said, but such a description is for others of greater powers than we possess. At this time it is pressing and necessary for us only to know their wiles against ourselves.

First, therefore, we must know this: that the demons have not been created like what we mean when we call them by that name; for God made nothing evil, but even they have been made good. Having fallen, however, from the heavenly wisdom, since then they have been groveling on earth. On the one hand they deceived the Greeks with their displays, while out of envy of us Christians they move all things in their desire to hinder us from entry into the heavens; in order that we should not ascend up there from whence they fell. Thus there is need of much prayer and of discipline, that when a man has received through the Spirit the gift of discerning spirits, he may have power to recognize their characteristics: which of them are less and which more evil; of what nature is the special pursuit of each, and how each of them is overthrown and cast out. For their villainies and the changes in their plots are many. The blessed apostle and his followers knew such things when they said, "for we are not ignorant of his devices" (2 Corinthians 2:11); and we, from the temptations we have suffered at their hands, ought to correct one another under them. Wherefore I, having had proof of them, speak as to children.

The demons, therefore, if they see all Christians, and monks especially, laboring cheerfully and advancing, first make an attack by temptation and place hindrances to hamper our way, to wit, evil thoughts. But we need not fear their suggestions, for by prayer, fasting, and faith in the Lord their attack immediately fails. But even when it does, they cease not but knavishly by subtlety come on again. For when they cannot deceive the heart openly with foul pleasures they approach in different guise, and thenceforth shaping displays they attempt to strike fear, changing their shapes, taking the forms of women, wild beasts, creeping things, gigantic bodies, and troops of soldiers. But not even then need you fear their deceitful displays. For they are nothing and quickly disappear, especially if a man fortify himself beforehand with faith and the sign of the cross. Yet are they bold and very shameless, for if thus they are worsted, they make an onslaught in another manner, and pretend to prophesy and foretell the future, and to show themselves of a height reaching to the roof and of great breadth; that they may stealthily catch by such displays those who could not be deceived by their arguments. If here also they find the soul strengthened by faith and a hopeful mind, then they bring their leader to their aid.

[St. Anthony] said they often appeared as the Lord revealed the devil to Job, saying, "his eyes are like the eyelids of the morning. Out of his mouth go burning lights; sparks of fire shoot out. Smoke goes out of his nostrils, as from a boiling pot and burning rushes. His breath kindles coals, and a flame goes out of his mouth" [Job 41:18–21]. When the prince of the demons appears in this way, the crafty one, as I said before, strikes terror by speaking great things, as again the Lord convicted him, saying to Job, "For he counts iron as straw, and bronze as rotten wood .... yea he counts the sea as a pot of ointment ...." and the depth of the abyss as a captive, and the abyss as a covered walk. [see Job 41] And by the prophet, the enemy said, "I will pursue, I will overtake" [Exodus 15:9], and again by another, "I will grasp the whole world in my hand as a nest, and take it up as eggs that have been left." Such, in a word, are their boasts and professions that they may deceive the godly. But not even then ought we, the faithful, to fear his appearance or give heed to his words. For he is a liar and speaks of truth never a word. And though speaking words so many and so great in his boldness, without doubt, like a dragon he was drawn with a hook by the Saviour [see Job 41:1], and as a beast of burden he received the halter round his nostrils, and as a runaway his nostrils were bound with a ring, and his lips bored with an armlet. And he was bound by the Lord as a sparrow, that we should mock him. And with him are placed the demons his fellows, like serpents and scorpions to be trodden underfoot by us Christians. And the proof of this is that we now live opposed to him. For he who threatened to dry the sea and seize upon the world, behold now cannot stay our discipline, nor even me speaking against him. Let us then heed not his words, for he is a liar: and let us not fear his visions, seeing that they themselves are deceptive. For that which appears in them is no true light, but they are rather the preludes and likenesses of the fire prepared for the demons who attempt to terrify men with those flames in which they themselves will be burned. Doubtless they appear; but in a moment disappear again, hurting none of the faithful, but bringing with them the likeness of that fire which is about to receive themselves.

Wherefore it is unfitting that we should fear them on account of these things; for through the grace of Christ all their practices are in vain.

[Demons] are treacherous, and ready to change themselves into all forms and assume all appearances. Very often also without appearing they imitate the music of harp and voice and recall the words of Scripture. Sometimes, too, while we are reading they immediately repeat many times, like an echo, what is read. They arouse us from our sleep to prayers; and this constantly, hardly allowing us to sleep at all. At another time they assume the appearance of monks and feign the speech of holy men, that by their similarity they may deceive and thus drag their victims where they will. But no heed must be paid them even if they arouse to prayer, even if they counsel us not to eat at all, even though they seem to accuse and cast shame upon us for those things which once they allowed. For they do this not for the sake of piety or truth, but that they may carry off the simple to despair; and that they may say the discipline is useless, and make men loathe the solitary life as a trouble and burden and hinder those who in spite of them walk in it.

Wherefore the prophet sent by the Lord declared them to be wretched, saying: Woe is he who gives his neighbors to drink muddy destruction. For such practices and devices are subversive of the way which leads to virtue. And the Lord Himself, even if the demons spoke the truth—for they said "You are the Christ, Son of God" [Luke 4:41]— still bridled their mouths and suffered them not to speak; lest haply they should sow their evil along with the truth, and that He might accustom us never to give heed to them even though they appear to speak what is true. For it is unseemly that we, having the Holy Scriptures and freedom from the Saviour, should be taught by the devil who has not kept his own order but has gone from one mind to another. Wherefore even when he uses the language of Scripture He forbids him, saying: But to the sinner said God, "Why dost thou preach My statutes, and takest My covenant in thy mouth?" [Psalm 49:16 LXX]. For the demons do all things—they prate, they confuse, they dissemble, they confound—to deceive the simple. They laugh madly, and whistle; but if no heed is paid to them, immediately they weep and lament as though vanquished.

The Lord therefore, as God, stayed the mouths of the demons: and it is fitting that we, taught by the saints, should do like them and imitate their courage. For they when they saw these things used to say: "When the sinner stood up against me, I was mute and held my peace; I kept silent even from good words" (Psalm 38:2 LXX). And again: " I was like a deaf man and heard not, and as one that is dumb who doth not open his mouth. and I became as a man who heareth not" (Psalm 37:14 LXX). So let us neither hear them as being strangers to us, nor give heed to them even though they arouse us to prayer and speak concerning fasting. But let us rather apply ourselves to our resolve of discipline and let us not be deceived by them who do all things in deceit, even though they threaten death. For they are weak and can do naught but threaten.

Already in passing I have spoken on these things, and now I must not shrink from speaking on them at greater length, for to put you in remembrance will be a source of safety. Since the Lord visited earth, the enemy is fallen and his powers weakened. Wherefore although he could do nothing, still like a tyrant, he did not bear his fall quietly, but threatened, though his threats were words only. And let each one of you consider this, and he will be able to despise the demons. If they were hampered with such bodies as we are, it would be possible for them to say, "Men when they are hidden we cannot find, but whenever we do find them we do them hurt." And we also by lying in concealment could escape them, shutting the doors against them. But if they are not of such a nature as this, but are able to enter in, even though the doors be shut, and haunt all the air, both they and their leader the devil are wishful for evil and ready to injure; and, as the Saviour said, "He was a murderer from the beginning, and does not stand in the truth" (John 8:44); while we, though this is so, are alive, and spend our lives all the more in opposing him; it is plain they are powerless. For place is no hindrance to their plots, nor do they look on us as friends that they should spare us; nor are they lovers of good that they should amend. But on the contrary they are evil, and nothing is so much sought after by them as wounding them that love virtue and fear God. But since they have no power to effect anything, they do naught but threaten. But if they could, they would not hesitate, but immediately work evil (for all

their desire is set on this), and especially against us. Behold now we are
gathered together and speak against them, and they know that when
we advance they grow weak. If therefore they had power they would
permit none of us Christians to live, for godliness is an abomination
to a sinner (see Sirach 1:25). But since they can do nothing they inflict
the greater wounds on themselves; for they can fulfil none of their
threats. Next this ought to be considered, that we may be in no fear
of them: that if they had the power they would not come in crowds,
nor fashion displays, nor with change of form would they frame deceits.
But it would suffice that one only should come and accomplish that
which he was both able and willing to do: especially as every one who
has the power neither slays with display nor strikes fear with tumult,
but immediately makes full use of his authority as he wishes. But the
demons as they have no power are like actors on the stage changing
their shape and frightening children with tumultuous apparition and
various forms: from which they ought rather to be despised as showing their weakness. At least the true angel of the Lord sent against the
Assyrian had no need for tumults nor displays from without, nor noises
nor rattling, but in quiet he used his power and immediately destroyed
a hundred and eighty-five thousand (see 2 Kings 19:35). But demons
like these, who have no power, try to terrify at least by their displays.

But if any one having in mind the history of Job should say, "Why
then has the devil gone forth and accomplished all things against him;
and stripped him of all his possessions, and slew his children, and smote
him with evil ulcers?" Let such a one, on the other hand, recognize that
the devil was not the strong man, but God Who delivered Job to him to
be tried. Certainly he had no power to do anything, but he asked, and
having received it, he has wrought what he did. So also from this the
enemy is the more to be condemned, for although willing he could not
prevail against one just man. For if he could have, he would not have
asked permission. But having asked not once but also a second time,
he shows his weakness and want of power. And it is no wonder if he
could do nothing against Job, when destruction would not have come
even on his cattle had not God allowed it. And he has not the power
over swine, for as it is written in the Gospel, they besought the Lord,

saying, "permit us to go away into the herd of swine" (Matt 8:31). But if they had power not even against swine, much less have they any over men formed in the image of God.

So then we ought to fear God only, and despise the demons, and be in no fear of them. But the more they do these things the more let us intensify our discipline against them, for a good life and faith in God is a great weapon. At any rate they fear the fasting, the sleeplessness, the prayers, the meekness, the quietness, the contempt of money and vainglory, the humility, the love of the poor, the alms, the freedom from anger of the ascetics, and chief of all, their piety[37] towards Christ. Wherefore they do all things that they may not have any that trample on them, knowing the grace given to the faithful against them by the Saviour, when He says, "Behold, I give you the authority to trample on serpents and scorpions, and over all the power of the enemy" (Luke 10:19).

'Wherefore if they pretend to foretell the future, let no one give heed, for often they announce beforehand that the brethren are coming days after. And they do come. The demons, however, do this not from any care for the hearers, but to gain their trust, and that then at length, having got them in their power, they may destroy them. Whence we must give no heed to them, but ought rather to confute them when speaking, since we do not need them. For what wonder is it, "if with more subtle bodies than men have, when they have seen them start on their journey," they surpass them in speed, and announce their coming? Just as a horseman getting a start of a man on foot announces the arrival of the latter beforehand, so in this there is no need for us to wonder at them. For they know none of those things which are not yet in existence; but God only is He who knows all things before their birth. But these, like thieves, running off first with what they see, proclaim it: to how many already have they announced our business—that we are assembled together, and discuss measures against them, before any one of us could go and tell these things. This in good truth a fleet-footed boy could do, getting far ahead of one less swift. But what I mean is this. If any one begins to walk from the Thebaid, or from any other district, before he begins to walk, they do not know whether he will walk. But when they have seen him walking they run on, and before he comes up report his approach. And so it falls out that after a few days the travelers arrive. But often the walkers turn back, and the demons prove false.

So, too, with respect to the water of the river, they sometimes make foolish statements. For having seen that there has been much rain in the regions of Ethiopia, and knowing that they are the cause of the flood of the river before the water has come to Egypt they run on and announce it. And this men could have told, if they had as great power of running as the demons. And as David's spy Husai (see 2 Kings 18:24) going up to a lofty place saw the man approaching better than one who stayed down below, and the forerunner himself announced, before the others came up, not those things which had not taken place, but those things which were already on the way and were being accomplished, so these also prefer to labor, and declare what is happening to others simply for the sake of deceiving them. If, however, Providence meantime plans anything different for the waters or wayfarers—for Providence can do this—the demons are deceived, and those who gave heed to them cheated.

Thus in days gone by arose the oracles of the Greeks, and thus they were led astray by the demons. But thus also thenceforth their deception was brought to an end by the coming of the Lord, who brought to naught the demons and their devices. For they know nothing of themselves, but, like thieves, what they get to know from others they pass on, and guess at rather than foretell things. Therefore if sometimes they speak the truth, let no one marvel at them for this. For experienced physicians also, since they see the same malady in different people, often foretell what it is, making it out by their acquaintance with it. Pilots, too, and farmers, from their familiarity with the weather, tell at a glance the state of the atmosphere, and forecast whether it will be stormy or fine. And no one would say that they do this by inspiration, but from experience and practice. So if the demons sometimes do the same by guesswork, let no one wonder at it or heed them. For what use to the hearers is it to know from them what is going to happen before the time? Or what concern have we to know such things, even if the knowledge be true? For it is not productive of virtue, nor is it any token of goodness. For none of us is judged for what he knows not, and no one is called blessed because he has learning and knowledge. But each one will be called to judgment in these points—whether he have kept the faith and truly observed the commandments.

Wherefore there is no need to set much value on these things, nor for the sake of them to practice a life of discipline and labor; but that living well we may please God. And we neither ought to pray to know the future, nor to ask for it as the reward of our discipline; but our prayer should be that the Lord may be our fellow-helper for victory over the devil. And if even once we have a desire to know the future, let us be pure in mind, for I believe that if a soul is perfectly pure and in its natural state, it is able, being clear-sighted, to see more and further than the demons—for it has the Lord Who reveals to it—like the soul of Elisha, which saw what was done (4 Kings 5:20–27 LXX) by Gehazi, and beheld the hosts standing on its side.

When, therefore, they come by night to you and wish to tell the future, or say, we are the angels, give no heed, for they lie. Yea even if they praise your discipline and call you blessed, hear them not, and have no dealings with them; but rather sign yourselves and your houses, and pray, and you shall see them vanish. For they are cowards, and greatly fear the sign of the Lord's Cross, since of a truth in it the Saviour "made a public spectacle of them, triumphing over them in it." (Colossians 2:15)

But if they shamelessly stand their ground, capering and changing their forms of appearance, fear them not, nor shrink, nor heed them as though they were good spirits. For the presence either of the good or evil by the help of God can easily be distinguished. The vision of the holy ones is not fraught with distraction: For "He will not cry out, nor raise His voice, nor cause His voice to be heard outside" (Isaiah 42:2). But it comes so quietly and gently that immediately joy, gladness and courage arise in the soul. For the Lord Who is our joy is with them, and the power of God the Father. And the thoughts of the soul remain unruffled and undisturbed, so that it, enlightened as it were with rays, beholds by itself those who appear. For the love of what is divine and of the things to come possesses it, and willingly it would be wholly joined with them if it could depart along with them. But if, being men, some fear the vision of the good, those who appear immediately take fear away; as Gabriel did in the case of Zacharias (see Luke 1:13), and as the angel did who appeared to the women at the holy sepulcher (Matt 28:5), and as He did who said to the shepherds in the Gospel, "Do not be afraid" (Luke 2:10). For their fear arose not from timidity, but from the recognition of the presence of superior beings. Such then is the nature of the visions of the holy ones.

But the inroad and the display of the evil spirits is fraught with confusion, with din, with sounds and crying such as the disturbance of boorish youths or robbers would occasion. From which arise fear in the heart, tumult and confusion of thought, dejection, hatred towards them who live a life of discipline, indifference, grief, remembrance of kinsfolk and fear of death, and finally desire of evil things, disregard of virtue and unsettled habits. Whenever, therefore, you have seen ought and are afraid, if your fear is immediately taken away and in place of it comes joy unspeakable, cheerfulness, courage, renewed strength, calmness of thought and all those I named before, boldness and love toward God—take courage and pray. For joy and a settled state of soul show the holiness of him who is present. Thus Abraham beholding the Lord rejoiced (see John 8:56); so also the babe John in the womb, at the voice of Mary, the God-bearer, leaped for gladness (Luke 1:41) But if at the appearance of any there is confusion, knocking without, worldly display, threats of death and the other things which I have already mentioned, know that it is an onslaught of evil spirits.

And let this also be a token for you: whenever the soul remains fearful there is a presence of the enemies. For the demons do not take away the fear of their presence as the great archangel Gabriel did for Mary and Zacharias, and as he did for those who appeared to the women at the tomb; but rather whenever they see men afraid they increase their delusions that men may be terrified the more; and at last attacking they mock them, saying, "fall down and worship." Thus they deceived the Greeks, and thus by them they were considered gods, falsely so called. But the Lord did not suffer us to be deceived by the devil, for He rebuked him whenever he framed such delusions against Him, saying: "Get behind me, Satan: for it is written, You shall worship the Lord your God, and Him only shall you serve" (Matthew 4:10, Deuteronomy. 13:4). More and more, therefore, let the deceiver be despised by us; for what the Lord has said, this for our sakes He has done: that the demons hearing like words from us may be put to flight through the Lord Who rebuked them in those words.

And it is not fitting to boast at the casting forth of the demons, nor to be uplifted by the healing of diseases: nor is it fitting that he who casts out devils should alone be highly esteemed, while he who casts them not out should be considered naught. But let a man learn the discipline of each one and either imitate, rival, or correct it. For the working of signs is not ours but the Savior's work: and so He said to His disciples: "Nevertheless do not rejoice in this, that the [demons] are subject to you, but rather rejoice because your names are written in heaven" (Luke 10:20). For the fact that our names are written in heaven is a proof of our virtuous life, but to cast out demons is a favor of the Saviour who granted it. Wherefore to those who boasted in signs but not in virtue, and said: Lord, in Your name did we not cast out demons, and in Your name did many mighty works?", He answered, "Verily I say unto you, I know you not" (see Matthew 7:22); for the Lord knows not the ways of the wicked. But we ought always to pray, as I said above, that we may receive the gift of discerning spirits; that, as it is written, we may not believe every spirit (see 1 John 4:1).

"I have become a fool [a]in boasting; you have compelled me. For I ought to have been commended by you; for in nothing was I behind the most eminent apostles, though I am nothing" (2 Corinthian 12:11), yet the Lord Who hears knows the clearness of my conscience, and that it is not for my own sake, but on account of your affection towards me and at your petition that I again tell what I saw of the practices of evil spirits. How often have they called me blessed and I have cursed them in the name of the Lord! How often have they predicted the rising of the river, and I answered them, "What have you to do with it?" Once they came threatening and surrounded me like soldiers in full armor. At another time they filled the house with horses, wild beasts and creeping things, and I sang: "Some put their trust in chariots, and

some in horses, but we will call upon the Name of the Lord our God"
(Psalm 19:8 LXX); and at the prayers they were turned to flight by the
Lord. Once they came in darkness, bearing the appearance of a light,
and said, "We have come to give you a light, Antony." But I closed my
eyes and prayed, and immediately the light of the wicked ones was
quenched. And a few months after they came as though singing psalms
and babbling the words of Scripture, "But I was like a deaf man, heard
not" (Psalm 37:14). Once they shook the cell with an earthquake, but I
continued praying with unshaken heart. And after this they came again
making noises, whistling and dancing. But as I prayed and lay singing
psalms to myself they immediately began to lament and weep, as if
their strength had failed them. But I gave glory to the Lord Who had
brought down and made an example of their daring and madness.

Once a demon exceeding high appeared with pomp, and dared to
say, "I am the power of God and I am Providence, what do you wish that
I shall give you?" But I then so much the more breathed upon him, and
spoke the name of Christ, and set about to smite him. And I seemed to
have smitten him, and immediately he, big as he was, together with all
his demons, disappeared at the name of Christ. At another time, while
I was fasting, he came full of craft, under the semblance of a monk,
with what seemed to be loaves, and gave me counsel, saying, "Eat and
cease from your many labors. Thou also art a man and art like to fall
sick." But I, perceiving his device, rose up to pray; and he endured it
not, for he departed, and through the door there seemed to go out as
it were smoke. How often in the desert has he displayed what resem-
bled gold, that I should only touch it and look on it. But I sang psalms
against him, and he vanished away. Often they would beat me with
stripes, and I repeated again and again, "Nothing shall separate me
from the love of Christ" (see Romans 8:35), and at this they rather fell
to beating one another. Nor was it I that stayed them and destroyed
their power, but it was the Lord, who said, "I saw Satan fall like lightning from heaven" (Luke 10:18); but I, children, mindful of the apostle's
words, "have figuratively transferred to myself" (1 Corinthians 4:6), that
you might learn not to faint in discipline, nor to fear the devil nor the
delusions of the demons.

And since I have become a fool in detailing these things, receive this also as an aid to your safety and fearlessness; and believe me for I do not lie. Once some one knocked at the door of my cell, and going forth I saw one who seemed of great size and tall. Then when I enquired, "Who are you?", he said, "I am Satan." Then when I said, "Why are you here?", he answered, "Why do the monks and all other Christians blame me undeservedly? Why do they curse me hourly?" Then I answered, "Wherefore do you trouble them?" He said, "I am not he who troubles them, but they trouble themselves, for I have become weak. Have they not read, 'The swords of the enemy are utterly broken, and Thou hast destroyed his cities' (Psalm 9:7 LXX)? I have no longer a place, a weapon, a city. The Christians are spread everywhere, and at length even the desert is filled with monks. Let them take heed to themselves, and let them not curse me undeservedly." Then I marveled at the grace of the Lord, and said to him: "You who art ever a liar and never speakest the truth, this at length, even against your will, you have truly spoken. For the coming of Christ has made you weak, and He has cast you down and stripped you." But he having heard the Savior's name, and not being able to bear the burning from it, vanished.

If, therefore, the devil himself confesses that his power is gone, we ought utterly to despise both him and his demons; and since the enemy with his hounds has but devices of this sort, we, having got to know their weakness, are able to despise them. Wherefore let us not despond after this fashion, nor let us have a thought of cowardice in our heart, nor frame fears for ourselves, saying, I am afraid lest a demon should come and overthrow me; lest he should lift me up and cast me down; or lest rising against me on a sudden he confound me. Such thoughts let us not have in mind at all, nor let us be sorrowful as though we were perishing; but rather let us be courageous and rejoice always, believing that we are safe. Let us consider in our soul that the Lord is with us, who put the evil spirits to flight and broke their power. Let us consider and lay to heart that while the Lord is with us, our foes can do us no hurt. For when they come they approach us in a form corresponding to the state in which they discover us, and adapt their delusions to the condition of mind in which they find us. If, therefore, they find us timid and confused, they immediately beset the place, like robbers, having found it unguarded; and what we of ourselves are thinking, they do, and more also. For if they find us faint-hearted and cowardly, they mightily increase our terror, by their delusions and threats; and with these the unhappy soul is thenceforth tormented. But if they see us rejoicing in the Lord, contemplating the bliss of the future, mindful of the Lord, deeming all things in His hand, and that no evil spirit has any strength against the Christian, nor any power at all over any one—when they behold the soul fortified with these thoughts— they are discomfited and turned backwards. Thus the enemy, seeing Job fenced round with them, withdrew from him; but finding Judas unguarded, him he took captive. Thus if we are wishful to despise the enemy, let us ever ponder over the things of the Lord, and let the soul ever rejoice in hope. And we shall see the snares of the demon are like smoke, and the evil ones themselves flee rather than pursue. For they are, as I said before, exceeding fearful, ever looking forward to the fire prepared for them.

And for your fearlessness against them hold this sure sign— whenever there is any apparition, be not prostrate with fear, but what-soever it be, first boldly ask, "Who are you? And from whence do you come?" And if it should be a vision of holy ones they will assure you, and change your fear into joy. But if the vision should be from the devil, immediately it becomes feeble, beholding your firm purpose of mind. For merely to ask, "Who are you? And from whence do you come?" (see Josh 5:13) is a proof of coolness. By thus asking, the son of Nun learned who his helper was; nor did the enemy escape the questioning of Daniel.[38]

Those ascetics who did not acquire the gift of discernment of spirits, nor realize their own fallen state, nor understand that Christ is everything for a Christian, nor understand that one must even reject the good aspects of the fallen nature and renounce one's own soul, and for these reasons were susceptible to conceit to a greater or lesser degree—these ascetics were subjected to great calamities and even perdition from physical appear-ances of spirits, which occurred as a result of the affliction of the body through physical labors that were not cleansed from conceit. When the spirits capture or trap a person in the secret places of his heart and mind, then it is much easier to do the same to the body.[39] Then a person trusts in falsehood, thinking he trusts the purest truth. St Isaac the Syrian wrote:

> There was another man in Edessa by the name of Jason, or Asimas, the composer of many triads chanted even to this day, who practiced a very lofty discipline and bound himself imprudently with very severe labors, until he was glorified [by men]. The devil deluded him, led him out of his cell, placed him on the summit of a mountain called Storios, made a pact with him, and showed him the forms of chariots and charioteers, saying to him, "God has sent me to take you into Paradise like Elias." In his childishness he was deceived and he sat in the chariot. Then the whole phantasy vanished, he fell from a great height to the earth, and died a death worthy of ridicule.[40]

It is clear that Asimas died because of his lack of spiritual knowledge concerning the fallen spirits, as well as the mystery of the redemption of mankind by the God-Man. For if he had this knowledge, he would have known that there is no place for conceit, which led him to believe the devil's lies. For this same reason, a terrible calamity fell upon two recluses of the Kiev Caves, Saints Isaac and Nikitas. To the first, the devil appeared as Christ himself, and to the second, in the form of an angel.[41] Entirely true are these words of St Peter: "your adversary the devil walks about like a roaring lion, seeking whom he may devour" (1 Pet 5:8). He devours the weak and the childish in spiritual wisdom; he does not consider it shameful to attack the great righteous ones either, hoping to delude them and cast them down in a moment of spiritual sleep or insufficient vigilance.

The tools that the devil used so effectively against Asimas he also tried to use on St Symeon the Stylite. In Asimas's case, he was able to kill him because of the man's own preliminary agreement; as for the Stylite, he wanted to catch him unawares: to destroy him, having taken away both the time and possibility to fully examine the delusion. This is what he said to the saint: "Listen, Symeon! The God of heaven and earth has sent me to you, as you see, with a fiery chariot and horses, to take you to heaven like

Elijah. You are worthy of such an honor for the holiness of your life. The hour has come in which you must reap the fruits of your labors, and to accept the crown from the hands of the Lord Himself. Go without tarrying, servant of the Lord, to see your Lord, to worship your Creator, Who created you in His own image. May the angels, archangels, prophets, apostles, martyrs also gaze upon you, for that is their desire."

While the tempter said this and other such things—the demons are garrulous and pompous—the saint at first did not realize he was the devil. This saint's character was remarkable for its simplicity and his inclination to obey without demur, as one can easily see by reading his remarkable life. Symeon said in answer, addressing God directly, "Lord! Is it true that You want to take me, a sinner, to heaven?" With these words, he already lifted his foot to enter the chariot, and then he crossed himself, at which point the devil and the chariot immediately disappeared.[42] Naturally, after this temptation, Symeon plunged himself even more deeply into humility and became even more afraid of conceit, which, though it was present in the most miniscule degree possible, still almost destroyed him. If the holy ones were subject to such dangers from the delusions of demons, then the danger for us is far greater. If the holy ones did not always recognize the demons that appeared to them in the form of saints or even Christ Himself, then how can we possibly believe that we will recognize them without making a mistake? The only way to salvation from these spirits is to reject any visions at all, and to turn aside from any communion with them, declaring ourselves to be incapable of any vision or communion with the spiritual world at all.

The holy instructors of Christian asceticism, who were illumined and taught by the Holy Spirit Himself, recognized the beneficial and wise reason for which human souls during their time on earth are covered by bodies as it were by veils or cloaks. They command righteous monks not to believe any phantom or vision if it suddenly appears, not to speak to it, not even to pay any attention to it. When such visions do occur, their command is simple: make the sign of the cross, close your eyes, and in a firm acknowledgment of your own unworthiness and incapacity to see holy angels, to pray God that He would protect you from all snares and delusions that are set for mankind by the spirits of evil, who are incurably infected with hatred and envy toward mankind. The fallen spirits so hate the human race that if it were allowed them by the hand of God that invisibly holds them back, they would instantly destroy all of us.[43] This teaching concerning the need for caution and for salvific doubt in the face of spiritual vision is accepted by the whole Church. It is one of those moral traditions that the children of the Church must hold to carefully and relentlessly. Saints Kallistos and Ignatius Xanthopoulos write, "Never accept anything that you see, either with your eyes or your mind within you or outside of yourself, even if that vision is of Christ or an angel or some saint, or an imaginary light. But abide in doubt and indignation concerning such visions."[44]

In the *Prologue*, we read the following instruction:

The devil appeared to a certain monk in the form of an angel of light, and he said to the monk, "I am Gabriel, send by God to you." The monk answered, "Look: haven't you been sent to someone else? I live in my sins and am unworthy of seeing an angel." Shamed by such an answer, the demon immediately disappeared. For this reason the elders say that if an angel does appear to someone, you shouldn't accept that vision, but humble yourself instead, saying, "I, living in sin, am unworthy of seeing an angel." A certain elder told a story of his own life, when he was praying in his cell: "I saw the demons openly, but I paid no attention to them." The devil, seeing his failure, once came to that elder in a vision of great light and sad, "I am Christ." The elder, however, having seen him, closed his eyes shut and said, "I am unworthy of seeing Christ, Who Himself said, 'Many will come in My name, saying, "I am the Christ," and will deceive many'" (Matthew 24:5). The devil, hearing this, disappeared; as for the elder, he praised God. The elders have said to us, never desire to see Christ or angels physically, lest you go completely mad, having accepted a wolf instead of the shepherd and having worshiped your enemies, the demons.[45] The beginning of the delusion of the mind is vanity. The vain ascetic is deluded by images and phantoms of the Divinity. You must also know that sometimes the demons vary their attacks. Sometimes some of them appear in their own forms, then others of their ranks appear in the form of angels, as though to help you against the demons.[46]

St Gregory of Sinai, in his instructions to hesychasts, writes the following:

> I wish you to have an exact understanding concerning delusion, to be
> protected from it, lest you, in your ignorance, having striven toward
> evil that hides behind a mask of good, not receive the worst harm or
> the destruction of your soul. Man's self-will easily inclines to commun-
> ion with the fallen spirits, especially the self-will of those who do not
> have spiritual knowledge, as those how are under the constant influ-
> ence of the spirits. The demons are close to beginners and to the self-
> willed, they surround them, casting nets of thoughts, digging pits of
> falls and imaginations, for their city (the mind and heart of the begin-
> ners and self-willed) are in the control of barbarians. They should not
> be amazed if one of these were to lose his mind or be deluded, if one
> of them accepted delusion or sees something that is contrary to truth,
> or says something untoward form their lack of experience and foolish-
> ness. It is not surprising if a beginner is fooled by delusion even after
> much labor, for this has happened to many ancient and recent ascetics
> ... And so never accept a vision, either physical or in your mind, either
> within or without, even if the image or Christ or an angel or other saint
> were to appear before you, or if you imagine a great light in your mind,
> for the mind is naturally inclined to imagination, and it easily creates
> whatever images it desires, especially if the ascetic is not vigilant over
> himself, thereby bringing great harm to himself ... Often that which is
> allowed by God for the acquisition of crows has led to great harm, for
> it pleases God that our self-will be challenged. If anyone will accept,
> without asking the experiences, whatever he sees with him mind or his
> senses, then he will be easily fooled, or he is inclined to delusion, as one
> who trusts too easily ... It requires much labor to find the truth exactly
> and to become purified of everything that is contrary to grace, for the
> devil usually offers delusion to the beginner in the form of truth, trans-
> forming his cunning into something seemingly spiritual. Therefore,
> the one who desires to acquire pure prayer in stillness must walk in
> great trembling and sorrow, always weeping for his sins, sorrowing
> and fearing lest he fall away from God, lest he be rejected in this or the
> future age. The devil, when he sees someone living in sorrow, does not
> remain there, for he fears the humility given by tears. If someone, led

by self-conceit, imagines himself capable of reaching an exalted state, he has acquired a demonic zeal, not a true one, and such a man is easily captured by Satan's nets, for he is Satan's servant. For this reason, it is a great weapon to combine prayer with tears ... Those who live brazenly and are led by their imaginations are easily cast down ... Man is in need of great discernment to learn the difference between good and evil. Do not quickly and frivolously believe in visions, but, remaining steadfast, preserve whatever good you have acquired by much testing, while also rejecting the bad, for you are required to test and discern, and only then to believe in that which is seems to be worthy of faith. Know that the activity of grace is evident. The devil cannot give grace, though he tries to transform himself. He can impart neither meekness, nor stillness, nor humility, nor hatred of the world, nor does he assuage the passions and lusts. All these are the activities of grace. The activity that comes from the devil is darkness, conceit, fear, and all forms of evil. From the action on your soul can you discern the nature of the light that arises in your soul, whether it is from God or Satan.[47]

In general, both the thoughts and the sensations of the heart, and physical appearances of the demons are known by their fruits, by the activity they produce in the soul, as the Saviour Himself said, "You will know them by their fruits" (Matt 7:16). Confusion and perplexity are true signs of demonic thoughts, sensations, and visions. But even such signs can only be accurately discerned by those who have studied the sensations of their souls for a long time, learning to distinguish good from evil (see Heb 5:14).

One time, the apostle Paul appeared to St Eleazar of Anzersky Island and gave him a certain mystical teaching. The next day, the same vision appeared before the eyes of the saint. When writing about this visitation in his diary, the saint noted: "I spit in his face and told him, 'Go away, deluder, and take your delusions with you!' Because I sensed him with my heart."[48] This is a model of one who has learned to discern good from evil! Exactly in the same way did Pachomius the Great rebuked the devil when he appeared in the form of Christ.[49]

However, for the inexperienced and the beginners, the only means to escape the delusion and the damage it brings is found in a firm rejection of any vision, due to our complete inability to discern visions properly.

What is the reason for the hypocrisy of the spirits, a hypocrisy terrible in both its beginnings and its ends? The reason is obvious. We can see it most vividly in ourselves, because man takes part in the fall of the rejected angels, and if we listen to the evil suggestions that they offer or that arise in our own fallen nature, then we become like demons. Among the qualities of our fallenness, we especially underline the desire to hide our sins, a desire that accompanies all human iniquity, and to justify ourselves. This is what Adam and Even did after they transgressed the command of God (see Genesis chapter 3); this is what their firstborn Cain did after he killed his brother Abel (see Genesis chapter 4). The further man goes from correction and virtue, the more strongly and subtly he desires to hide himself with hypocrisy. The most hardened criminals are often at the same time unscrupulous hypocrites. Shut behind the mask of hypocrisy, hiding behind the mask of virtue and holiness, they prepare and perpetrate the worst evils. And the more well-crafted the mask, the better they are able to accomplish their crimes. Even the fallen angels hide behind the mask of hypocrisy. They are hardened, constant, incorrigible villains, but they perpetrate their evildoings most often while hiding under the guise of the holy angels, prophets, martyrs, apostles, and even Christ Himself. They try to fit themselves into the circumstances, the mindset, the inclinations, the impressions of a human being. To some ascetics they offer visions of coffers of gold and silver and other objects of luxury and earthly greatness, with the intention of finding a resonance in the imagination of the person, which may activate his hidden love of money and avarice. To others they offer images of feasting with much food and drink; to still others they show halls filled with music and crowds of people dancing. To yet others they appear in the form of women to awaken their lust. When the fallen angels want to bring an ascetic down through fear, they appear in the form of wild beasts, executioners or prison guards, and warriors with shining weapons, with lit torches, any figures that had previously frightened the ascetic in life. Still others try to delude with beautiful singing, as though it were angelic, through harmonious music that seems to come from heaven. And others are deluded by voices that sound as though they come from the lips of God Himself. To others they appeared as departed relatives and friends, or in any other human form, trying to convince the ascetic by all means necessary that they are not fallen spirits, but human souls whose fate is yet to be determined, and who for this reason wander the earth without harbor, and often in such cases they invent some interesting tale that makes the frivolous monk curious and makes them trust the lie, offering it blithely as the whole truth. This last method of delusion is especially used by spirits in our own time. These "wandering spirits" are believed even by those who do not believe in the existence of evil spirits. This is exactly what the evil spirits need: those thieves and murderers then can perpetrate all the evils they desire when those whom they will to destroy do not even believe in their existence. As St Macarius the Great said, "We must carefully look around everywhere for the snares, delusions, and evil actions of the enemy. For just as the Holy Spirit through Paul 'became all things to all men, that [he] might by all means save some,' (1 Corinthians 9:22) so the evil spirit through hatred of all tries to become all things, that he might destroy everyone."[50]

Man willingly rejected communion with God and the holy angels, willingly entered communion with the evil spirits, standing together with them in the same ranks, the ranks of those creatures rejected by God, at enmity with God. By doing this, mankind has subjected himself to those evil spirits. Salvation is given to fallen man "freely" by God; however, it is left to our will to accept or reject this salvation. Man is given a chance, given the power of grace to tear himself from the ranks of the fallen spirits, to cast off their yoke; however, he is also given the choice to remain in his previous state of communion with them, of subjugation to them. For us human beings, either warfare or slavery is inevitable. Pious labors are nothing other than the active acceptance of salvation, the revelation of our free will, demonstrated and proved by experience, by our very life.

It is therefore natural for the fallen spirits to try to keep us imprisoned within their communion when we come to desire to end that communion, to be freed from bondage. As for us, it is necessary to prove our sincere desire to cast off the yoke by bringing into action all the means that we have at our disposal. By entering the world of the spirits through asceticism for the purpose of being freed, we naturally encounter the fallen spirits first of all. Though the divine grace given to us at baptism (without which any battle with the demons or freedom from their bondage would be impossible) secretly guides us, helps us, and fights together with us, at first, we still are surrounded by the demons. Since we have been in communion with them due to our fallen state, we must forcefully cut off this communion. Because of the fallenness of our nature, all good and correct thoughts and emotions in us are intermixed with evil and false ones. Because of that intermixing, any good that we have in us is useless. The fallen spirits try to keep us in our fallen state, in which we are inevitably imprisoned by them, and so they offer us various sinful thoughts and images that resonate with our fallen nature, forcing it to take pleasure in them. Or sometimes they offer such evils that even the fallen nature rejects, hiding them behind a mask of goodness and truth.

Acting thus through our thoughts and imaginations, the spirits do exactly the same when they begin to appear to our physical senses. The general rule of Christian monastic asceticism is that as soon as the monk enters the fray, he is met and surrounded by fallen spirits, who first act upon him through thoughts and images, then later in physical form. This is clearly seen in the lives of Anthony, Macarius, Pachomius the Great, Mary of Egypt, Andrew the Fool for Christ, John the Much-suffering, and all other Christian ascetic saints. At first, they had to battle thoughts, imaginations, and sensations that were obviously evil or deviously evil. After a long time, after many constant efforts expended, such saints are then sent holy thoughts and sensations. When they reach the physical vision of spirits, then at first the ranks of fallen angels encounter them head-on, and only after a violent battle do the holy angels approach them for communion, since now such ascetics have actively rejected their initial communion with the demons and have shown their ability for subsequent communion with the angels. This order of asceticism was demonstrated by Jesus Christ Himself, our Saviour, Who took upon Himself all our weakness, save sin. At first, the tempting devil approached Him in the desert, and only after the Lord defeated him did the angels approach the Lord and "ministered to Him" (Matt 4:11).

Young monks who have not yet acquired the necessary knowledge of spirits through the invisible warfare of the mind and senses have been forbidden by experienced monastic leaders any overly zealous labor of fasting, vigil, reclusion, for during such labors the spirits quickly begin to appear physically and can easily delude the ascetic, to his harm and even perdition.[51] Only a small number of monks are capable of battle with demons, even among those who have acquired detailed knowledge in the invisible war. Such ascetics have trained the sensations of their heart to discern good from evil, with the help of spiritual sensations that have been illumined by divine grace through their ascetic labors.[52] The only correct entry point into physical vision of spirits is Christian perfection. But such perfection, and therefore the physical vision of Spirits, is only possible for those brought to it directly by God Himself. Those who force their way into physical vision of spirits willfully act incorrectly, unlawfully, contrary to the will of God. For such a person, it is impossible to avoid being deluded and becoming spiritually deceived and damaged. The very desire to see spirits is itself the beginning of the lie and the self-deception.

The Spiritual Vision of Spirits

Far less onerous for a person is the limitation of his physical vision, or blindness as compared with man's primal vision, blindness produced by the fall, than the blindness of the spirit, produced by that same fall.[53] What is this blindness of the spirit? This question might especially be asked by the wise of this world, who, without waiting for an answer, will immediately call any reference to the blindness or death of the human spirit to be nothing more than empty rhetoric and foolishness. That is exactly the blindness of spirit we are speaking of! It is no mistake to call it a kind of death. "Are we blind also?" (John 9:40) This is what the proud and blind Pharisees asked of the Lord. A lack of knowledge concerning their blindness is not a sign of vision. Fallen people, having no desire to acknowledge their blindness, remain blind, and even those who were born blind, when they acknowledged their blindness, came to see through the Lord Jesus Christ (see John chapter 9).

Let us try, through the light of the Holy Spirit, to see the blindness of our own spirit. This blindness has stricken both our minds and our hearts. Because of this blindness, the mind cannot distinguish between true and false thoughts, and the heart cannot distinguish between spiritual and emotional (sinful) sensations, especially when the latter are not overtly sinful. Because of this spiritual blindness, all of our actions become false. For this reason, the Lord called the scribes (that is, the educated of that time) and the Pharisees "fools and blind" ... leading the blind (see Matt 23:17), those who themselves do not enter the kingdom of heaven, but also prevent others from entering as well.

During true spiritual labor, the grace of God, which was planted within us by Baptism, begins to heal us, little by little, from this blindness of spirit through the process of compunction. In contrast to our previous state of blindness, we begin to enter a state of vision. Since, in the state of vision, the mind is the viewer, the Holy Fathers call this state "the vision of the mind," noetic. Since this state of vision is given by the Holy Spirit, it is also called spiritual vision, being a gift of the Holy Spirit. This is the primary difference between this state and a state of contemplation. Contemplation is natural for all human beings; each person contemplates whenever he wishes. Vision, however, is natural only to those who have purified themselves through repentance. It appears not by man's will, but by the touch of the Spirit of God to our own spirit. Consequently, it occurs exclusively by the all-holy will of the All-holy Spirit. The hieromartyr Peter of Damascus has an especially clear and detailed teaching concerning spiritual vision, that is, vision of the mind.[54]

Compunction is the first spiritual sensation given to the heart after grace illumines it. This sensation includes God-pleasing sorrow, diluted with grace-filled consolation, and a previously unseen reality becomes evident to the mind. From this spiritual sensation then comes spiritual vision, as the Scriptures witness: "O taste, and see" (Ps 33:9). This vision then further intensifies the sensation: "If we force ourselves with compunction, this invites unlimited warmth that arises in the heart from the warm thoughts that appear to the mind for the first time. Acquiring and preserving such a state makes the mind subtle with warmth, capable of sight. From this, warm thoughts, as we have already said, arise in the depths of the soul, and this is called 'vision'. This vision then gives birth to the warmth that gave birth to it. From this warmth, which grows from the grace of vision, an abundance of tears come to life."[55]

As long as the sensation persists, so does the vision. With the end of the sensation, vision ends as well. It comes unexpectedly, and it leaves unexpectedly, depending not on our will, but rather on our disposition. The gates to spiritual vision are humility.[56] Constant abiding in compunction is accompanied by constant vision. This vision is the reading and the acceptance of the New Testament by the spirit. With the end of compunction, this communion with the New Testament also ends, and we begin to commune with the Old; instead of humility ["whoever slaps you on your right cheek, turn the other to him also"] (Matt 5:39) that does not resist an evil person in the heart, what comes to rule is harsh justice that strives to pluck out "an eye for an eye and a tooth for a tooth" (Matt 5:38). For this reason, St Sisoes the Great said with great sorrow: "I read the New Testament, but I keep returning to the Old."[57] Whoever desires to constantly remain in compunction and spiritual vision must strive to constantly remain in humility, casting out of himself all self-justification and condemnation of others, letting in humility by self-condemnation and the acknowledgment of one's own sinfulness before God and man.

The first spiritual vision is the vision of one's own sins, which to this point have been hidden by forgetfulness and ignorance. Having seen them through compunction, the ascetic immediately receives experiential knowledge of the preceding blindness of his spirit, which caused things that existed to appear to him to have no existence whatsoever. However, this vision of things existent once again fades when compunction fades. But when compunction appears again, so does that vision.

The ascetic's experience allows him to pass from recognition of his sins to acknowledgment of a sinfulness that has stricken his nature. From that, he passes to a knowledge of his passions or the various illness of his nature. From this vision of his fallenness, he passes gradually to a vision of the fall that has gripped all mankind. Then, the world of the fallen spirit slowly reveals itself to him; he examines the spirits through the light of his own passions, through battle with them, through the thoughts, images, and sensations that they offer to him. Then, the delusional and false sense that the earthly life is limitless is taken from him, and he begins to see its end—his own death. He begins to be exalted, that is, to be carried in spirit and sensation to the very moment of his death, to the hour of the impartial judgment of God.

From this state of fallenness, the ascetic then realizes the need for a Redeemer, and by applying the commands of the Lord to his own illness and by examining the healing and life-giving properties of the commandments on his sicknesses and his stricken soul, he then acquires a living faith in the Gospel, and his whole life becomes a confession of the Gospel. In the Gospel, as in a mirror, he sees his fallen nature even more vividly, as well as the fall of mankind in general and the fall of the evil spirits.

We will limit our survey of spiritual vision to what has already been said, since this is what is essentially necessary and easily attainable to the assiduous monk. We will conclude this survey with the words of St Maximus the Confessor: "It is impossible for the mind (i.e. the spirit) to achieve dispassion from action alone (that is, from *podvig* or spiritual struggles alone). Dispassion is only acquired (or 'accepted') through much and varied vision."[58] The word used here ("accepted") makes it clear that these visions are not like contemplation, which is a willful state of the imagination. Another way of translating the word "accepted" is "visited upon."

It is entirely natural for our spirit to acquire dispassion, a state in which the sensations of our fallen nature will be replaced by spiritual sensations, which are preceded and accompanied by compunction. The reason of our fallen nature will be then replaced by spiritual reason that is formed from knowledge given by spiritual visions. To distract us from living by the commandments of the Gospel, from humility in emulation of Christ, from compunction, from spiritual vision, from freedom from slavery to our passions, from dispassion, from the resurrection of the soul, and to keep us in blindness and death, in bondage to themselves—the fallen spirits battle ascetics fiercely. In this warfare, they let loose all their natural hatred, all the evil that they possess. This cunning and evil are here called "natural" to the fallen spirits not because they were given them at the moment of their creation—NO! The fallen spirits were created good, unfamiliar with evil, as we have already read in the teaching of Anthony the Great. They became evil because they willingly, through their willful fall, assimilated evil to their very nature. We repeat here what we wrote before: the fall of man consists of the intermixing of good with evil, while the fall of the demons consists of the complete rejection of good, in the complete assimilation to evil.[59]

"Therefore have I held straight to all Thy commandments; I have hated every wrong way" (Ps 118:128). This is what the Holy Spirit says concerning His leading mankind to salvation. On the contrary, the spirit of evil counteracts any command of the New Testament, hating every image of a life pleasing to God. But in this opposition to the commandments of the Gospel, in their cooperation with every sinful inclination, the warring ascetic comes to know the fallen spirits, examining them and studying them. After this hard-won knowledge of experience, if physical vision of spirits is granted, it can only supplement that knowledge. In exactly the same way, knowledge of man occurs, as well. Detailed knowledge of mankind is acquired by studying man's way of thinking and feeling, his way of action; the more detailed this examination, the more firm the knowledge. Face-to-face interaction only adds to this knowledge; however, personal acquaintance itself has almost no meaning with reference to this essential knowledge of man's nature.

The fallen spirits act on us through various thoughts, various images, even physical touch. In these actions, they are examined and studied. Holy Scripture mentions all of these. The Gospel depicts the devil as initially placing into Judas Iscariot's heart the thought of betraying the God-man (see John 13:2), and only later does Satan enter into Judas (see John 13:27). From the Gospel, it is made clear that Judas had an inclination toward avarice (see John 12:6), which he tried to hide under a positive mask, but which was no more than a hypocritical care for the welfare of the poor. On the foundation of this passion, the devil began to offer him the thought of betrayal. When Judas accepted and assimilated the demonic thought into himself and decided to act upon it, then the devil took total control over him. As St Theophylact of Bulgaria wrote, "Look! Satan entered into him, that is, he entered into his very heart, he enveloped his soul. Before, he chilled him from outside by the passion of love of money, but now he has come to control him completely."

How terrifying it is to agree with a demonic thought! Because of this agreement, God steps away from man, and man perishes. This is what happened to Ananias and Sapphira, mentioned in the Book of Acts, who, by accepting the thoughts of the devil, agreed to lie before the Holy Spirit. Immediately after their sinful act, they were stricken with death.

"But Peter said, 'Ananias, why has Satan filled your heart to lie to the Holy Spirit and keep back part of the price of the land for yourself?'" (Acts 5:3) The fact that the devil tempts mankind through the imagination is evident from the devil's tempting of the God-Man Himself: the devil showed the Lord "all the kingdoms of the world" and their glory "in a moment of time" (Luke 4:5), that is, in the imagination. Our mind has the ability to think and the ability to imagine; through the latter, the mind assimilates the images of objects to itself. The devil uses the former to try to offer sinful thoughts to us, and he uses the latter to impress those sinful thoughts on our mind through seductive images.

"As a small and gentle child rejoices and runs after a magician when he performs a trick, so our soul, which is simple and good, being created thus by the all-good Master, finds joy in the fantasies of the devil. Being seduced, it attaches itself to evil as though it were good, and then it combines its thoughts with the fantasies of the devil."[60]

Demonic fantasy acts on the soul very deleteriously, arousing a sympathy with sin through the imagination. If it occurs frequently, its impression can be permanent, and disastrous for the soul.

As for how the devil acts on man through the physical senses, we find examples in the Book of Job chapters 1 and 2, and the case of the woman in the Gospels who had "a spirit of infirmity eighteen years" being physically bound by the devil through a strange illness (Luke 13:10). From this touch of the demonic, lusts of the flesh are aroused and various physical illnesses can appear that typically human medicine cannot heal. All these examples of demonic attacks against humanity can be studied if we read the lives of the saints and the works of the Holy Fathers, especially those written by monks. However, learning by reading is insufficient; true knowledge is only acquired by experience. When the human spirit begins to sense divine grace, then the person gradually passes from knowledge of the spirits to spiritual vision of them. This vision is accomplished by the mind and the heart, and is given by the Holy Spirit. It is natural to the renewed mind and heart, just as physical vision is natural to the physical organ of the eye. The eye does not see because it was instructed to do so by reading, but because it naturally does so.

Spiritual vision of spirits is accomplished by the mind and the heart. The heart accuses the evil spirits; the mind is not sufficient to do this, for the mind alone cannot distinguish images of truth from images of falsehood that hide behind a mask of truth. Spiritual discernment is founded on spiritual sensations, as St Isaac the Syrian said, "Spiritual reason is the sensation of eternal life."[61] This is further shown in the admission of the two disciples concerning the sensation of their heart and the meaning of that sensation when they met the Lord on the road to Emmaus. In other words, they did not understand with their minds, but they knew with their hearts: "Did not our heart burn within us while He talked with us on the road, and while He opened the Scriptures to us?" (Luke 24:32) This same heart, which witnessed so faithful concerning the Lord, also has the capacity to discern spirits accurately, testing them, "whether they are of God" (1 John 4:1) or of the kingdom of darkness and hatred.

Only a heart purified by repentance, renewed by the Holy Spirit, is capable of such discernment. But a heart that is still imprisoned by its passions and the demons is only capable of false and deluded discernment. For this reason, St Barsanuphius the Great said to a monk who asked him how to discern thoughts coming from God from thoughts coming from the fallen nature or the demons: "That which you ask only belongs to people who have acquired a great measure of spiritual maturity. If the inner eye will not be purified by much medicine, then it will not be able to rid itself of tares and thistles and to gather the grapes that fortify and rejoice the heart. If a person does not reach this level, he will not be able to distinguish [between these thoughts], but he will be ridiculed by the demons and will fall into delusion, having come to believe them, for they can change things as they like, especially for those who do not know their snares" (see Romans 16:18).

Later in that same letter, the great old man said, "Know, brother, that any thought that is not preceded by the silence of humility does not come from God, but is clearly from the left side. Our Lord comes with quietness; everything from the enemy comes with confusion and noise. Though the demons can show themselves as though enveloped in light, but being ravening wolves in their essence, they are revealed through the confusion that they sow, for it is said, 'You shall know them by their fruits.' May the Lord enlighten all of us, lest we be enticed by their false truth."

We will conclude our homily with the spiritually wise instruction of St Macarius the Great:

> The lover of virtue must assiduously strive to acquire discernment so that he may fully discern good from evil, to be able to examine and know the many different demonic snares that the devil uses to seduce, hiding behind various apparently good thoughts. It is useful to be always careful to avoid dangerous consequences. Do not quickly admit, in your frivolity, the inspiration of any spirit, even if it be a heavenly angel, but remain indomitable, subjecting everything to the most careful examination, and when you will find something truly good, accept it, but whatever seems to you evil, reject it. Evident are the actions of the grace of God, which sin, though it puts on the mask of good, can never give. Even though, according to the apostle, Satan himself can appear as an angel of light (see 2 Corinthians 11:14) to seduce man, but these beautiful illusions can give no good action, which is a clear sign that it is evil. It can give neither love for God nor love for neighbor, neither meekness nor humility, joy, peace, the curbing of thoughts, hatred for the world, calmness of the spirit, desire for heavenly gifts. Neither can it cut off passions and lusts, which is an evident activity of grace, for it is said, 'the fruit of the Spirit is love, joy, peace, longsuffering, kindness, goodness, faithfulness' (Galatians 5:22). On the contrary, Satan can very easily give man pride and conceit, for he is very capable of both. Thus, you can know the noetic light in your soul by its fruits, whether it is from God or Satan. Basically, the soul itself, if it has a health discernment and can tell the difference between good and evil, can immediately recognize both the former and the latter through noetic sensation (spiritual sensation). Just as vinegar and wine look the same on the outside, but the tongue can immediately tell one from the other, so also the soul, by its own power, by its own spiritual sensation, can discern the gifts of the Good Spirit from the fantasy of the evil one.[62]

The heart that is illumined by divine grace is resurrected into a spiritual life. It acquires spiritual sensation that was unknown to it in the state of the fall, in which the noetic sensations of the human heart were dulled by being mixed together with the sensations of irrational beasts. Spiritual sensation can truly be called noetic or "reasoning," because He Who gives it is "The Holy Spirit, Light and Life, Living Noetic Source, Spirit of Wisdom, Spirit of Reason, God and Deifier."[63] "O taste, and see" (Ps 33:9), we say once again in the words of the Holy Scriptures. Spiritual vision, from which comes spiritual discernment, comes about as a result of spiritual purification.[64] "Solid food belongs to those who are of full age, that is, those who by reason of use have exercised their senses to discern both good and evil" (Heb 5:14). And so, spiritual discernment is found in perfected Christians; those who have succeeded in their pious ascetic struggles take part in this good gift. It is not the lot of the beginner or the inexperienced one, even if they are elders of advanced physical age.

So what must the beginner do? When he enters the monastic life, he enters the arena of battle against the spirits. And so, what rules should guide him, lest be become a victim of his own ignorance or of the hatred and cunning of the spirits? The Holy Fathers of the Orthodox Church answer this question thus:

> True discretion, said he, is only secured by true humility. And of this humility the first proof is given by reserving everything (not only what you do but also what you think), for the scrutiny of the elders, so as not to trust at all in your own judgment but to acquiesce in their decisions in all points, and to acknowledge what ought to be considered good or bad by their traditions. And this habit will not only teach a young man to walk in the right path through the true way of discretion, but will also keep him unhurt by all the crafts and deceits of the enemy. For a man cannot possibly be deceived, who lives not by his own judgment but according to the example of the elders, nor will our crafty foe be able to abuse the ignorance of one who is not accustomed from false modesty to conceal all the thoughts which rise in his heart, but either checks them or suffers them to remain, in accordance with the ripened judgment of the elders. For a wrong thought is enfeebled at the moment that it is discovered: and even before the sentence of discretion has been given, the foul serpent is by the power of confession dragged

out, so to speak, from his dark under-ground cavern, and in some sense shown up and sent away in disgrace.[65]

The revelation of thoughts and guidance by an experienced elder and brother used to be the common work of ancient monasticism. It is part of the tradition of the Apostles. As the apostle James wrote, "Confess your trespasses to one another, and pray for one another, that you may be healed" (Jas 5:16), while the apostle Paul revealed that he took great care to edify every Christian, trying to lead each one to Christian perfection, and that this is how the grace of the Holy Spirit worked within him (see Col 1:28–29). The holy teachers of ancient monasticism acted likewise: being vessels of the Holy Spirit, they could quickly raise their disciples to perfection, making them into temples of God. We can be assured of this by reading what remains of their writings. It was not gray hair or number of years or earthly erudition, but rather communion with the Holy Spirit that raised these monks to the level of guide and attracted hearers of the word to one who spoke the word of God, not his own, human word.

As St John Cassian wrote in the same Conference, it is good not to hide one's thoughts from one's elders; however, one should not reveal them to just anyone, but only to spiritual elders who have the gift of discernment, not those who are merely old and gray-haired. Many who have trusted old age and confessed their thoughts have received not healing, but have fallen into despair from the inexperience of those who accepted their confession. St Moses of Sinai asked the counsel of a young monk named Zacharias, who lived in Sketis. Zacharias fell at the feet of the elder and said, "Father! Do you ask *me* this?" The elder answered, "Believe me, my son Zacharias, that I saw the descent of the Holy Spirit on you, and so I find it necessary to ask you."[66] The revelation of thoughts and a life under the direction of a spirit-bearing elder were considered by ancient monastics to be so indispensable that monks who rejected such a path were considered to live a life outside of possible salvation.[67] With the gradual weakening of Christianity, monasticism itself began to weaken. Living vessels of the Holy Spirit grew more and more rare. Many hypocrites began to pretend to be holy and spiritual, desiring to acquire riches or human glory, and they began to attract to themselves many inexperienced monks by the apparent beauty of their mask. The hypocrites began to damage and even destroy these unfortunate monks.

Even in the tenth century, St Symeon the New Theologian wrote the following: "Study the divine Scriptures and the writings of the Holy Fathers, to compare their teachings with the teachings of your own guide and elder, so that you may see their actions and teachings as in the mirror of his own life. As for anything false or evil, recognize it and reject it, lest you be deluded. Know that in our days many charlatans and false teachers have appeared."[68]

With the passage of time, fewer and fewer spirit-bearing teachers have arisen, as the later Holy Fathers admit with great sorrow. "Today such guides have become almost nonexistent," said Nilus of Sora, who lived in the fifteenth century. Because of this weakening of the spiritual guidance of living Holy Fathers, later Fathers, inspired by the Holy Spirit Who in timely fashion and with discernment has anticipated the spiritual needs of monks in the last times, wrote down many instructive works that when combined can sufficiently describe the nature of the monastic life.[69]

These holy writings, to a certain degree, fill out the lack of living vessels of the Spirit. These latest ascetic fathers put much more emphasis on the guidance of the Holy Scriptures and the writings of the Father, as Symeon the New Theologian suggested, without, at the same time, rejecting very careful conversation with, and guidance by, contemporary fathers and brethren, all the while avoiding the modern temptation of wandering about and seeking acquaintances both within and outside the monastery and preserving constantly the mind in the heart and in humility and repentance. It is very difficult and dangerous to succeed as a monk using this method; however, this is the method given by God to us in our time, and we must with reverence use the gift of God given to us for our salvation. This difficulty in success, and the many different snares along the way, humble our spirits whether we like it or not, since our spirits incline so much to vanity and self-aggrandizement. Thus, we come to that previous knowledge of our own weaknesses, which leads us to hope exclusively on the mercy of God. Such "hope does not disappoint" (Rom 5:5).

Why are we not given the same fiery wings of ancient monasticism, by which those monks quickly and powerfully flew over the sea of the passions (this image comes from a vision of one of those ancient fathers[70])? These are the judgments of God that surpass our understanding. To examine them is forbidden, for such a labor would be in vain, an arrogant and iniquitous endeavor, for "unsearchable are His judgments and His ways past finding out! For who has known the mind of the Lord? Or who has become His counselor? ... to whom be glory forever. Amen" (Rom 11:33–34, 36).

Conclusion

O you who have been called by the mercy of God to the monastic life! Let us use all our efforts to acquire spiritual knowledge and spiritual states, which are so necessary for our salvation. Let us not satisfy empty curiosity or vain and useless learning. It is terrible to allow frivolity in this holy labor, for the fruit of such frivolity can be terrible, difficult-to-heal wounds, sometimes even spiritual death. Let us try to find poverty of spirit, tears, meekness, and a desire for heavenly righteousness. Let us beg God that He reveal our sins to us, and that He vouchsafe us to offer true repentance! Let us pray God that He reveal our passions and grant healing from them! Let us pray God that He reveal to us the fall of mankind, the God-Man's redemption, the purpose of our earthly wandering and the eternity that awaits us either in unending bliss or sufferings, that He prepare us and make us capable of receiving this heavenly blessedness, that He take off us those seals and destroy those manuscripts on which are written the deeds that will cast us into the prisons of hell! Let us beg God that He grant us purity and humble-mindedness, the fruits of which are spiritual discernment that faithfully distinguishes good from evil! Spiritual discernment tears off the mask from the actions of our passions, which often seem to the inexperienced and the passionate to be actions of great good or even the manifestation of divine grace! Spiritual discernment tears the mask off the fallen spirits, who had hoped to hide themselves and their snares behind it.

Let us pray God that He grant us spiritual vision of spirits, through which we may see them in the thoughts and images they offer to us, so that we may cease communing with them in our spirits, so that we may cast off their yoke, so that we may escape from their bondage! This communion with the fallen spirits and bondage is the essence of our fall. Let us avoid the ignorant and dangerous desire and striving for physical visions that lie outside the order of things as established by God. With submission and reverence let us follow the teachings of the Holy Fathers, the tradition of the Orthodox Church! With reverence let us obey the commands of God, Who has covered our souls with the thick veil of the flesh for the time of our earthly wandering, Who separated thereby the world of the created spirits from us, Who protected us through hour bodies from the fallen spirits. We do not need physical vision of spirits to complete our difficult earthly life. We need a different guiding light, and it is already given us: "Thy law is a lamp unto my feet, and a light unto my paths" (Ps 118:105).

Those who travel by the constant light of this guiding lamp—the law of God—will be deluded neither by their passions nor the fallen spirits, as the Scripture reveals: "Great peace have they who love Thy Law, and nothing can trip them" (Ps 118:165). This light reveals all the hidden and obvious dangers on our path; it reveals not only our fallenness, not only the fallen spirits, but the miracles of God as well: "Thou through Thy commandment hast made me wiser than my enemies," the prophet says (Ps 118:98). "Depart from me, ye wicked" (Ps 118:115), there is no place for you here, for I constantly exercise myself in the study of the law of my God. His Law is a teaching for all day (see Ps 118:97) and all night, for my entire life, which in all fairness may be called a day, since it is illumined by the law of God, and also can justly be called night, for human society is wrapped in gloom that comes from the lord of this world. The Law of the Lord is light, it illumines the spiritual eyes (see Ps 18:8–9), and sin cannot hide from that light, even if it pretends to be virtue. Nor can the dark demon hide, though he wear a mask of a bright angel.

In God's own good time, we will enter the world of the spirits. This time is not distant from any of us! May the all-good God allow us to live in such a way that we will terminate communion with the fallen spirits and enter communion with the holy spirits, even before death, so that we, having on such a foundation laid aside the body, may be joined to the ranks of those holy spirits, not to the rejected fallen spirits. Then, in unutterable joy, we will see the ranks of the holy angels and the ranks of holy saints in their wondrous uncreated mansions, at their eternal spiritual feast. Then we will come to know and see the fallen cherub with his dark armies; then the God-given vision of demons—those most unfortunate of creatures—will satisfy fully our desire to know, without any danger for us, since we will be sealed by the finger of God in unchangeableness and in inability to be deluded or damaged by evil. Amen.

CHAPTER 2

A Homily on Death

"Remember the day in which you came out of the land of Egypt all the days of your life" (Deut 16:3).

Death is a great sacrament. It is the birth of a person from this earthly, temporary life into eternity. Upon completion of this sacrament of death, we cast off ourselves our crude covering of our body, and we pass with our subtle, ethereal spiritual being into another world, into the realm of beings that are of the same nature as our soul. This world is inaccessible for the crude organs of our physical body, through which our senses have acted throughout the time of our life on earth, although they belong, properly, to the realm of the soul. The soul, when it leaves the body, is invisible and inaccessible to us, like other objects of the invisible world. All we see at the moment of the final sacramental exhalation is the sudden lifelessness of the body; then, it begins to decay, and we hurry to cover it with earth. There, it becomes food for corruption, worms, and forgetfulness. In this way, countless generations of people have died and been forgotten. But what occurred and occurs with the soul after it leaves the body? This remains unknown to us, limited as we are by our human reason.

Death is an intimate sacrament! Before people were illumined by the light of Christianity, for the most part they had the crudest understanding concerning the immortality of the soul. The greatest wise men of paganism could do little more than guess and speculate. However, the heart even of a fallen person, no matter how dark or blunted, constantly sensed, so to speak, its own immortality. All the pagan teachings are proof of this: they all promise man some kind of life after death, either a joyful or a terrible life, depending on the manner of one's earthly life.

It is absolutely necessary for us, short-lived wanderers on this earth, to come to know our fate in eternity. If our cares during this short life are focused on avoiding all sorrow and surrounding ourselves with pleasant things, all the more must we attend to our eternal fate. What does death do to us? What awaits the soul beyond the pale of the material? Can it be possible that there is no justice for good or evil actions performed by people, whether willingly or unwillingly? Is it possible that there is no justice there, just as for the most part on earth evil triumphs and succeeds, while good is persecuted and suffers? It is vitally important for us to reveal the mystery of death, to see the invisible fate of man's future with physical eyes.

The sacrament of death is revealed to us by the word of God, and it becomes open and accessible, through the actions of the Holy Spirit, to senses that have been purified and made subtle by grace. As the apostle Paul writes, "The Spirit searches all things, yes, the deep things of God" (1 Cor 2:10), not only of man.

The Fate of the Body after Death

Death is the separation of the soul from the body which were united by God's will and will be sundered also by God's will. Death is the separation of the soul from the body because of our fall, which caused our body (originally incorruptible) to become corruptible. Death is the execution of immortal man, a punishment for rebellion against God. Through death, man is painfully sundered and torn apart into two halves, which are his constituent parts. After death, then, there is no longer a human being. There are two parts of him, existing separately: the soul and the body.

Yes, the body does continue to exist, even though we can see it fall apart and transform into the earth from which it was taken. It continues to exist, even in its corruption, like a seed in the earth that awaits the second union with the soul, after which it will become untouchable by this visible death. The bodies of those especially chosen by God resist this corruption, being filled generously with the grace of God, and even in the valley of the shadow of death, they reveal the beginnings of their future, glorious resurrection. Instead of stinking, they exude a sweet fragrance; instead of spreading noxious infection, they pour out healing of all illnesses. They pour out life itself. Such bodies are simultaneously dead and alive. They are dead to human nature, but they are alive through the presence of the Holy Spirit in them. They witness to the greatness and holiness in which God created man, and that that greatness and holiness have been returned by the Redeemer.

The Fate of the Soul after Death

While the body sleeps the sleep of death, what happens to the soul? The Word of God reveals that our souls unite—depending on the good or evil qualities acquired during earthly life—with the angels of light or the fallen spirits. Together with the angels, the souls comprise in their nature a single kind of being, being divided only in quality. That is, the souls' state is determined by the good or the evil they assimilated to by their free will to a nature that was primally incorrupt and holy. We find indubitable proofs of this in the Holy Scriptures and the writings of the Holy Fathers. The Lord promised the repentant thief immediate passage for his soul from the cross to paradise: "Assuredly, I say to you, today you will be with Me in Paradise" (Luke 23:43). The much-suffering poor man Lazarus was borne, after death, by the angels into a part of paradise that was called the bosom of Abraham, while the unmerciful rich man, who rejoiced during his earthly life and "fared sumptuously every day" (Luke 16:19-31), was cast down into hell.

The souls of the righteous, upon being separated from their bodies, enjoy blessedness in heaven in expectation of the resurrection of their bodies, as the seer St John the Theologian wrote, while the sinners await the same resurrection in terrible sufferings (see Rev 6:10-11 and 20:13). When the trumpet of the resurrection sounds, then heaven will present its inhabitants for a glorious reunion with their bodies, which will come to life at "the voice of the Son of God" (John 5:25), just as the four-day-dead and stinking Lazarus heard it and came back to life. Hell will present its inhabitants also, for the dread judgment and the final verdict. After the utterance and fulfillment of that final verdict, the blessedness of the righteous will increase, and the sinners will return to their hell for even worse sufferings (see Ps 9:18).

The Lord Himself described the righteous after the resurrection, that they "are like the angels of God in heaven" (Matt 22:30). When predicting His own second coming and dread judgment, the Lord said that then He will tell the righteous who stand at His right: "Come, you blessed of My Father, inherit the kingdom prepared for you from the foundation of the world." As for those who stand at His left, he will say, "Depart from Me, you cursed, into the everlasting fire prepared for the devil and his angels" (Matt 25: 34, 41). It is also true that the fate of individual righteous people and sinners will be quite different. The justice of God will give to each person according to his deeds (see Rev 22:12). It is not only heaven that has a countless number of mansions, as the Saviour Himself said, but hell also has countless prisons and various kinds of tortures: those who sinned knowingly "shall be beaten with many stripes," while those who sinned without knowing it "shall be beaten with few" (Luke 12:47-48).

Only Orthodox Christians, and even then only those who led an earthly life of piety or who purified themselves of their sins through sincere repentance, confession before a spiritual father, and self-improvement, will inherit eternal blessedness together with the bright angels. On the contrary, the impious (those who do not believe in Christ), the evil-minded (the heretics), and those among the Orthodox who lived a life of sin or fell into some mortal sin without healing themselves through repentance, will receive eternal suffering together with the fallen angels. The patriarchs of the Eastern Catholic Church said as much in their epistle:

> The souls of people who fell into mortal sins and who did not despair at their death, but repented before passage from this life, though they did not have time to offer any fruits of repentance such as prayer, tears, prostrations during prayer, compunction of heart, consolation of the poor, and expressing their love for God and neighbor by their actions (all of which the Catholic Church from the beginning admitted to be God-pleasing and beneficial)—the souls of such people descend into hell and suffer punishments for their sins, without losing the hope of being released from them. This aid to those who suffer after death is received through God's mercy, through the prayers of priests and for good deeds performed in memory of those who died, but especially by the power of the Bloodless Sacrifice, which the priests offer for all Christians every day of the year. (Article 18)[1]

"The death of sinners is evil" (Ps 33:22), while for the righteous and the holy it passes from the rumors and confusion of life to unconquerable calm, from constant sufferings to unending blessedness, passing from earth to heaven together with a countless host of holy angels and holy people. In insatiable contemplation of God and in constant fire of love for Him is found the highest and most essential joy of the inhabitants of heaven. St Macarius the Great wrote concerning this subject in the following manner:

> When the soul of a man departs out of the body, a great mystery is there accomplished. If it is under the guilt of sins, there come bands of devils, and angels of the left hand, and powers of darkness take over that soul, and hold it fast on their side. No one ought to be surprised at this. If, while alive and in this world, the man was subject and compliant to them, and made himself their bondman, how much more, when he departs out of this world, is he kept down and held fast by them. That this is the case, you ought to understand from what happens on the good side. God's holy servants even now have angels continually beside them, and holy spirits encompassing and protecting them; and when they depart out of the body, the bands of angels take over their souls to their own side, into the pure world, and so they bring them to the Lord.[2]

The mere fact that the same place of habitation, the same joy and the same punishment, as the angels is intended for the souls of human beings indicates that souls are beings that in all ways are similar to angels. This is evident from the afore-mentioned words of the Lord, Who said that the righteous after the resurrection would be like angels in heaven. Angels have appeared to the ancient righteous ones Abraham, Lot, Jacob, and others. Noteworthy is the fact that these righteous people did not immediately recognize that those who visited them were not men, but bodiless beings. After Christ's resurrection, angels appeared to the myrrh-bearing women in the form of men dressed in shining white robes (see Luke 24:4, John 20:12). During the ascension, they appeared to the Apostles also in the form of men in white robes (see Acts 1:10).

The Holy Father often saw the angels as wearing white robes, while the demons appeared as foul and dark creatures. The Lord, after His resurrection, suddenly appeared before the Apostles, who were gathered together in an upper room. The Apostles were initially afraid, thinking

they saw a ghost, but the Lord reassured them, explaining the difference between the appearance of a spirit and His own appearance in His
glorified body. "Why are you troubled? And why do doubts arise your
hearts? Behold My hands and My feet, that it is I Myself. Handle Me and
see, for a spirit does not have flesh and bones as you see I have" (Luke
24:38–39). Here it is not said that a spirit has no form. More than that, it is
made quite clear that spirits (i.e., angels and souls) do have a form; what
they do not have is flesh and blood, which the body of Christ did have
even in his glorified state. This same understanding is expressed by the
Christians of the Jerusalem community when they thought that the girl
Rhoda, who saw Peter knocking at the gate, had actually seen his guardian
angel ("So they said, 'It is his angel'" [Acts 12:15]).

St Macarius the great says that angels have a visible form, just as the
soul also has its image and form, and this image (both of the angel and
the soul) is the image and form of the external man in his body.[3] He also
teaches that angels and souls, though very subtle in their essence, are still
ethereal and subtle bodies. They are different from the material and crude
bodies of our earthly flesh. The crude human body is a covering for the
subtle body of the soul. The soul has eyes, ears, hands, and feet, and similar organs of the physical body are laid on top of these.[4] When the soul
leaves the body after death, it casts the body off like clothing. St Macarius writes that the most perfected of Christians, purified and illumined
by the Holy Spirit, see the form of the soul, but such perfection and vision
only very few among the saints achieve.[5] In those who pray the prayer
of the Spirit, sometimes the soul leaves the body through an especially
inconceivable action of the Holy Spirit.[6]

In the time of exalted monastic asceticism when St Macarius lived in
Sketis in Egypt, only a few among these holy ones were given the gift of
seeing the form of the soul; all the more today are such saints rare. But they
do exist even in our times, by the great mercy of God and by the unerring promise of the Lord Jesus to remain with His faithful disciples until
the end of the age. According to the personal account of one such saint of
God, who suddenly saw his own soul leave his body and stand in the air
during the abundant action of prayer, the soul is an ethereal, very subtle,
airy body that has the image of our crude body, that is, all its members,

including the hair and the expressions on the face. In other words, the soul has total similarity with the body. It was not merely the powers of the mind and heart that were present in the soul, but it was the entirety of life, while the body remained during prayer on the chair, as though dead, like a suit of clothes cast off, until, by God's command, the soul returned into the body just as inconceivable it left it.[7]

Angels are similar to the soul: they have members including eyes, a head, mouths, hands and fingers, feet, and hair. In a word, they look like physical people in their bodies. The beauty of virtue and God's grace shine in the faces of the holy angels. This same character is stamped on the faces of the most virtuous Christians as well. As for the fallen angels, desperate hatred comprises their character; their faces look like the disfigured faces of the worst villains among human beings. This is what those who have seen both angels and demons witness.

Both the angel and the soul are called "bodiless," since they do not have flesh as we do, and so are spiritual, beings of subtlety that completely differ from objects in our material world. This is how they are called in everyday human language, as well as in the sacred Scriptures and the writings of the Fathers.[8] Their essence is incomparably more subtle than the essence of earthly objects that we can see. In our usual fallen state, we cannot see spirits, but we sense their influence over us if we lead an attentive, virtuous life. A grace-filled, living, noetic sense of spirits—this is spiritual vision of spirits (see 1 John 5:18).[9] Wind, air, various vapors and gases are usually called, even in the Scriptures and writings of the Fathers, "spirit."[10] However, in the most essential, exact meaning of the term, only God is Spirit. He, as perfect Being, is completely different in His essence from the essences of created things, no matter how spiritual or subtle those essences may be compared to material creatures. There is no creature one in essence with God! And so, other than God, there is no other spiritual being that is spiritual in essence.[11] "God is Spirit" (John 4:24). "Who makes His angels spirits and His ministers a flame of fire" (Heb 1:7), and He became man "to send fire" into our hearts (Luke 12:49) that have been deadened by sin and frozen by sin. He made us flame and fire, untouchable by corruption and the devil, through union with Him. Completely alien to true life and true spirituality are the fallen angels, as well as the souls of rejected sinners.[12]

The future home of the soul corresponds to its nature, that is, to its ethereal composition. Eden was ethereal, just as heaven is, just as hell is as well. In addition to the spiritual joy and inner peace of the holy soul that reveals itself already in this life, depending on the measure of the soul's purification, it is also placed after death into a country that is appropriate for a soul that has been found worthy of eternal blessedness by the mercy of God. A sinful soul, rejected by God, not only suffers in conscience and through its state of being rejected in this life, but it is also imprisoned in a horrifying underground prison, variously called "hell, Tartarus, or Gehenna," where it is subject to horrible tortures that are capable of tormenting its ethereal nature. All this is spoken of by the Holy Scriptures, and is revealed by the Holy Spirit, by His choice and wisdom, to people who are worthy of such revelation, a revelation that is beneficial to their souls.

Often, when we want to examine some object of the physical world in detail, we choose a comfortable place for ourselves, from which that object may be seen and examined better. We do this not because the object itself requires this posture of us, but because we need to work within the limitation of our physical bodies. Similarly, it would not be in the least superfluous to choose a comfortable metal place for this discussion of ours. We can easily find such a place, and then standing in it, we will be able to see and come to acknowledge our worthlessness amid the majesty of creation, the worthlessness of our means to acquire knowledge, and even the worthlessness of our own knowledge. In such a posture, we will have no choice but to admit the need, the essential need, of divine revelation, even for accurate self-knowledge. We see neither heaven nor hell with our physical eyes; what do we see with them? What do we see with them in this physical world (I say nothing of the world of the spirits!) that we insist on calling the visible world? We see in it only the smallest portion of objects, nothing in comparison with the entire reality. The telescope and the microscope incriminate us; even our smell and touch, which are aware of gases that are invisible to the eye, incriminate us. Matter itself, limiting and hindering our gaze through the constantly shifting horizon, proves the impenetrableness of the earth and many other objects on its surface. We are further incriminated by the limitation, the extreme limitation, of our own vision, which cannot see any object in its actual form.[13] Our eyes cannot see gases because of their subtlety; they cannot pierce the depths of crude matter because of its density. We cannot even see one side of an object without the other side (or many other facets) becoming invisible to us. So what do we actually see of the visible nature? A miniscule part of the whole!

And still, our familiarity with our own limitation causes us to consider our vision to be complete and satisfactory. Instead, let this limitation give us a humble and true knowledge, and then let us raise up the gaze of our mind to those objects that are hidden from our crude senses, but which are revealed to us by the mercy and grace of God.

Paradise and Heaven

The God-seer Moses, who described the creation of the world in Genesis, says that the Lord simultaneously planted a garden of delights in Eden (see Gen 2:8) and placed two people there, the founders of the race of mankind. "Then the Lord God took the man He formed and put him in the garden to tend and keep it" (Gen 2:15). According to this account, the Lord Himself witnessed that the kingdom of heaven was prepared for man from the foundation of the world. The forefathers rebelled against the command of God in Eden; after this sin, they immediately transformed in both soul and body, becoming no longer capable of inhabiting Eden. Then God, as the God-inspired writer says, "sent him out of the garden of Eden to till the ground from which he was taken." The Slavonic version of the Bible has an interesting turn of phrase here, "next to the garden of delights," which leads us to the thought that nature itself is like Eden in its beauty, and so when we see nature, we fallen human beings are reminded of our lost Eden. When we see the beauty of nature, we can not help but exclaim, "it is like Eden!" A similar expression is used in the Holy Scriptures to describe the fruitful land of Sodom before its fall: it was said to be "like the garden of God" (Gen 13:10).

Moses describes Eden as a beautiful and extensive garden (see Gen 2:9). Many saints of the New Testament Church saw Eden in the same way. It is indeed thus in actual fact; however, Eden's essence and its nature are subtle, corresponding to the nature of its inhabitants—the spirits, and so it is inaccessible to our senses, which have become crude and blunted by the fall. When man was cast out of Eden, having originally been its care-taker, he lost his position of authority, and God gave it to "the cherubim and the fiery sword" (Gen 3:24). The soul of the thief who confessed the Lord on the cross was placed in this Eden (see Luke 23:43), and many souls of Christians who have been found worthy of salvation have been placed in Eden as well. This explains the nature of Eden as garden. As St Macarius the Great said:

> But as a merchant on a voyage of many stages, in the multiplication of his merchandise, sends to his friends to procure him houses, gar-dens, clothes that he requires, and when he sets out for home, brings with him great wealth, and his friends and kinsfolk welcome him with great rejoicing, so in spiritual things, if any are making the heavenly wealth their merchandise, their fellow citizens, the spirits of saints and angels, are aware of it, and say with admiration, "Our brethren on the earth have come into great wealth." So they, having the Lord with them at their departure, come with mighty rejoicing to those above, and those who belong to the Lord receive them, having prepared for them there houses, and gardens, and clothes all bright and costly.[14]

St Gregory of Sinai, when speaking of those who saw Eden and told of their vision, notes that there is a lower heaven, which is filled with sweet-smelling gardens planted by God Himself, that the trees of these gardens are constantly covered with flowers and fruits, that through this garden a river flows that nourishes the garden and separates it into four quarters.[15] These rivers are found in Scripture as well: "a river went out of Eden to water the garden, and from there it separated into four heads" (Gen 2:10). The holy prophet David also speaks of the waters that are found above heavens (see Ps 148:4). The place of Eden, according to Scripture, is in the East. That is the direction of Eden from the reference point of the Earth. St Theodora recounted that after her soul left her body, she, together with angels accompanying her, directed their travel to the East, where she was to receive her heavenly reward.[16] God's great saint, Symeon of the Holy Mountain, saw Eden to the East, as did St Euphrosyne of Suzdal in a miraculous vision.[17] This is why all Orthodox churches are oriented

Eastward; the bodies of the dead are also laid toward the East, "near the garden of delights." To those who still consider the Scriptures' eastward placement of Eden as insufficient evidence of its being there, we answer with the words of Gregory of Sinai: "Scripture generally makes simple and straightforward statements about matters that are still obscure."[18]

The apostle Paul was taken up into Eden, and then to the third heaven, "whether in the body or out of the body I do not know, God knows," as he said, and there he heard "inexpressible words, which it is not lawful for a man to utter" (2 Cor 12:3-4). The nature of Eden, the beauty of heaven, the abundance there of grace-filled blessedness so transcend everything beautiful and pleasant on earth that the holy apostle, to express what he saw in his holy vision, used the following phrase: "Eye has not seen, nor ear heard, nor have entered into the heart of man the things which God has prepared for those who love Him" (1 Cor 2:9-10). In these words of the apostle we find a sorrowful truth: the fall of man is so profound that in his fallen state he can no longer by himself even conceive of the blessedness he lost; his sin-loving heart has lost all sympathy with spiritual pleasures.

However, these words, which denounce the calamitous state of our fall and those who abide in that fall, at the same time also announce the joyful truth of the Holy Spirit's renewal of those people who by faith and repentance have entered the spiritual tribe of the New Adam, our Lord Jesus Christ. The Holy Spirit, having entered into a person, destroys within him the kingdom of sin, ceases the invisible internal warfare and disorder, installs the peace of Christ, which produces such a spiritual pleasure that the heart, filled with it, dies in its sympathy to sin. That heart then begins to constant abide with God and in God. Having established this kingdom of God in man, the Holy Spirit often then raises the worthy among his servants to peaceful climes, to mansions prepared for the righteous for their eternal feast. Many of the holy ones of God were transported in ecstatic vision to Eden while still alive, and from it they even entered heaven, to the heaven of heavens, to the very Throne of the Lord, surrounded by the fiery Seraphim and Cherubim. All these eye-witness accounts agree concerning Eden itself. Thus, Symeon of the Holy Mountain saw beautiful gardens in Eden, as well as the soul of the forefather Adam and the soul of the thief, the first of men led by the God-Man, after redemption, into Eden.[19]

Among the visions of Eden that we know of, the vision of St Andrew the Fool for Christ is the most vivid and detailed. He remained supernaturally in ecstatic vision for two entire weeks, contemplating the invisible world. Then, he confided to his friend, Priest Nicephorus, concerning the vision in the following words:

> I saw myself in a beautiful and wondrous Eden, and, ecstatic in spirit, I thought, what is this? I know that I live in Constantinople; how did I arrive here? I do not know. I saw myself dressed in the brightest clothing, as though it were woven from lightning itself. There was a crown on my head, woven from great flowers, and I wore a king's girdle. Rejoicing in this beauty, wondering with my mind and heart at the unutterable splendor of God's Eden, I walked in it and was glad. There were many gardens there with tall trees; their tips shook and gave joy to the sight. A pleasant fragrance wafted from their flowers. Some of these trees constantly flowered, others were covered by golden leaves and had on them various fruits of inconceivable beauty and pleasantness. It is impossible to compare any of those trees to earthly trees: God's hand, not man's, planted these trees. There was a countless multitude of birds in these gardens. Some of these had golden wings, others had white wings like snow, while others were multicolored. They sat in the branches of the Edenic trees and sang beautifully; from the splendor of their singing I nearly lost myself, so ecstatic was my heart. It seemed to me that the voice of their singing reached even the heights of heaven. These wondrous gardens of Eden stood in ranks like an army arrayed against an army. While I walked among them in joy of heart, I saw a great river that flowed among them, filling them. On the other bank of this river was a vineyard, whose vines, decorated with golden leaves and golden grapes, grew abundantly. Quiet and sweet breezes breathed there from four sides; from their breath, the garden shook and produced a wondrous sound by the movement of their leaves.[20]

Similarly, St Theodora told St Basil the New of her vision of the country of Eden. It was filled with glory and had many gardens of golden leaves and many different fruit-bearing trees. St Theodora was shown Eden in detail by the angels that guided her:

When I saw all this I marveled and was very joyous and happily looked at everything. A holy angel who was showing these things to me explained, "This is the abode of the apostles; that one—of the prophets and other martyrs; those others—of the holy bishops, holy monks, and the holy righteous." All these were in their breadth and length like a king's city.

"When we entered and found ourselves inside these lovely dwellings, the saints met us and kissed us in spirit and rejoiced in my salvation."[21]

We repeat: the natural beauty of this world is only a pale imitation of Eden, whose beauties are incorrupt, indescribably delicate, filled with holy peace and grace. The earth itself, after the sin of our fathers, was cursed by the Creator, and it constantly expressed this curse in its confusions and its disorders. Either it quakes, swallowing entire cities and villages, or fierce waters overwhelm it, submerging entire countries, or terrifying storms tear through it with thunder, lightning, and hail leaving nothing but devastation in their wake. Mankind, living on this earth, finds itself in constant conflict, both individual and social, presenting a massive spectacle of suffering, unending toil, countless sins, horrifying crimes, Babylonian idolatry. Virtues can barely find a small and sorrowful place in this world. Implacable and insatiable death walks on this earth and constantly destroys entire generations of mankind, which are replaced by new generations through the law of multiplication, established for the human race by its Creator. And death will continue to walk about and devour people until it itself will be destroyed together with the dying world.

The beasts that inhabit the world have also risen up one against the other, mercilessly destroying each other. Even the elements seem to be in constant warfare among themselves. Everything battles on earth, everything suffers, everything hurtles toward mutual destruction. What a horrifying and constant disorder! What a ubiquitous and cruel conflict! It is either invisible or barely visible to those who are in the midst of it; however, from the solitude and quiet of the monastery, it is evident for the wanderer whom God has placed next to the closest approximation of Eden (the monastery) for constant sighing and sorrowing concerning its loss.[22] If this earth, cursed by God, this earth of our exile, this land of sorrows, delusions, evil-doing, death, an earth convicted by God to be destroyed by fire (see 2 Pet 3:10) still has its beauties that can delight us, then how incredible must be the Eden prepared by God for His beloved as an eternal home for their eternal pleasure?

No fleshly eye has seen, no fleshly ear has heard, being occupied only by sensuality, "nor have entered into the heart of man the things which God has prepared for those who love Him. But God has revealed them to us through His Spirit" (1 Cor 2:9-10). St Andrew was raised not only to Eden, but, like the apostle Paul, to the third heaven. In addition to the already-quoted witness concerning Eden, he continued his account thus:

> After this a kind of fear fell upon me, and it seemed to me that I was standing at the peak of the firmament of heaven. Before me a youth was walking with a face as bright as the sun, clothed in purple ... When I followed in his steps I saw a great and splendid Cross, in form like a rainbow, and around it stood fiery singers like flames and sang sweet hymns, glorifying the Lord Who had once been crucified on the Cross. The youth who was going before me, coming up to the Cross, kissed it and gave me a sign that I should also kiss the Cross ... In kissing it I was filled with unutterable sweetness, and smelled a fragrance more powerful than that of paradise. Going past the Cross, I looked down and saw under me as it were the abyss of the sea ... My guide, turning to me, said, "Fear not, for we must ascend yet higher."
>
> "And he gave me his hand. When I seized it we were already above the secondfirmament. There I saw wondrous men, their repose, and the joy of their feasting which cannot be communicated by the human tongue ... And behold, after this we ascended above the third heaven, where I saw and heard a multitude of heavenly powers hymning and glorifying God. We went up to a curtain which shone like lightning, before which great and frightful youths were standing, in appearance like fiery flames ... And the youth who was leading me said to me: 'When the curtain opens, you shall see the Master Christ. Bow down to the throne of His glory.' Hearing this, I rejoiced and trembled, for I was overcome by terror and unutterable joy ... And behold, a flaming hand opened the curtain, and like the Prophet Isaiah I beheld my Lord, sitting upon a throne, high and lifted up, and above it stood the Seraphim (Isa.

6:1). He was clothed in a purple garment; His face was most bright, and His eyes looked on me with much love. Seeing this, I fell down before Him, bowing down to the most bright and fearful throne of His glory. The joy that overcame me on beholding His face cannot be expressed in words. Even now, remembering this vision, I am filled with unutterable joy. In trembling I lay there before my Master, wondering at the greatness of His mercy that allowed me, a sinner and an impure man, to stand before Him and see His divine glory. I was filled with compunction, thinking of my own unworthiness and looking at the majesty of my Master, repeating within myself the words of Isaiah the prophet, "Woe is me, for I am undone! Because I am a man of unclean lips, and I dwell in the midst of a people of unclean lips; for my eyes have seen the King, the Lord of hosts" (Isaiah 6:5). And then I heard that the all-merciful Creator spoke to me with all-pure and sweetest lips three divine words, which so sweetened my heart and so inflamed it with love for Him, that I seemed to be melting like wax from the warmth of the spirit, and the words of David were fulfilled in me: "my heart is even like melting wax" (Psalm 21:15) ... After this all the heavenly host sang a most wondrous and unutterable hymn, and then—I myself do not understand how—again I found myself in paradise."[23]

When St. Andrew reflected that he had not seen the Mother of God in heaven, an angel told him: "Did you wish to see here the Queen who is brighter than the heavenly powers? She is not here; she has gone away to the world which lies in great misfortune, to help people and to comfort the sorrowing. I would have shown you her holy place, but now there is no time, for you must again return to where you came from. This is the command of the Master." As he spoke to me, it seemed that I sweetly slept; having awoken, I saw that I was in the same place as I was before.[24]

From this vision of St Andrew, it is evident that paradise is the closest heavenly land to earth, or the "first heaven," above which other heavens are found, which the spirit-inspired David sang a bout, calling them the "heaven of heavens" (Ps 148:4). In these upper mansions, the souls of the righteous abide now, corresponding with their worthiness; this is where the righteous will rise after their souls are reunited with their bodies in the general resurrection, "shall be caught up together with them in the clouds to meet the Lord in the air. And thus we shall always be with the Lord" (1 Thess 4:17). The Lord will repeat, with these saints, the raising of Adam from earth to Eden. Their holy bodies, not only their souls, renewed and recreated by the God-Man, will become capable of such ascent to the heavens, as the body of the first-created Adam originally was.[25]

The vision of St Andrew, like all similar visions of other saints, is a proof and an explanation of the already-quoted opinion of St Macarius the Great that the angels and the souls of men have their own image and form, and that this form is the form of the external man. So much are they alike, in fact, that St Andrew did not know for sure if he was raised up in the body or out of the body. Here are the saints own words, as offered in the expansive life of St Andrew, written by Priest Nicephorus: "I saw myself, as though I had no body, because I did not feel the body." Then the holy man explains the clothing that was on him, and in doing so he mentions the members of the body. Returning to an explanation of his state, the holy man said, "Evidently I was in the body, but I did not feel the heaviness of the body; I felt no physical needs for the entire two weeks of my vision. This leads to the thought that I was outside the body. I do not know what to say definitively. Only God, the knower of hearts, can answer this question." St Andrew saw the angels as bright men and youths. He talked to them. The angel that led him offered him his hand several times; the angels who stood before the veil had the form of very tall young men with stern faces, fiery swords in their hands. When describing these angels, St Andrew mentions their members: face, eyes, hands, feet, as though having difficulty himself in discerning their nature. He concluded that they were fleshless bodies, or, in a more modern formulation, gaseous bodies. St Andrew saw the manner and nature of the mansions on high, and they also transcended everything that carnal man knows or can even imagine, for carnal man is nailed to the earth, not renewed or taught by the Holy Spirit, and so incapable of piercing through the mystery of the age to come.

Hell

Hell is found within the earth.[26] God, upon uttering Adam's sentence after his expulsion from Eden, at first listed the earthly punishments allotted for the one who rebelled against the Edenic command, then he announced that Adam would be subject to these punishments until he returned to the earth from whence he was taken. "Earth you are, and to earth you shall return" (Gen 3:19). Here is not said that he will go into the earth with his body only: the sentence for one who dared rebel against God is worse than it seems to a superficial glance.[27] The righteous of the Old Testament, as is evident from the Scriptures, constantly refereed to the center of the earth as the place of hell. "I shall go down into the grave to my son in mourning" (Gen 37:35), said the holy Patriarch Jacob when he was brought the false news of his son Joseph's death. The righteous and much-suffering Job begged God to let him rest for a time from the many temptations surrounding him, "Before I go to the place from which I shall not return, to an obscure and dark land, to a land of eternal darkness where there is no light, neither can anyone see the life of mortals" (Job 10:21–22). The God-inspired lawgiver Moses, when announcing God's wrath against Korah and his followers, said, "If these men should die naturally like all men, or if they are visited by the common visitation of all men, then the Lord has not sent me. But if the Lord will show by a sign from heaven that opening its mouth the earth shall swallow them down with their houses, their tents, and everything belonging to them; and they shall go down alive into Hades. Then you shall know these men provoked the Lord" (Num 16:29–35).

King David glorified the Lord: "For great is Thy mercy toward me, and Thou has delivered my soul from the nethermost hell" (Ps 85:13). When the soul of Prophet Samuel was called up from the dead by the witch of Endor, she said, "'A man is coming up, standing up, and he is covered with a mantle.' And Saul discerned it to be Samuel" (1 Kgdms 28:14). Prophet Isaiah said to Satan, "Now you shall descend to Hades, to the foundations of the earth" (Isa 14:15). Ezekiel uses similar language when speaking of the fallen angel: "I cast him down to Hades. together with those who descend into the pit. All the trees of splendor ... all that drink water, comforted him in the earth" (Ezek 31:16). In this passage, the prophet calls the fallen angel "Pharaoh" and likens him to the tree of Eden; other angels, led by the chief fallen angel into perdition, were also compared to other trees of Eden, their state before their fall.

The New Testament likewise gives the depths of the earth as the place of hell. When speaking of His imminent descent into hades with His soul and the divinity that was inseparable from it, the God-Man said, "so will the Son of Man be three days and three nights in the heart of the earth" (Matt 12:40). When explaining these words of the Saviour, Blessed Theophylact of Bulgaria says that the Lord fulfilled this prophecy by going down into the nethermost parts of the earth, to hell. The Lord, according to the apostle Paul, "descended into the lower parts of the earth" (Eph 4:9). And the apostle Peter writes, "by whom also He went and preached to the spirits in prison" (1 Pet 3:19).

St John of Damascus writes, "The deified soul of Christ descends into hell so that the light of the sun of righteousness, which had shone forth for those living on earth, would also shine forth for those sitting inside the earth, in darkness and the shadow of death."[28] In his fourteenth exegetical homily, St Cyril of Jerusalem writes:

> Our Lord Jesus said in the Gospel, "For as Jonah was three days and three nights in the belly of the great sea monster, so will the Son of Man be three days and three nights in the heart of the earth." If we examine the story of Jonah, we find in it actions very similar to the actions of Jesus. Jesus was sent to preach repentance, so was Jonah. But he fled from his charge, not knowing the future: Jesus, however, willingly came to preach salvific repentance ... Jonah was cast out into the belly of the sea monster, but Jesus willingly descended to the place of the noetic sea monster, so that death would cast out those it had eaten, as the Scripture declared, "I will deliver them out of the hand of Hades and will redeem them from death" (Hosea 13:14). Jonah prayed in the belly of the sea monster, saying, "Out of the belly of Hades, You he≈ard my cry of my voice" (Jonah 2:2). And this he said while still inside the beast. But being inside it, he said to himself that he was 'in Hades' because he was a type of Christ who had to go down into hell. A little later, he clearly prophecies, speaking on behalf of Christ, "my head plunged into the crefts of the mountains"[29] (Jonah 2:5). If he was in the belly of the beast, what sort of mountains could there be? I know this, he answers; however, I am an image of the One Who will be placed

inside a mountainous tomb. Being in the midst of the sea, Jonah said, "I descended into the earth, the bars of which are everlasting barriers" (Jonah 2:6), because he bore the image of Christ who descended into the earth.[30]

Similarly, Epiphanius of Cyprus indicates very clearly that the physical location of hell is within the earth, describing in his homily for Holy Saturday the salvation of man by the God-Man. We add this homily here, with certain sections excised:

What is this? Today, great silence in the earth. What is this? Great silence and great stillness. Great silence, for the King sleeps. The earth feared and was still when God fell asleep in the flesh. God died in the flesh, and Hell trembled. God slumbered a short spell, and woke up out of Hell those of times past who were sleeping. Today is salvation for those on earth, and those of ages past beneath the earth. Today is salvation for the world, both seen and unseen. Twofold is the Master's coming today, twofold the dispensation, twofold the love of man, twofold the descent, and likewise the condescension, twofold the visitation unto men—from heaven to earth, and from earth to under the earth. God draws nigh, Hell's gates open wide. O ye of times past who are fallen asleep, rejoice! Ye that sit in darkness and the shadow of death, receive the great Light! The Master is with his slaves, God with the dead, the Life with mortals, the Guiltless with the guilty, the unwaning Light with those in darkness, the Liberator with the captives, the One far above the heavens with those in the lowest depths. Christ is among the dead, let us go down with him. Let us learn the mysteries there, let us come to know the wonders of the hidden God hid beneath the earth, let us learn how the preaching appeared even to those in Hades. Let us then make haste and journey in mind to Hades, that we may see how there at last, he masters with masterly might the most mighty master and tyrant, and with his brilliant lightning, as with a whole army, effortlessly subdues the ranks of that immortal infantry; Then said He to Adam, Again I bid thee, *Awake thou that sleepest*: for I did not make thee, that thou shouldest be held captive in Hell. *Arise from the dead*: for I am the Life of mortals. Arise, my creation; arise, my form, made in mine own image. Again I bid thee, *Awake thou that sleepest*: for I did not make thee, that thou shouldest be held captive in Hell. *Arise from the dead*: for I am the Life of mortals. Arise, my creation; arise, my form, made in mine own image. Wherefore arise, all of you, let us go hence, from decay to incorruption, from death unto life. Arise, let us go hence, from darkness to everlasting light. Arise, let us go hence, from grief to joy. Arise, let us go hence, from bondage to liberty, from prison to the Jerusalem above, from bonds to God, from straightness to the bliss of Paradise, from earth to heaven.[31]

During the triumphant services of Holy Saturday and Pascha, the Church, celebrating and hymning the salvation of mankind by the God-Man Who suffered for us, who trampled down death by death, Who destroyed the gates and prisons of hell, Who raised mankind in Himself and with Himself, uses very clear language about the physical place of both hell and Eden. The Church does not give the precise geographical location of either, but while praising the Lord and speaking of hell and heaven, the church in passing does express its opinion about their location, speaking about it as though the fact were universally acknowledged. During Matins of Holy Saturday, after the reading of the six psalms and the great litany, two profoundly consoling and extremely poetic troparia are sung. In the first, the burial of the Lord is hymned, in the second, his descent into hell: "Noble Joseph, taking down Thy most pure body from the Tree, wrapped it in clean linen with sweet spices, and laid it in a new tomb .... Going down to death, O Life immortal, Thou hast slain hell with the dazzling light of Thy divinity. And when Thou hast raised up the dead from their dwelling place beneath the earth, all powers of heaven cried aloud 'Giver of Life, O Christ our God, glory to Thee.'"[32]

After this, all the clergy, and in some monasteries all the monks, come out with lit candles to the middle of the church, stand before the shroud, and begin to sing the Lamentations, combining them with the verses of Psalm 118. From these lamentations, I will include those that most clearly mention that hell is found within the earth.

"The Light-bearer of righteousness entered under the earth, and He raised the dead as from sleep, dispelling all the darkness in hell."

"He who holds the earth in the palm of his hand, though dead in body, is now held under the earth in order to save the dead from hell's bondage."

"O Master, you descended to earth to save Adam, but you did not find him on earth, and so you have descended even to hell in search of him."

"O what joy! O what great sweetness filled those in hell, as light shone forth in the dark depths!"

"Willingly did you descend under the earth, O Savior, to give life to dead mankind, and you raised them up in the glory of the Father."

"Having listened, O Word, to Your Father, You descended even to harrowing hades, and You resurrected the race of man."

"You Who created man with Your own hand entered under the earth, so that you raise from the fall the hosts of mankind with Your all-powerful might."

"Once Adam feared the sound of God walking in Eden; but now he rejoices at the One who descends into hell. For before he fell, but now he is raised up again."

"O gracious One, You remained inseparable from the bosom of the Father, thought You deigned to become man as well, and You descended into hell, O Christ!"

"Rise up, gracious One! Raise us from the pits of hell!"

"With a desire for the underworld, as a dead man you descended, lead the fallen from earth to heaven, O Jesus!"

"Though You were seen as a dead man, Jesus, but as living God you raised those who fell from earth to heaven."[33]

In the last two lamentations, the Church not only declares the place of heaven to the universal hearing of the congregation, but also the place of Eden. Since mankind, in the person of our forefathers, fell from Eden to earth, the Church indicates in its figurative language that mankind fell from "heaven." In the canon from Matins of Holy Saturday, we hear these words: "Fill with Your glory all who descended into the depths of the earth." Later we find the following phrases sprinkled throughout the canon: "The Lord revealed Himself to those living in hell ... He communed with those in hell ... Hell, O Word, met You, grieving that Your soul would not remain in hell ... Hell from below wailed at being wounded, having accepted into its heart the One Wounded with a spear in the ribs ... The Lord descended even to the treasure-houses of hell."

In the Synaxarion of Holy Saturday, we read that in this day we celebrate the burial of the Lord and His descent into Hell, that He descended into hell with His incorrupt and divine soul, after it was separated from His body by death. Various expressions concerning hell as a deep pit are used here. Evidently, throughout this service, the assumption is that hell is the underworld, being located deep within the earth.

The same opinion concerning the place of hell and paradise we also find in the service of Holy Pascha. In the Eirmos of sixth ode of the Paschal canon, we find the following words: "You descended into the depths of the earth, and you destroyed the eternal bonds that held the prisoners, O Christ." In the Synaxarion for Pascha, we read the following phrases: "The Lord today stole human nature from the treasure-holds of hell, leading man to the heavens, to the primordial state of incorruption. And so, He descended into hell, not to resurrect all the dead, but only as many as willed to believe in Him. The holy ones from before the ages, held by need, He freed from hell, and allowed all of them to enter the heavens."

Here again, we find that the "primordial state," that is, Eden, is "in the heavens." "Through Your resurrection, O Lord, Eden was opened again, and You renewed the path to heaven for us."

We also find other references to hell being within the earth in many services of the Orthodox Church. Everywhere, this reference is made as though the fact is entirely obvious and universally known, and so precision in language is rare in this case. However, we do find it occasionally, and since it appears as a universally known fact, it serves as a very compelling proof of the fact: "The veil was torn apart when You were crucified, O our Saviour, ... "

There is a similarly passing reference to the location of hell as a universally known fact in The Ladder of St John. He advises the ascetic to constantly remember the endless pit of nether flames, the "underground" terrifying places and pits, the narrow passageways, so that through such thoughts and images, his soul might tear itself away from the sensuality that had become natural to it.[34]

In other words, the teaching that hell is found within the earth is the teaching of the Orthodox Church; we find this teaching in many writings of the Holy Fathers.[35] No Holy Father rejects this teaching.[36]

In the first centuries of Christianity, when the hardened and blind zeal of the pagans led to rivers of Christian blood flowing, in Prusa, the central city of Bithynia, Patricius, the bishop of the city, was tortured and executed near some natural springs that were located near the city. The temperature and healing properties of the water were ascribed by the pagans to the gods, but St Patricius explained that the heat of the water resulted from hell being found within the earth.

St Theodora, whom we have already mentioned above, was taken to the depths of the earth after having visited the mansions of Eden. There she saw the horrifying tortures prepared for sinners in hell.

A soldier who died and came back to life, named Taxiotis, told that he had been taken by demons in the toll house of lust. They took him from the aerial realm down, into the earth. The earth parted, and he was taken through narrow and foul-smelling passageways into the nether prisons of hell, where the souls of the sinners are imprisoned in eternal darkness and torment.[37]

The Parting of the Soul from the Body

The manner of the soul's departure from the body and the circumstances surrounding it are described by the Holy Fathers for our edification and salvation. St Theodore the Studite, in his third catechesis, says,

> Brethren! Will we always remain here? No! No! Woe is us, brethren! How terrifying the mystery of death! We must always be so attentive, filled with repentance, discerning, thinking that death stands before us at this moment, thinking about how the body will be separated from the soul, how the angels will come, to say nothing of the demons. And the demons come, attracted to those addicted to passions. Think of how terrible will be the labor and suffering when we see their terrifying forms and hear the command, "Soul, come out!" At that moment, we can offer great help, consolation, and joy to those who are dying by our good deeds and the purity of our conscience. Then obedience will have great power; then humble-mindedness will bring great consolation,

then tears will help, then good deeds will make the demons disperse, patience will aid, and the enemies will turn back without any success. Then, the soul will go with great joy together with the angels directly to the Savior. But souls that have become addicted to passions and have been defeated by sins will be terrified greatly; then, the demons will be victorious and will bear that accursed soul with themselves into the nether hell, into darkness and Tartarus, for torture.

Once, two angels appeared to St Macarius of Alexandria (who was a contemporary of St Macarius the Great). This holy man abounded with gifts of the Spirit. In this conversation, one of the angels said,

> Hear, Macarius, how the souls are separated and taken away from the body, both for the righteous and the unfaithful. Imagine warriors sent by a king seizing someone, tying him up and detaining him, even if that one had no desire to be taken and even opposes it. Such a man is afflicted with terror; he shakes and fears the presence of those who take him without any mercy on a road he wishes not to travel. Just so, when the angels are sent to take the soul of some person out of his body, the soul is terrified and fears the presence of the terrifying and stern angels. Then the soul finally realizes how useless riches, good connections, or friends are in such a moment; it hears and understands the tears and weeping of the people that surround it, but it cannot utter a single word, nor raise its voice, because never before was it forced to listen to such a command. It is terrified also by the unutterable distance of the journey and the utter change in its manner of life; it is also terrified by the sight of those that now control it and show it no amount of compassion or mercy. Moreover, it is overwhelmed by sorrow because of its connection to the body; it sorrows at the imminent separation, since it is natural for them to dwell together in unity. No consolation of conscience accompanies it or helps it, except if the soul knows that it has performed good deeds. Therefore, the soul, even before the judgment of the Most High Judge, is judged by conscience.

St Cyril of Alexandria speaks extensively about the circumstances accompanying death in his homily on the departure of the soul. We present a short excerpt from it here:

What fear and trembling await you, O soul, in the day of your death! You will see terrifying, wild, cruel, unmerciful, and shameless demons surrounding you. Just this vision alone is worse than any torture. The soul, seeing them, will come into confusion, worry, seeking to hide, to run to the angels of God. The holy angels will hold the soul; together with them it rises up into the air, where it encounters the toll houses that guard the path from earth heaven, that hold the soul and prevent it from going further. Each toll house tests the soul for specific sins; each sin, each passion has its own testers. What terror and fear and confusion will await the soul seeing all this, until the final judgment is uttered that frees it from this torture! Terrible and filled with groaning is this hour of uncertainty. The divine powers stand against the impure spirits and offer the good thoughts and deeds that belong to the soul, while it, in fear and trembling, standing between the angels and demons that fight over it, awaits either its justification and freedom or its condemnation and perdition. If it lived a pious life, pleasing to God, and was made worthy of salvation, then the angels will take it, and it will calmly continue its path to God, having the holy powers as its fellow travelers. Then will be fulfilled the words: sorrow, sickness, and sighing have fled away. Then, having been freed form the evil, rotten, and terrifying spirits, it will continue to unutterable joy. However, if it becomes clear that the soul lived in lust and lack of attention, then it will hear the horrifying voice: "Let the iniquitous be taken, lest he see the glory of the Lord!" Then will begin the days of wrath, sorrow, need, and pain, days of darkness ... The soul is abandoned by God's angels and seized by the black spirits of evil. They begin to beat it mercilessly and take it to the earth, having opened the cracks of the earth, they cast the soul, tied with unbreakable bonds, into the dark country, the nether prisons of hell, where the souls of sinners are imprisoned, as Job said, in a land that is terrible and dark, a land of eternal murk, where there is no light, nor life for man, but only eternal sickness and sorrow and weeping and gnashing of teeth without end and never-ending groaning. There we hear the constant "Woe is me! Woe is me!" There the souls cry out, but there is no one to help; there they cry out, and no one delivers them. There is no opportunity to know the degree of that calamity. There is no chance to express the degree of that sickness to which the souls imprisoned there are subjected. All human language falls silent when trying to explain the terror and fear that possess the inhabitants of hell; no human words can express the pain and the sorrow; constantly and eternally they cry out, and no one has mercy on them. They sigh profoundly, but no one hears them. They weep, but no one redeems them. They cry out, but no one has compassion on them. Where is the glory of this world? Where is vanity? Where is pleasure? Where is satiety? Where is nobility? Where is the courage of the flesh? Where is feminine beauty, so delusive and dangerous? Where is shameless brazenness? Where are the beautiful ornaments and clothing? Where is the sweetness of sin, so impure and vile? Where are those who cover themselves with perfumes and fine oils? Where are those who feast with music? Where is the passion for money and inheritance and all the lack of compassion that comes from them? Where is inhuman pride that abhors everyone and that teaches only to respect oneself? Where is the empty and vain glory of man, where are the spectacles and games? Where are those who blaspheme or live idly? Where are their soft clothes and soft beds? Where are their tall buildings and wide gates? Where is the wisdom of the wise, the oratory of the speakers, and the vanity of education? Alas! All these will fall, utterly surprised, and their wisdom will be swallowed up. Brethren! Listen how we must live, for we must give account for our every action, both small and great! We must even answer for every idle word to the Righteous Judge![38]

The aforementioned warrior Taxiotis had this to say about his own death:

When I was dying, I saw the demons surrounding me. Their appearance was terrifying; my soul, as it looked at them, was in great confusion. Then I saw before myself two beautiful youths, and my soul jumped into their arms. We began to ascend into the air to a great height, as though flying, and we came to the toll houses that guard the entrance to heaven and detain every human soul. Every toll house tested a certain kind of sin: there was one for falsehood, another for envy, another for price. Each sin had its own testers. And I saw that the angels held all my good deeds in a treasure box, taking them out and comparing them with my evil deeds. Thus, we passed the toll houses. As we approached the gates of heaven, we came to the toll house of lust. Those who guard that toll house detained me, and showed to me all my sins of the flesh from my childhood. The angels who led me said, "All the sins of the flesh that you committed in the city God has forgiven you, because you repented of them." But the enemies retorted, "But when you left the city, you sinned with the wife of your landowner." The angels, having heard this, and not finding a good deed that might counteract this sin, abandoned me. Then the evil spirits sized me, and beating me with whips, they took me to the earth. The earth opened up, and I was taken through narrow and foul-smelling descents into the nether prisons of hell.

Theodora, the disciple of the great saint of God Basil the New, gave an especially detailed account of her own death. Here we offer an excerpt of her vision:

"My child Gregory," she said, "you have asked me about a terrible thing, which it is frightening even to recollect."

"When the hour of my death came, I saw faces such as I had never seen before, and heard words such as I had never heard. What shall I say? Cruel and hard-to-endure evils, of which I formerly had no idea, encountered me then because of my evil deeds. However, through the prayers and the assistance of our common spiritual father Basil, I was saved from these hardships. But how shall I tell you about that physical pain, that stress and close feeling which the dying experience? Like a man who, entirely naked, falls into a great fire, burns, melts, and turns into ashes; so the dying are destroyed by their deathly illness in the bitter hour when the soul parts from the body."

"When I drew near the end of my life and the time of my departure had come, I saw a great multitude of demons who had surrounded my couch. Their faces were dark like soot and pitch, their eyes were like glowing coals, their entire appearance was as frightening and evil as fiery hell itself. They began to grow indignant and to make noise like dogs; others howled like wolves. As they looked at me, they were full of anger; they threatened me kept rushing at me and gnashing their teeth, and appeared ready to devour me. Yet they seemed to wait for a Judge who had not yet come but would do so; they were making ready charts and unrolling scrolls on which were written all my evil deeds. My miserable soul was taken by great fear and trembling. Not only the bitterness of death tormented me but even more the terrible appearance and the cruel demeanor of the frightening demons; these were to me like another death, only a worse one. I kept turning away my eyes in all directions so as not to see their terrible faces, and wished not to hear their voices, but I was unable to be rid of them. They turned everywhere and there was no one to help me."

"When I was at the end of my strength I saw two radiant angels of God, who were like youths of inexpressible beauty. They were coming toward me. Their faces were shining, their gaze was full of love; their hair was like snow, white with a golden tinge; their garments glistened like lightning and were girded with gold. When they came near me, they stopped on the right side of my couch and entered into a quiet conversation between themselves. As I saw them I was filled with joy and looked at them with pleasure."

"The black demons shuddered and retreated some distance. One of the radiant youths, angrily addressing the black ones, said, 'O shameless, cursed, dark, and evil enemies of the human race! Why do you always come first to the dying, and frighten and confuse every parting soul by your words? You have no reason to rejoice, for here you will find nothing. God is merciful to this soul, and you have no part and no allotment in her.' When the angel ceased speaking, the demons tottered, began to cry out, and mutter, and point to all my evil deeds, committed from my youth on. They exclaimed, 'We have no part in her, you say! Whose sins then are these? Did she not do such and such?' With such exclamations they kept their position and were waiting for death. When death came, it was roaring like a lion and was very frightening in appearance. It looked like a human being but had no body; instead it consisted of human bones. Death brought various instruments of torture, such as swords, arrows, javelins, sickles, saws, and others unknown to me. When I saw these, my humble soul trembled with fear. The holy angels said to death, 'Do not tarry, free this soul from its bodily ties, and do it

fast and quietly, for she has but a small burden of sins.' Death stepped up
to me, took a small axe and separated my legs, then my arms; then with
its other instruments it weakened all the rest of my limbs, separating
them joint by joint. I lost the use of my arms and legs, my whole body
grew numb, and I no longer was able to move. Finally death cut off my
head, and I no longer could move it, for it felt as if it belonged to someone else. Lastly, death dissolved in a cup some kind of mixture, and putting the cup to my lips, made me drink. The potion was so bitter that my
soul was unable to endure it. It shuddered and went out of my body."

"The light-bearing angels immediately took it in their arms. When I
looked back I saw my body lying breathless and immovable. I looked at
my body like someone who has taken off his clothes and thrown them
down; this was a strange feeling. Meanwhile, although the holy angels
were holding me, the demons surrounded us and cried: 'This soul has a
multitude of sins—let her answer for them!' They kept pointing to my
sins, but the holy angels sought out my good deeds; and indeed, with
God's help they found all that, by God's grace, I ever did of good. The
angels gathered together everything that was good: all those instances
when I gave alms to the needy, or fed the hungry, or gave drink to the
thirsty, or clothed the naked, or brought into my house and rested
there the homeless, or served the servants of God, or brought comfort
to the sick or those who were imprisoned; or when I went with diligence to God's house and prayed with all my heart and shed tears, or
when I attentively listened to what was read and sung in church, or
brought to church incense and candles, or filled with oil the church
lamps before the icons, or kissed the icons with awe and reverence; or
when I fasted and abstained on Wednesdays, Fridays, or during other
fasts, or when I prostrated myself before God and spent nights awake
in prayer, or when I sighed to God and wept for my sins, or confessed
my sins before my spiritual father with great regret for what I had
done, and then tried with all my strength to balance my sins with good
deeds; or when I did anything good to my neighbors, when I bore no
anger to my enemies, bore no grudges and meekly endured hurts and
reproaches, did good in return for evil, humbled myself, felt sorry for
those who suffered and commiserated with those to whom anything

bad happened, comforted those who were weeping and rendered them assistance, supported any good beginning and tried to turn people away from what was bad; or for myself turned my eyes away from vanity and kept my tongue from oaths, lies, or bearing false witness, or speaking without need—and all my other good deeds, even the least important ones, did the holy angels gather and make ready to put on the scale in order to balance my evil deeds."

"The demons, however, saw this and gnashed their teeth at me. They wanted to tear me instantly from the angels' arms and to carry me down to the bottom of hell. At this time, holy Basil himself appeared unexpectedly and said to the holy angels: 'Holy angels! This soul did great service to ease my old age, and therefore I prayed for her to God, and God has given her to me.' Having said this, he took something out that appeared like a little bag of gold and gave it to the angels with the words, 'Here is the treasure of prayers before the Lord for this soul! As you pass through the torments of the air and the evil spirits begin to torment her, pay her debts with this.'"

"He then disappeared, but the evil spirits, when they saw the gift from holy Basil, at first stood dumbfounded. Then they raised plaintive cries and became invisible. Then Basil, the man who had pleased God, came again. He bore many vessels of pure oil and precious myrrh, and all these, one after the other, he poured on me. I was filled with spiritual fragrance and felt that I had changed and become very light. Once more the holy man said to the angels: 'When, holy angels, you will have done for this soul all that is needed, lead her to the dwelling that the Lord has prepared for me, and let her remain there.' Then once more he became invisible. The holy angels took me up, and we went eastward through the air."[39]

In the Holy Gospel, we see an indication that the circumstances surrounding human death are the same as those offered in these writings of the Fathers. The Lord said that the soul of the poor man Lazarus "was carried by the angels to Abraham's bosom" (Luke 16:22). The avaricious rich man who imagined that he would live a long life because of his earthly successes, heard the following from God: "Fool! This night your soul will be required of you; then whose will those things be which you have provided?" (Luke 12:20). The Lord says "required," according to the interpretation of these words of the Gospel by Blessed Theophylact who writes that the soul is required by the unmerciful toll-collecting angels, who tear out the soul of the sinner in a terrifying manner. The soul of the righteous man is not torn out of him; he, rejoicing, gives his spirit to his God and Father.

Even though the death of the righteous or repentant sinners completely, or at least in most ways, differs from the death of rejected sinners or sinners who have not repented enough, still, fear and trembling are natural for every man at the moment of his death. This is how it must be, for death is an execution. Even the God-Man, preparing to accept his willing death for the salvation of man, greatly sorrowed and suffered. The sweat that fell from his brow was as blood pouring from a wound: "My soul is exceedingly sorrowful, even to death" (Matt 26:38), He said to the apostles who had fallen asleep from their confusion and who did not feel the nearness of the danger. "O My Father, if it is possible, let his cup pass from Me; nevertheless, not as I will, but as You will" (Matt 26:39). This is how He prayed to His Father. The most holy Virgin Theotokos also felt terror before her death, even though she had been warned of her coming death by Archangel Gabriel and told of the mansions above and the glory that awaited her, even though the Holy Spirit, who abounded in her, had already taken all her thoughts and desires to heaven in advance.[40]

All the saints prepare themselves for the fateful hour of death with fear and weeping, for they understand the significance of this moment fully. When St Agathon's death was about to come, he spent three days in intense attention to himself, not speaking to anyone. The brethren asked him, "Abba Agathon, where are you?"

And he answered, "I am standing before the judgment of Christ."

The brethren responded, "Is it possible, father, that you are afraid?"

He answered, "I tried to live by the commandments of God, but I am a man and how can I know whether my deeds were pleasing to God?"

The brothers then asked, "Do you not trust in your own life, which was lived in accordance with the will of God?"

"I cannot trust in it," he answered, "because the judgments of man are not the same as the judgments of God."

They wanted to ask him more questions, but he said, "Show me your love, and do not speak to me anymore, for I am not free."

And he died with joy. "We saw him rejoicing," his disciples said, "as though he were greeting dear friends."

This saint of God constantly and strictly attended to himself and said that without intense self-examination, no person can achieve success.[41] This is the path to salvation. The saints of God, who constantly examined themselves, constantly found within themselves new failing, and once they found them, they plunged ever deeper into repentance that purified them and prepared them for heaven. On the contrary, evil inattentiveness and busyness are always connected with a profound ignorance concerning oneself; not surprisingly, such self-ignorance is always very self-satisfied and proud of itself. "Many delude themselves," said Blessed Theophylact, "with vain hope, thinking that they will receive the kingdom of heaven, and they in advance add themselves to the ranks of those who rose up because of their virtue, imagining great things about themselves ... Many are called, because God calls many, even all, but there are few chosen, few who are saved, few who are worthy of being chosen by God. To call is God's work, but to be chosen is ours: the Jews were called, but were not chosen, for they were not obedient to the One Who called."[42]

St Arsenius, who was great among monks, during the entire course of his life, whenever he did manual labor, put a kerchief on his knees because of the amount of tears that fell from his eyes. He died. Abba Pœmen, a father who was gifted with unusually profound spiritual discernment, said upon hearing of this man's death, "You are blessed, Arsenius, for you wept for yourself during this life. Whoever does not weep for himself here will weep eternally. It is impossible to run away from weeping. Either you weep here willingly, or you will weep there unwillingly, in tortures." Hearing of this death, Patriarch Theophilus of Alexandria said, "Blessed are you, Abba Arsenius! You constantly remembered the hour of your own death."[43]

The Death of the Righteous and the Sinner

Here is a comforting account of the death of the righteous, which is edifying and salvific in its description of the proper compunction and humility of heart that the saints had in preparation for death. A certain father lived so purely that he was never denied any request he made of God. This elder once desired to see the separation of the soul from the body, both of a righteous man and a sinner. Brought by the hand of God to a certain city, he stopped at the gates in the monastery in which lived a rather famous recluse. At that moment, the recluse was sick and awaited death. The elder saw that a great preparation was being made of candles and oil lamps for the recluse, as though it was because of him that the Lord gave this city bread and water and protected it. The city dwellers even said to one another, "If this recluse dies, we will all perish at once."

In the meantime, the hour of this recluse's death arrived. The elder saw an emissary from hell with a fiery trident in his hands descending on the recluse, and he heard a voice saying, "Since this soul never comforted Me in himself for a single hour, you may tear the soul out without mercy." The demon pierced the heart of the recluse with his fiery trident, and having tortured him for several hours, pulled out his soul.

After this, the elder came into the city, where he found a certain sick wanderer who lay on the street. There was no one to serve this wanderer. The elder saw that the Archangels Michael and Gabriel themselves came down to take his soul. One of them sat at his right, the other at his left side, and they began to ask the soul to leave the body. It did not want to leave and refused to come out. Then Gabriel said to Michael, "Let us take this soul and go." Michael answered, "It is commanded us by the Lord to take this soul without pain. We cannot take it by violence." After these words, Michael exclaimed with a loud voice, "Lord! What do you command us to do with this soul? It will not listen to us and does not want to come out." And a voice came down from heaven, "Behold! I send down David with his Psalter and a choir of God's heavenly Jerusalem, so that the soul, hearing their psalmody and voices, will come out." They came down and surrounded the soul, singing hymns, and only then did the soul come out into Michael's arms, and was received with joy.[44]

Who will not wonder at God's love and mercy to the human race? Unfortunately, to our great misfortune, we hard-heartedly push away all the mercies of God and with foolish blindness stand in the rows of the servants and followers of the enemy of God and mankind.

The end of the chosen ones of God is filled with glory. When Sisoes the Great approached his death, his face lit up, and he said to the fathers who sat with him: "Here comes Abba Anthony!" Then he sat for a while in silence and said, "Here comes the choir of the apostles." And his face brightened even more; he began to speak with someone. The elders asked him to tell them with whom he was speaking. He answered, "The angels have come to take me; but I am begging them that they leave me a little more time for repentance." The elders said to him, "Father, you are not in need of repentance." But he answered, "Truly, I do not know if I have even begun to repent." And then, they all knew that he was perfect. This is how a true Christian sees himself, in spite of the fact that during his own life he resurrected the dead with a single word and was filled with the gifts of the Holy Spirit. And then, his voice was illumined even more, shining like the sun. All present were afraid. And he said to then, "Look! The Lord has come, and He has said, 'Bring Me my chosen vessel from the desert.'" With these words, he died. Lightning flashed at that moment, and the room was filled with a sweet fragrance. This is how one of the great saints ended his earthly life.[45]

But even sinners who offer sincere repentance of their sins are found worthy of God's mercy. During the reign of the Roman Emperor Maurice, there lived in Thrace a cruel and savage robber. No one could capture him, no matter how hard they tried. The blessed emperor, hearing of this, had his own personal cross sent to the robber with a message that he should not be afraid, that with this sign all his evil deeds were forgiven under the condition of his complete reformation. The robber was brought to compunction by this act, came to the king, and fell at his feet, repenting of his crimes. After some days, he grew ill and was placed in home for wanderers, where he saw a dream of the final judgment. Having woken up and noticed that his disease was worse and that he was nearing his end, he turned to prayer with tears:

Lord King and Lover of mankind, You Who saved a thief like me, show Your mercy on me as well. Accept these tears on my deathbed. As You accepted those who came to work at the eleventh hour, though they had done nothing worthy until then, so accept my bitter tears, cleanse and baptize me with them. Expect nothing more of me than this; I have no more time, and the creditors approach. Do not test me or seek more from me; You will find in me nothing good; my iniquities have preceded me, and I have come to my evening. Countless are my crimes. As You accepted the tears of the apostle Peter, so accept these, my small tears and erase the manuscript of my sins. With the power of Your mercy, destroy my iniquities.

Praying thus for the space of several hours, wiping away his tears with a napkin, the thief passed away. In the hour of his death, the chief physician of that house saw a dream: black demons approached bedside of the thief with sheets of paper filled with the many sins of the thief; then, two beautiful young noblemen brought a pair of scales. The demons put all the sins on one side, and the scales dropped to the ground. Then the holy angels said, "Do we not have anything here? What can we possible find here, considering that it is no more than ten days since he stopped killing people? Still, we will find something." One of them found the handkerchief of the thief, filled with his tears, and said to the other, "Look, this handkerchief is filled with his tears. Let us put it on the scales, together with the Love of God for mankind, and let us see what happens."

No sooner had they placed the kerchief onto the scales than they tipped to the other side. The holy angels said in one voice, "Truly the love of God for man has triumphed!" Taking the soul of the thief, they led it away. The demons wailed and left in shame. When the physician woke up, he went to visit the thief. He saw the body still warm, just recently deceased. The handkerchief, soaked with tears, lay on his eyes. When he heard from the other wanderers in the house about the nature of the thief's repentance, the physician took the handkerchief and gave it to the emperor, saying, "Lord! Let us glorify God, for in your reign also was a thief saved." However, the final words of the writer of this account are very wise in their warning: it is better to prepare yourself for death in good time than to hope for a last-minute repentance at the terrible hour of passing.[46]

True are the words of St John of the Ladder, when he said that evil that turns from frequent repetition into an essential quality of a person becomes impossible to heal.[47] "An evil habit rules as a tyrant, even over those who weep."[48] To this we must add that repentance is only possible if a person has a correct, even if simple, understanding of the Orthodox

Christian Faith, free of any heresy or false wisdom. Those who have their worldview formed by the virtues and rules found in novels and other soul-corrupting heretical books cannot have true repentance. Such people dismiss many mortal sins that lead to hell as negligible, forgivable mistakes, and tend to excuse fierce sinful passions as frivolous and pleasant weaknesses. They do not even fear to fall into these passions even at the very gates of death. The ignorance of such Christians is a horrible tragedy!

The Lord calls people to repentance and salvation until the last moment of their lives. In this final moment, the doors of God's mercy are still open to anyone who wants to enter. Let no one despair! While the field is still open, all the labor counts. The last minutes of a person's life can redeem his entire life. In Egypt, there lived a certain virgin named Thaïs, an orphan, who decided to turn her house into a refuge for traveling monks from the Egyptian desert. Many years passed, during which she gave refuge to many fathers. Finally, all her money ran out. She began to suffer from want. Certain ill-willed people befriended her and turned her away from virtue; she began to lead a sinful life, even a debauched one. The fathers, hearing of this, were very saddened. They called Abba John Kolobos ("the Dwarf") and said, "We heard that Sister Thaïs has turned aside from a virtuous life. When she had money, she showed us love; now we must do the same and help her." Abba John came to her and asked the old woman who guarded the front door to tell Thaïs of his arrival. But she answered, "You monks wasted all her inheritance!" Abba John said, "Tell her that I have something to her great advantage."

The old woman did so. Thaïs said to the old woman, "These monks who constantly walk by the shores of the Black Sea sometimes find pearls and precious stones; come, bring him to me." Abba John came to her and sat next to her. When he looked at her face, he lowered his head and began to weep bitterly. She said to him, "Father, why are you crying?" He answered, "I see that Satan is playing on your face, and so how can I fail to weep? Did Jesus displease you so much that you turned to deeds that are abhorrent to him?" When she heard this, she began to tremble, and said, "Abba! Is there any repentance for me?" He said, "There is."

"Take me, wherever you will," she said to him, and getting up, she followed him. John, noticing that she said nothing about the care of her home, was amazed. When they reached the desert, it grew dark. He made a hole for cover out of the sand for her and for himself. Making the sign of the cross over her makeshift home, he said, "You will sleep here." Having finished his prayer rule, he lay down to sleep. At midnight, John woke up and saw that a path appeared from the place where Thaïs slept to heaven, and the angels of God were taking her soul up that path. He got up to wake her up, but she had already died. John fell on his face in prayer, and he heard a voice, "One hour of her repentance is accepted over the long repentance of many others who did not show such self-rejection in their repentance."[49]

"Lord! For Your servants who abandon their bodies and come to you, our God, there is no death, but only a passage from sorrow to what is pleasant and sweet, to consolation and joy."[50]

Truly, the separation of the soul from the body is not death; it is only the consequence of death. There is a much more horrifying death. There is the death that is the source of all human sickness, both of soul and body, as well as the physical death that we call death. St Macarius the Great explains: "True death is hidden in the heart, and through it the external man passed from life to death. If anyone in the hidden places of his heart passes from death to life, then such a person will truly live for all ages, and will never die. Though for such people the bodies part for a time from their souls; however, they are sanctified, and they will rise again in glory. This is why we call the death of the saints 'sleep.'"[51]

Spiritual Death

The very word and understanding of death first astonished the hearing and thought of mankind when they entered Eden. Among the trees of Eden were two especially notable trees: the tree of life and the tree of the knowledge of good and evil. As the Lord led man into Eden, He commanded him, "You may eat food from every tree of the garden; but of the tree of the knowledge of good and evil you may not eat, for in whateverday you eat from it, you shall die by death" (Gen 2:16–17). In spite of this terrifying threat of death, man disobeyed the commandment, and, after this rebellion, immediately died; that is, death immediately appeared in all the movements of the soul and the sensations of the body. The Holy Spirit that lived in mankind, that imparted him immortality of soul and body, that was the source of man's life, left mankind, since they broke communion with God by their willful rejection of His command and by their equally willing entry into communion with Satan.

St Gregory Palamas said:

> As the separation of the soul from the body is the death of the body, so the separation of God from the soul is the death of the soul. And this death of the soul is the true death. This is made clear by the commandment given in paradise, when God said to Adam, "On whatever day you eat from the forbidden tree you will certainly die" (cf. Gen 2:17). And it was indeed Adam's soul that died by becoming through his transgression separated from God; for bodily he continued to live after that time, even for nine hundred and thirty years (cf. Gen 5:5). The death, however, that befell the soul because of the transgression not only crippled the soul and made man accursed; it also rendered the body itself subject to fatigue, suffering and corruptibility, and finally handed it over to death. For it was after the dying of his inner self brought about by the transgression that the earthly Adam heard the words, "Earth will be cursed because of what you do, it will produce thorns and thistles for you; through the sweat of your brow you will eat your bread until you return to the earth from which you were taken: for you are earth, and to earth you will return" (Gen 3:17-19).[52]

Signifying the death of the soul, St John the Theologian wrote, "There is sin leading to death .... and there is sin not leading to death" (1 John 5:16-17). Sin leading to death is sin that kills the soul, the kind of sin that completely separates man from divine grace and makes him a victim of hell if he does not heal himself with active and powerful repentance that is capable of restoring his union with God. With such repentance the apostle Peter healed his mortal sin of denying Christ, while King David showed similar repentance of his two mortal sins: adultery and murder. Repentance is only effective when man, having turned away from his sin and confessed it, then abandons it completely.[53] This is the repentance of those harlots, adulterers, publicans, and thieves that took the kingdom of heaven by violence; this is the repentance leading to resurrection of death of the soul, to which the apostle Paul calls us, "Awake, you who sleep, arise from the dead, and Christ will give you light" (Eph 5:14).

But who listens to this call, this spiritual trumpet that calls to the resurrection of the soul, to a resurrection more necessary for salvation than the raising of the body? We all remain in our deadness, fulfilling all our sinful desires that not only war against the soul, but being fulfilled, kill the soul as well. Indicating this death of the soul, this essential death, the Saviour of the world labeled all His contemporaries who did not listen to His all-holy teaching (a teaching necessary for salvation, the "one thing needful" [Luke 10:42] for true human life) as walking dead men: "Let the dead bury their own dead, but you go and preach the kingdom of God" (Luke 9:60). This is what He said to one of His followers who asked permission to leave the Lord and His holy teaching for a time, in order to bury his recently deceased parent. The Lord called those who lived by the flesh "dead" men, since they were truly dead, dead in spirit.[54] Those among such dead people who remain distant from Christ during their earthly lives and pass on to eternity in the same state will not know resurrection during the entire course of time given for this resurrection (that is, between the two comings of Christ): "But the rest of the dead did not live again until the two thousand years were finished" (Rev 20:5).

The son of spiritual thunder continues: "Blessed and holy is he who has part in the first resurrection. Over such the second death has no power, but they shall be priests of God and of Christ, and shall reign with Him a thousand years" (Rev 20:6). The Church's generally received interpretation of this prophecy is that the thousand years is not an exact number of years, but a symbol for the very long time allotted by the mercy and long-suffering of God for all the fruits on earth who are worthy of heaven to grow ripe and ready for the granaries of heaven and not to be lost.

When the saints of God in the early Church had come to consider that the sins of the world were too great for the world to continue, making the final judgment of God necessary and imminent, this is what they heard from God: "It was said to them that they should rest a little while longer, until both the number of their fellow servants and their brethren, who would be killed as they were, was completed" (Rev 6:11). This is how long-suffering and great is the mercy of God! According to the interpretation of St Andrew of Cæsarea, "The thousand years indicate the time from the incarnation of Christ until His glorious second coming ... This is the thousand years during which the Gospel is to be preached."

There is need to stumble over the precise number of one thousand years. Such numbers have no literal meaning, neither in the Song of Songs: "Solomon had a vineyard at Baal Hamon": and everyone "was to bring a thousand silver coins for its fruit." "You, O Solomon, shall have a thousand, and those who keep its fruit, two hundred" (Song of Songs 8:11–12), nor in the words of the Lord Jesus: "But others fell on good ground and yielded a crop: some a hundredfold, some sixty, some thirty" (Matt 13:8). Such round numbers symbolize abundances and completeness. From the beginning of this "millennium," and even until this day, the first, mystical, essential resurrection of the dead is being revealed; it will continue to the end of time. "Most assuredly, I say to you, he who hears My word and believes in Him who sent Me has everlasting life, and shall not come into judgment, but has passed from death into life" (John 5:24).

Interpreting this passage, Blessed Theophylact writes that those who believe in Christ will not come to judgment, that is, to torment, but will live with an everlasting life, not being ever subjected to the eternal, spiritual death, even if he tasted in his nature the temporary death of the body. The Lord's words to Martha at Lazarus's resurrection have the same meaning: "I am the resurrection and the life. He who believes in Me, though he may die, he shall live. And whoever lives and believes in Me shall never die" (John 11:25–26). The sons and daughters of the old Adam, born in the image and likeness of his fallenness, born for eternal death, pass through faith in the New Adam to eternal life. This passage, this resurrection, is invisible for the physical eyes, inconceivable to the carnal mind, but it is clear and evident for the soul that is resurrected. As St Macarius the Great said,

> When you hear that Christ, having descended to hell, freed the souls imprisoned there, do not think that this event occurred at such a distance from what occurs now. Know this: the tomb is your heart, and there your mind and thoughts are buried and imprisoned in utter

darkness. The Lord comes to the souls that cry out to Him from hell, that is, He comes to the depths of the heart and there commands death to release the imprisoned souls that implore Him, the only One Who can free them, to be freed. Then, having cast aside the heavy stone lying on the soul, He opens the tomb, He raises the dead soul, and He leads it from prison to the light.[55]

The first resurrection is accomplished thanks to two sacraments: baptism and repentance. Through holy baptism, the soul is raised from the tomb of unbelief and iniquity, or from the stain of original sin and one's own personal sins committed in ignorance. Through repentance, the faithful soul rises from the death of mortal sin, or a frivolous and sensual life, after baptism. The one who resurrects is the Holy Spirit.

St John the Theologian saw those who were raised from spiritual death, and he said of them, "And I saw thrones, and they sat on them, and judgment was committed to them. Then I saw the souls of those who had been beheaded for their witness to Jesus and for the word of God, who had not worshiped the beast or his image, and had not received his mark on their foreheads or on their hands. And they lived and reigned with Christ for a thousand years .... This is the first resurrection" (Rev 20:4-5). This first resurrection is the revitalization of the soul from its death through faith in the Lord Jesus Christ, through the washing away of sin by Holy Baptism, through a life lived according to the commandments of Christ and through the purification, in confession, of sins committed after baptism. The thrones of the saints represent their mastery over their passions, the demons themselves, the limitations of mankind, storms, and beasts. They represent the abundance of their spiritual gifts.

They are given judgment, that is, spiritual discernment, through which they accuse and reject sin, no matter how well it hides under a mask of good. This judgment allows them to condemn the demons of darkness who assume the image of angels of light, and not to allow them to delude them. They bow neither to the Beast nor to his idol, not to antichrist nor to the forerunners of antichrist who persecute Christianity, who demand that Christians deny Christ and reject His all-holy commandments. They did not allow the mark of the enemy of God to be impressed on their forehead or their right hand, but having assimilated the mind of Christ, they constantly expressed it in their manner of thinking and their way of life, not sparing even their blood to prove their faithfulness to Christ, and so they reigned with Him.

For them, there is no death! For them, the separation of the body and soul (we repeat the aforementioned thought of St Basil the Great) is not death, but passage from a sorrowful earthly wandering to eternal joy and consolation. "The second death," that is, the final condemnation to eternal hellish tortures, "has no power" over those who were raised by the first resurrection. These resurrected ones "shall be priests of God and of Christ, and shall reign with Him a thousand years" (Rev 20:6).

This reigning of the priests of God in the Holy Spirit cannot be interrupted by the separation of the soul from the body; on the contrary, it develops and becomes all the more established. "Now when the thousand years have expired" (Rev 20:7), the time will come, the noetic fruit of the earth will ripen, and then will follow the second resurrection, the resurrection of the body. After it, the blessedness of the righteous, who were raised in good time with the first resurrection, will become even greater. However, the death of the rejected sinners, who were denied the first resurrection, will become even worse.

Eternal Death

Even though at the regeneration to come, in the resurrection of the righteous, the bodies of the godless and sinners will also be raised up, yet they will be given over to the second death, age-long chastisement, the unsleeping worm (cf. Mark 9:44), the gnashing of teeth, the outer, tangible darkness (cf. Matt. 8:12), the murky and unquenchable fire of Gehenna (cf. Matt. 5:22), in which, as the prophet says, the godless and sinners "will be burned up together and there will be none to quench the flame" (Isa. 1:31). For this is the second death, as St John has taught us in the Revelation (cf. Rev. 20:14). Hark, too, to the words of the Great St Paul, "If you live in accordance with your fallen self, you will die, but if through the Spirit you extirpate the evil actions of your fallen self, you will live" (Rom. 8:13). Here he speaks of life and death in the age to be: life is the enjoyment of the everlasting kingdom, death age-long chastisement.

Thus the violation of God's commandment is the cause of all types of death, both of soul and body, whether in the present life or in that endless chastisement. And death, properly speaking, is this: for the soul to be unharnessed from divine grace and to be yoked to sin. This death, for those who have their wits, is truly dreadful and something to be avoided. This, for those who think aright, is more terrible than the chastisement of Gehenna. From this let us also flee with all our might. Let us cast away, let us reject all things, bid farewell to all things: to all relationships, actions and intentions that drag us downward, separate us from God and produce such a death. He who is frightened of this death and has preserved himself from it will not be alarmed by the oncoming death of the body, for in him the true life dwells, and bodily death, so far from taking true life away, renders it inalienable.

As the death of the soul is authentic death, so the life of the soul is authentic life. Life of the soul is union with God, as life of the body is its union with the soul. As the soul was separated from God and died in consequence of the violation of the commandment, so by obedience to the commandment it is again united to God and is quickened. This is why the Lord says in the Gospels, "The words I speak to you are spirit and life" (John 6:63). And having experienced the truth of this, St Peter said to Him, "Thy words are the words of eternal life" (John 6:68). But they are words of eternal life for those who obey them; for those who disobey, this commandment of life results in death (cf. Rom. 7:10). So it was that the apostles, being Christ's fragrance, were to some the death-inducing odor of death, while to others they were the life-inducing odor of life (cf. 2 Cor 2:16).

And this life is not only the life of the soul, it is also the life of the body. Through resurrection the body is also rendered immortal: it is delivered not merely from mortality, but also from that never-abating death of future chastisement. On it, too, is bestowed everlasting life in Christ, free of pain, sickness and sorrow, and truly immortal.

The death of the soul through transgression and sin is, then, followed by the death of the body and by its dissolution in the earth and its conversion into dust; and this bodily death is followed in its turn by the soul's banishment to Hades. In the same way the resurrection of the soul—its return to God through obedience to the divine commandments—is followed by the body's resurrection and its reunion with the soul. And for those who experience it the consequence of this resurrection will be true incorruption and eternal life with God: they will become spiritual instead of non-spiritual, and will dwell in heaven as angels of God (cf. Matt. 22:30).

As St Paul says, "We shall be caught up in the clouds to meet the Lord in the air, and so we shall be with the Lord for ever" (1 Thess. 4:17). The Son of God, who in His compassion became man, died so far as His body was concerned when His soul was separated from His body; but this body was not separated from His divinity, and so He raised up His body once more and took it with Him to heaven in glory. Similarly, when those who have lived here in a godly manner are separated from their bodies, they are not separated from God, and in the resurrection they will take their bodies with them to God, and in their bodies they will enter with inexpressible joy there where Jesus has preceded us (cf Heb. 6:20) and in their bodies they will enjoy the glory that will be revealed in Christ (cf. 1 Pet. 5:1). Indeed, they will share not only in resurrection, but also in the Lord's ascension and in all divine life. But this does not apply to those who live this present life in an unregenerate manner and who at death have no communion with God. For though all will be resurrected, yet the resurrection of each individual will be in accordance with his own inner state (cf. 1 Cor 15:23). He who through the power of the Spirit has extirpated his materialistic worldly proclivities in this life will hereafter live a divine and truly eternal life in communion with Christ. But he who through surrendering to his materialistic and worldly lusts and passions has in this life deadened his spiritual being will, alas, hereafter be co-judged with the devil, the agent-provocateur of evil, and will be handed over to unbearable and immeasurable chastisement, which is the second and final death.

Where did true death—the death that produces and induces in soul and body both temporal and eternal death—have its origin? Was it not in the realm of life? Thus was man, alas, at once banished from God's paradise, for he had imbued his life with death and made it unfit for paradise. Consequently true life—the life that confers immortality and true life on both soul and body—will have its origin here, in this place of death. If you do not strive here to gain this life in your soul, do not deceive yourself with vain hopes about receiving it hereafter, or about God then being compassionate towards you. For then is the time of requital and retribution, not of sympathy and compassion: the time for the revealing of God's wrath and anger and just judgment, for the manifestation of the mighty and sublime power that brings chastisement upon unbelievers. Woe to him who falls into the hands of the living God (cf. Heb. 10:31)! Woe to him who hereafter experiences the Lord's wrath, who has not acquired in this life the fear of God and so come to know the might of His anger, who has not through his actions gained a foretaste of God's compassion! For the time to do all this is the present life. That is the reason why God has accorded us this present life, giving us a place for repentance.[56]

The eternal sufferings that await sinners in hell are so horrible that no person living on earth can have any clear understanding of it, outside of a special revelation from God. All our horrifying physical illnesses and dangers, all the worst earthly sufferings and sorrows are nothing compared to the suffering in hell. In vain do the sensual epicureans cry out, "It is not possible that the sufferings of hell, if it even exists, can be that horrible or eternal! This is incompatible with either the mercy of God or human reason. Man exists on this earth for pleasures; he is surrounded by objects of pleasure: why should he not use them? What is so evil or sinful about that?"

Leaving this challenge to the conscience of those who utter it and contrast it to the divine revelation and teaching, the son of the holy Church, who lives on earth for the sake of repentance, cultivates a worldview considering the sufferings of hell that is inspired by the word of God. After all, there is no limit to what the much-passionate human heart will reject, the better to give itself up to debauchery! It has used human reason as a blind tool of its own sinful desires, all the while calling its own reason healthy and robust. For the sake of sinful freedom, it has rejected the teaching about God and His commandments, which was announced on earth by the Son of God Himself. It has rejected the sweet spiritual pleasure that is given by the love of God. Is it any wonder that it has rejected the reins and the threatening that stops a sinner in his tracks, rejecting even hell and eternal sufferings? But they do exist.

Any sin of a limited creature before its unlimited and perfect Creator is an eternal sin. Such a sin demands eternal retribution. Any punishment of a creature for a sin against its Creator must completely dissolve that sin's existence: hell with its terrible and eternal sufferings satisfies this requirement of implacable justice.[57]

The Sufferings in Hell

The sacred Scriptures everywhere call the sufferings in hell eternal. This teaching has constantly been preached and continues to be preached by the holy Church. Our Lord Jesus Christ several times in the Gospels confirmed this terrible truth. Declaring that rejected sinners would share the fate of the fallen angels, he announced what He would say to them at His final judgment: "Depart from Me, you cursed, into the everlasting fire prepared for the devil and his angels" (Matt 25:41). After the final judgment over the human race, the perished will go "into everlasting punishment" (Matt 25:46).

In the parable of the cruel rich man and the poor man Lazarus, the Lord showed that between the mansions of eternal blessedness and the prisons of hell "there is a great gulf fixed, so that those who want to pass from here to you cannot, nor can those from there pass to us" (Luke 16:26). The "worm" of hell "does not die, and the fire" of hell "is not quenched" (Mark 9:48). The nether prisons demonstrate a strange and terrifying annihilation of life together with a preservation of life. There is a complete cessation of any activity; there is only suffering there. The worst of the diseases of the heart rules there: despair. Crying and wailing that attract no consolation of the soul are present there. There are unbreakable bonds there and a darkness that cannot be pierced, despite the great amount of fire. It is the kingdom of eternal death. The sufferings of hell are so horrible that the worst of earthly sufferings is nothing in comparison.

The Saviour of the world, when prophesying to his disciples that they would be persecuted, said, "My friends, do not be afraid of those who kill the body, and after that have no more that they can do. But I will show you whom you should fear: Fear Him who, after He has killed, has power to cast into hell; yes, I say to you, fear Him!" (Luke 12:4-5) Gazing with the eye of faith at the unutterable blessedness prepared for the faithful servants of God, as well as the equally unutterable sufferings awaiting unfaithful servants, the holy martyrs disdained the most terrifying tortures that the maddened fury of the persecutors could invent for them, and so through countless sorrows and deaths they trampled on their own eternal death.

The holy monks (who are the inheritors of the martyrs) constantly looked at the tortures of hell with their mind, and by this remembrance they cast down the thoughts and images of the tempter, who so vividly and alluringly played on the sensual imagination of the desert dwellers. St Anthony the Great used this tool—the remembrance of death and the sufferings of hell—especially in the beginning of his labors. During the night, the devil would assume the appearance of beautiful women, and appearing to Anthony in this form, would try to arouse sinful desire within him. But Anthony countered these images of the devil with his own vivid imagination concerning the flames of hell, the worm that never sleeps, and other hellish horrors, and through this weapon, he put out the fire of sensuality and destroyed the images of the tempter.[58] We are only defeated by our passions because we forget about the sufferings that follow. We only consider earthly sufferings to be terrible because we have not studied the sufferings of hell. A certain monk of ascetic life said to a holy elder: "My soul desires death." The elder answered, "You only say that because you desire to avoid sorrows, but you do not know that the future sorrows are incomparably worse than the ones here." Another brother asked the elder, "Why do I remain inattentive, though I remain in my cell?" The elder answered, "That is because you have not come to know neither the expected consolation nor the future sufferings. If you knew them as you should, then you would endure everything and would not falter, even if your cell was filled with worms and you stood in them up to the neck."[59]

The Lord, by His great mercy, revealed part of the eternal sufferings to some of His chosen ones for their salvation and spiritual growth. Through their accounts, our own understandings about the tortures of hell have become clearer and more detailed. Here is one of these accounts:

> There once were two friends. One of them, touched by the Word of God, entered a monastery and led his life in tears of repentance. Another remained in the world, leading a distracted life. Finally, he became so spiritually hardened that he began even to mock the Gospel. This man died in such a hardened state. When his friend heard of his death, the monk began to pray God that He would reveal his friend's fate after death. After some time, his friend appeared in a dream. "Well, how is it over there? Are you well?" asked the monk. "Do you wish to know this?" answered the dead man with a groan. "Woe is me, an unfortunate one! The worm that never sleeps gnaws at me, he does not give me any rest, nor will he leave me alone for all eternity." "What sort of sufferings are they?" asked the monk. "They are unbearable!" the dead man exclaimed. "But there is no opportunity to avoid the wrath of God. For the sake of your prayers, I am given momentary reprieve, and if you wish, I will show you my tortures. You would not be able to bear it if I showed them to you as they truly are; but you may at least see part of it." Saying this, the dead man raised his clothing up to his knees. O what a horrible sight! His entire leg was covered in a horrifying worm that was eating it alive, and the wounds gave off such a horrifying stench that the shocked monk woke up immediately. But the stench of hell had filled his cell with such pungency that the monk ran out of it in terror, forgetting to close his door. The stench then spread to the entire monastery; all the cells were filled with it. It would not fade with time, so the monks were eventually forced to abandon the monastery and move to a different place, while the monk who saw the prisoner of hell and his horrible tortures could not get rid of that stench in his nostrils for his entire life, neither could he wash it off his hands, nor cover it with any perfumes.[60]

There are many other reports from ascetics that corroborate this account. They could not remember their visions without horror, and in constant tears of repentance and humility, they sought to find the only possible joy: confirmation of salvation. This is what happened to

St Hesychius of Horeb. During a severe illness, his soul left his body for an entire hour. Having returned to his body, he begged everyone who was near him to leave him alone. Then he locked the door of his cell, and remained for twelve years in complete solitude, not speaking to anyone, not eating anything except for bread and water. In this solitude, he descended deep with his mind into what he saw during his vision and constantly shed silent tears. When it came time for him to die, he said one thing to the brothers who came to him after repeated requests: "Forgive me! Whoever has acquired the remembrance of death can never sin."[61]

Like this recluse of Horeb, Russia's own recluse of the Kiev Caves, Athanasius, died and resurrected after having lived a holy and God-pleasing life. After a long disease, he died. The brothers took away his body, according to monastic custom, but he remained unburied for two days because of some unforeseen circumstances. On the third night, the abbot saw a divine vision, and he heard a voice, "Athanasius, the man of God, lies unburied for two days, and you are not taking care of him!" In the early morning, the abbot came with the brethren to the dead man, with the intention of burying him, but they found him seated and weeping. They were terrified, seeing him alive. Then they asked him, "how did you come back to life? What did you see and hear during the time that your body was parted from your soul?" But the monk only had one answer to all their queries: "Save yourselves!"

When the brethren continued to ask him for an edifying word, he commanded them obedience and constant repentance. After this, Athanasius shut himself in a cave and remained there without leaving for twelve years, day and night remaining in constant tears, eating a little bread and water once every two days, and not speaking with anyone the entire time. When the time came for him to die, he repeated the same instruction he gave twelve years before about obedience and repentance, and then he peacefully departed to the Lord.[62]

As the apostle Paul wrote, "but a certain fearful expectation of judgment, and fiery indignation which will devour the adversaries. Anyone who has rejected Moses' law dies without mercy on the testimony of two or three witnesses. Of how much worse punishment, do you suppose, will he be thought worthy who has trampled the Son of God underfoot, counted the blood of the covenant by which he was sanctified a common thing, and insulted the Spirit of grace? For we know Him who said, 'Vengeance is Mine, I will repay,' says the Lord. And again, 'The Lord will judge His people.'[31] It is a fearful thing to fall into the hands of the living God" (Heb 10:27–31).

The space between heaven and earth, a space that separates the Church triumphant from the Church militant, is usually called "the air" in the Scriptures and in the writings of the Holy Fathers. Let us leave the study of the component parts of this "air" to the chemists. Instead, we will study that which is essential and necessary for our own salvation.

What is the blue sky that we see about us and call the sky? Is it the same thing as heaven? Or is it only a huge depth of air, boundless, colored with blue and hiding heaven from our gaze? The latter is most likely. It is a natural proper of air to assume a bluish color at a great distance, even to color objects of different hues with the same bluish tint if viewed from far away. Anyone can see this using personal experience. All you need to do is stand at a high place on a clear day and look to the distance. The groves of trees, the fields of wheat, the buildings—in a word, everything ceases to take its natural color at great distance, but takes on a bluish hue, which is an effect of the air between our eyes and the objects that we look at. The farther the objects, the bluer they appear. Finally, at an extreme distance, everything becomes the same blue-colored, indistinct horizon. This is perhaps a sorrowful, yet true expression of our own limitation produced by sin! However, it is better to acknowledge it than to delude oneself in ignorance through various false opinions concerning unlimited vision or knowledge.

Perfected Christians, who have purified their senses, have seen heaven with their eyes, and have in heaven and in the air that which we cannot see with our crude physical vision. Thus, by the action of the Holy Spirit, the protomartyr Stephen suddenly saw, before his martyrdom in the midst of a crowd of Jews that hated Christ and Christian, heaven opening up before his eyes. According to the Scripture, Stephen "being full of the Holy Spirit, gazed into heaven and saw the glory of God, and Jesus standing at the right hand of God, and said, 'Look! I see the heavens opened and the Son of Man standing at the right hand of God!'" (Acts 7:55–56)

The disciples of Macarius the Great saw heaven and their elder's entrance into it, also by the inspiration of the Holy Spirit.[63] St Isidore of Scetis, who was present at the death of the young ascetic Zachariah, saw the gates of heaven open for the dead man, and he exclaimed, "Rejoice, my son Zachariah, the gates of heaven open for you!"[64] As we have already mentioned before, St John Kolobos saw a light-covered path rise from earth to heaven, on which the angels raised the soul of the dead Thaïs.[65] The mother of St Paisius Velichkovsky saw, when her spiritual eyes were opened, that heaven's gates opened and a lightning-bearing angel leaving to console her after she was disconsolate at her son's decision to become a monk.[66]

When the senses are freed from the shackles of the fall, they become profoundly sensitive, and their field of action becomes very broad. In fact, space ceases to be a barrier. The previously mentioned visions of the saints are enough proof of this; however, we will offer even more examples of such spiritual experience. St Anthony the Great, who lived in one of the deserts of Egypt, not far from the Black Sea, saw the soul of St Amon being raised to heaven by the angels, even though that saint lived in the Nitrian Desert, on the other side of Egypt. The disciples of Anthony the Great noted the day and hour of this vision, then they ascertained from monks who visited from Nitria that St Ammon died at that exact hour and day in which St Anthony saw the vision. The distance between the two monasteries took thirty days of travel by foot to cross.[67]

Evidently, the vision of Christian who has been renewed by the Holy Spirit and has acquired an exalted degree of perfection, extends far beyond the limits of human sight in its natural state; the same is true of the hearing of a perfected man. It was not difficult for the saintly disciples of Macarius the Great to see his soul ascending the heights and to hear the words that he uttered in those high places, and upon his entry into the gates of heaven. A certain woman was once brought to Macarius, and her appearance had been changed because of her being possessed by a demon. However, some of his disciples could not see the alteration in her appearance, though it was evident to him. Then he explained to them that the reason for their lack of vision was the carnal state of their senses, which were incapable of seeing the spirits and their effects.[68] This is the state in which we find ourselves, as though in prison and in bondage.

However, most people do not sense their bondage or their imprisonment. It seems to them that they are sufficiently free. The acknowledgment and sensation of this state is a gift of God. This state was revealed
to King David by the Holy Spirit, and David uttered, on behalf of all mankind, a most touching prayer to God for deliverance from this terrible
state: "Bring my soul out of prison, that I may confess Thy name" (Ps 141:8).
The apostle Peter calls the carnal and emotional state of humanity, even
of pious people, to be a dark place. This place can be not only a physical
one, but, in a figurative sense, both a mental and a moral dark place, as the
Scriptures make clear: "His place (that is, God's place) hath been at Salem
(meaning peace)" (Ps 75:3 LXX). Those who are imprisoned in the dark place
and desire to be saved must be guided by the Holy Scriptures as by a lan-
tern, at least until the Holy Spirit descends on them and makes them living books of divine teaching, always open and never silent: "And so we
have the prophetic word confirmed, which you do well to heed as a light
that shines in a dark place, until the day dawns and the morning star rises
in your hearts" (1 Pet 1:19).

O you who have been imprisoned in the prison of earthly wisdom!
Let us hear those who have acquired spiritual freedom in the Lord and
have been illumined with spiritual reason! O you who have been born
blind! Let us hear those who have had their eyes opened by the touch of
the hand of God, those who have seen the light of truth, those who have
seen and come to know, in the radiance of that light, all that is unseen
and unknowable for carnal minds. The word of God and the Spirit that
cooperates with the Word reveal to us, through the vessels that He
chooses, that the distance between heaven and earth, all the visible blue
expanse of sky, the air and the aerial realm, are the habitation of the
fallen angels that have been cast out of heaven. "And war broke out in
heaven: Michael and his angels fought with the dragon; and the dragon
and his angels fought, but they did not prevail, nor was place found for
them in heaven any longer" (Rev 12:7–8). This casting out from heaven of
the devil and the spirits that followed him, as the prophet Ezekiel wrote
and St Andrew of Cæsarea explains followed their first sin, when they
were banished from the angelic hosts and thrown out of heaven (see Ezek
28:16).

In the book of Job, the fallen angel is already depicted as wandering in the limitless space of the realm under heaven; he wanders there, crossing it quickly, driven forward by his insatiable hatred for the race of man (see Job 1:7). The holy apostle Paul calls the fallen angels the "spiritual hosts of wickedness in the heavenly places" (Eph 6:12), while their head he calls "the prince of the power of the air" (Eph 2:2). The fallen angels are scattered in their multitude throughout the transparent abyss that we see above ourselves. They never cease to agitate all human societies and every human being individually; there is no crime or sin that they would not defend or take part in; they incline and instruct man in sinfulness by any means necessary.[69] "Your adversary the devil walks about like a roaring lion, seeking whom he may devour" (1 Pet 5:8). This he does both during the time of our earthly life and after our soul is separated from the body. When the soul of a Christian, having left the earthly habitation, begins to travel through the aerial realm into its fatherland on high, the demons stand in its way, trying to find anything in common that it has with them, their sinfulness, their fallenness, and to take it to the hell that is prepared for the devil and his angels. This they do by rights that they have acquired.

God, having created Adam and Eve, gave them lordship over the earth. He blessed them, as the Scriptures say, "Be fruitful and multiply; fill the earth and subdue it, and have dominion over the fish of the sea, over the birds of heaven, and over every living thing that moves on the earth" (Gen 1:28). It was not only the earth that was given to primal man, but even Eden itself, which they were commanded to cultivate and protect (see Gen 2:15). They had only God as their Master. And what did they do in Eden? Alas, what tragic blindness! Alas, what inconceivable blindness and madness! Having listened to the cunning and murderous advice of the fallen angel, they cast off themselves the light burden of obedience to God and laid on their shoulders the heavy yoke of slavery to the devil. Alas! Our forefathers disobeyed the command of God and fulfilled the advice of their own hateful enemy, a dark spirit, a blasphemous spirit, and they ruined their communion with God, not only by entering communion with the devil but by willingly subjugating themselves to him, and with them that part of the created world that was created for their and over which God had made them lords.

"The enemy, having seduced Adam," said Macarius the Great, "and in this way having gained lordship over him, deprived him of all authority, and was declared the prince of this age. At the beginning, God placed man in the position of prince of this age and lord of all the visible world."[70] Our forefathers were cast out of Eden to the earth, an earth that was cursed because of them, and one of the cherubim with a fiery sword was placed at the gate to guard the way to the tree of life (Gen 3:24). But another cherub[71] stood in the way of man's return to Eden, the cherub that did not care about his wondrous might as one of the cherubim, but as the author and father of evil and death fell into the abyss of perdition, leading with him many other angels and the entire race of man. This cherub, by God's just allowance and providence, became the prince of the air, together with his host of fallen angels, the prince of this world and this age, the prince and the head of those angels and men who willingly submit to him. He makes his stand between earth and Eden, and from the moment of the fall until the salvific suffering and life-creating death of Christ did not allow a single departed soul of man to ascend along those paths. The gates of heaven were closed for mankind forever. And both the righteous and sinners descended into hell.

Both the eternally closed gates and the impassable way were opened before our Lord Jesus Christ, Who, having accepted willing death, descended with His all-holy soul and His divinity (which never departed from Him) into Hades. There, He destroyed the gates of hell, freed its prisoners,[72] and, having then raised His body, crossed the aerial realm with His body and sat on the throne of God. The dark powers were horrified in their blindness, seeing the coming of the God-Man who destroyed all their power. In spiritual joy, with great majesty, the hosts of the holy angels opened the gates of heaven before Him.[73] Then horror once again possessed the demons when they saw the thief—who confessed Christ as Lord—ascend after Christ into paradise. Then, they understood, with wonder, the power of the redemption. By the inconceivable wisdom of God, after the Lord Jesus Christ's redemption of the human race, mankind is once again given the freedom to choose life or death, to accept the Redeemer and His redemption or to reject it. And many, unfortunately, very many, have chosen to remain in communion with Satan, in his bondage and slavery, and have declare themselves open enemies of the Saviour and His divine teaching. Also very many, having conscripted themselves into His army and having declared themselves His servants, have subsequently turned back on their oaths of fidelity to Him, and by their actions, both hidden and obvious, they forge alliance with the spirits of evil. All who have openly rejected the Redeemer become the property of Satan; their souls, after death, go directly into hell. But even Christians who inclined toward sin are unworthy of immediate transfer from the earthly life into blessed eternity. Justice demands that those inclinations toward sin, those betrayals of the Redeemer, be weighed and valued. Judgment and analysis are required to determine the level of inclination toward win, to determine what predominates in a human soul—eternal life or eternal death. Finally, every Christian soul, after death, must stand before the impartial judgment of God, as the apostle Paul said, "It is appointed for men to die once, but after this, the judgment" (Heb 9:27).

The Aerial Toll Houses

God's justice judges Christian souls that have left their bodies, through the mediation of the angels, both holy and fallen. The former, during the earthly life of each person, note all his good deeds, while the latter note all his sins. When the soul of a Christian begins ascending into heaven, guided by the holy angels, the dark spirits accuse it of various sins that were not wiped away by repentance as offerings to Satan, as proof of communion with him and as worthy of receiving the same eternal fate as they.

To test the spirits that cross the aerial realm, the dark powers have set up various testing stations and guardhouses in wondrous sequence. All along the way from earth to heaven, hosts of evil spirits stand guard. Each station tests for a specific kind of sin as the soul approaches that station. The aerial demonic guards and stations are called toll houses in the writings of the Fathers, while those who man them are called publicans. The reason this name is given has to do with the fact that publicans were tax collectors in the Roman Empire during the time of Christ and the early centuries of the Church's existence. Since this responsibility was often (due to the simplicity of ancient customs) given to people without positive qualities or virtues, publicans allowed themselves all manner of violence

and cunning to steal money for themselves. They usually set up their stations at the gates of cities, in marketplaces, and other public places, lest
anyone avoid their piercing gaze. The actions of publicans made them
despised and hated by the common people. Even the title publican began
to mean simply any person who had no feelings or principles, someone
capable of any sort of violence or demeaning action. Publicans were
accursed, rejected people. It is in this sense that Christ uses the term to
indicate anyone who refuses to listen to the Church: "let him be to you like
a heathen and a tax collector"(Matt 18:17). For Old Testament worshipers
of the true God, there was nothing more abhorrent that worship of idols;
however, publicans were hated just as much as idol-worshipers. The name
"publican" thus passed from people to the demons who guard the aerial
ascent from earth to heaven, since their responsibility, and the manner of
fulfilling it, resemble the profession of publican so closely. As the sons of
falsehood, demons accuse human souls not only of sins they committed,
but even of sins they never committed. They come up with various lies and
delusions, combining slander with baseless insolence, all for the sake of
tearing the soul from the hands of the angels and increase the number of
prisoners of hell.[74]

The teaching of the aerial toll houses is the teaching of the Church.
There is no doubt that the apostle Paul spoke of them when he told that
Christian had to battle against the principalities and powers of the air.
This teaching is found in the most ancient Christian tradition and in the
prayers of the Church. The most holy Virgin, when told of her impending
death by Archangel Gabriel, prayed with tears to her Lord that He would
deliver her soul from the foul spirits of the aerial region. When the hour
of her holy death approached, when her own Son descended with hosts of
angels and the souls of the righteous, she prayed to Him in the following
words before committing her spirit into His hands: "Accept now my spirit
in peace, and protect me from the dark regions, lest any attack of Satan
greet me there."[75]

St Athanasius the Great, the Patriarch of Alexandria, in his life of
St Anthony the Great, writes the following:

For once, when about to eat, having risen up to pray about the ninth
hour, he perceived that he was caught up in the spirit, and, wonderful

to tell, he stood and saw himself, as it were, from outside himself, and that he was led in the air by certain ones. Next certain bitter and terrible beings stood in the air and wished to hinder him from passing through. But when his conductors opposed them, they demanded whether he was not accountable to them. And when they wished to sum up the account from his birth, Antony's conductors stopped them, saying, "The Lord has wiped out the sins from his birth, but from the time he became a monk, and devoted himself to God, it is permitted you to make a reckoning." Then when they accused him and could not convict him, his way was free and unhindered. And immediately he saw himself, as it were, coming and standing by himself, and again he was Antony as before. Then forgetful of eating, he remained the rest of the day and through the whole of the night groaning and praying. For he was astonished when he saw against what mighty opponents our wrestling is, and by what labours we have to pass through the air. And he remembered that this is what the apostle said, "according to the prince of the power of the air" [Ephesians 2:2]. For in it the enemy has power to fight and to attempt to hinder those who pass through. Wherefore most earnestly he exhorted, "Take up the whole armour of God, that you may be able to withstand in the evil day" [Ephesians 6:13], that the enemy, "having no evil thing to say against us, may be ashamed" [Titus 2:8].[76]

St John Chrysostom said that every dying person, though he be the greatest emperor on earth, is filled with fear and bewilderment when faced with the terrifying ranks of angels and the demons who come to his deathbed.[77]

St Macarius the Great said, "Having heard that under the heavens there are rivers filled with serpents and the jaws of lions, the powers of darkness, an unquenchable fire, and having all one's members terrified by this news, do you not know that if you do not accept the pledge of the Spirit at your death, they will seize your soul and will prevent it from entering the heavens?"[78]

The great martyr Eustratius, after enduring many terrible tortures and sufferings, and after performing many wondrous miracles, uttered this prayer to God before his death for his firm and persistence confession of

Christ, in which he first thanks God, Who beheld him and granted him during his earthly sufferings to defeat the invisible enemy, the devil; he then transitions to the coming separation of his soul from the body and says:

> O Master, let Thy hand cover me, and let Thy mercy come upon me, for my soul is troubled and pained over its departure from this, my wretched and defiled body, lest the wicked council of the adversary meet it and detain it in darkness, because of the many sins, known and unknown, which I have committed in this life. Be Thou merciful unto me, O Master, and let not my soul behold the dark visages of the evil demons, but let Thy radiant and most luminous angels receive it. Give glory to Thy holy Name, and by Thy might lead me up to Thy divine judgment seat. When my time cometh to be judged, let not the hand of the prince of this world seize me to drag me down to the abyss of hell, but stand Thou before me and be my Saviour and Helper, for these bodily torments are gladness for Thy servants. [Have mercy, O Lord, upon my soul, which hath been defiled by the passions of this life, and receive it purified by repentance and confession, for blessed art Thou unto the ages of ages. Amen.][79]

Similarly, St George, after defeating all the terrible tortures invented by his torturer, after raising a dead person back to life before everyone's eyes, after throwing down the idols with the name of the Lord alone, prayed thus before his moment of execution: "Blessed be the Lord my God, who did not abandon me to the jaws of my captors, who did not not give joy to my enemies at my expense and who delivered my soul as a bird from the snare of the fowler! Lord! Hear me now: stand before Me in this hour of my death and deliver my soul from the snares of the prince of the air, that horrifying enemy, and his impure spirits. Do not remember the sin of those who sin against me in ignorance, but give them Your forgiveness and love, that they, having known You, may also receive a portion with Your chosen in the Kingdom."

The great ascetic of God, the seer of mysteries, St Nephon, Bishop of Constantia, a city on Cyprus, once stood at prayer, and saw the heavens opened and a multitude of angels, among whom some descended to the earth, others ascended into heaven, raising human souls into the heavenly mansions. He began to attend to this vision, and he saw two angels strive upward, holding a human soul. When they approached the tollhouse of lust, the publican-demons came out and said angrily, "This is our soul! How dare you carry it past us when it is ours?" The angels answered, "On what grounds do you call this soul yours?" The demons said, "It sinned until death, not only in natural, but even unnatural sins; moreover, it condemned its neighbor, and what is worse, it died without repentance. What do you say to that?" The angels answered, "We will believe neither you nor your father Satan until we have asked this soul's guardian angel." The guardian angel said, "Yes, this person sinned much; but once he grew ill, he began to weep for his sins and confess them before God. Did God forgive him? Only God knows. It is His authority, and to His righteous judgment we give glory."

Then the angels, disdaining the accusations of the demons, entered the heavenly gates with the soul. Then St Nephon saw another soul being carried by the angels. The demons stopped them, exclaiming, "Why are you carrying this soul up without our knowledge, when this person was avaricious, lustful, angry, and violent?" The angels answered, "We know that this soul, though it sinned in these ways, wept, sighed, confessed, and gave alms, and so God forgave it all." The demons retorted, "If such a soul is worthy of God's mercy, then go ahead and take all the sinners of the entire world; there's no point in us toiling away here." The angels answered, "All sinners who confess their sins with humility and tears will receive God's mercy; those who die without repentance are subject to God's judgment." Thus having shamed the demons, they moved on.

Then the saint saw a third soul being raised, this one belonging to a certain God-loving man, a pure, generous, and merciful person. The demons stood at a distance and ground their teeth at this soul; the angels of God came out of heaven to greet it, singing, "Glory to You, Christ God, that You did not give this soul to the enemy and rescued it from the nether hell!"

Then St Nephon saw that a certain soul was being carried down to hell. This was the soul of a certain slave who was tortured by his master with hunger and beatings; not being able to bear the constant abuse, the man killed himself according to the devil's inspiration. His guardian angel remained at a distance and wept; the demons rejoiced. Then a command came from God to the guardian angel to go to Rome, to take care of a certain newly baptized infant. Then St Nephon saw a soul taken from the grasp of the angels at the fourth tollhouse and cast down into hell. That was the soul of a man committed to lust, magic, and violence, who had died suddenly without repentance.[80]

St Symeon the Fool for Christ, who reached the height of Christian perfection, told his fellow ascetic Deacon John concerning his death and of the great reward awaiting him in heaven, which he learned of through a vision from on high. He said, "I don't know of anything in myself that would be worthy of heavenly rewards; it must be that the Lord wants to have mercy on me through an abundance of His grace. Know that you also will be taken from here soon, and so take care as much as you can about the state of your soul, so that you may pass without trouble through the aerial region and avoid the evil hand of the prince of darkness. My Lord knows that I am filled with great sorrow and terror while I pass through those places where all the words and acts of man are tested."[81]

Blessed John the Merciful, Patriarch of Alexandria, constantly spoke about death and the passage of the soul from the body, as it was revealed to him by St Symeon the Stylite:

When the soul leaves the body and begins to ascend to heaven, the hosts of demons meet it and subject it to various difficulties and tests. They test it in falsehood, slander, anger, envy, wrath, remembrance of evils, price, foul language, disobedience, dishonest gain, love of money, drunkenness, overeating, resentment, dabbling in magic, hatred of neighbor, murder, thievery, lack of mercy, lust, and adultery. During this passage of the soul from earth to heaven, even the angels cannot help the soul. Only repentance, good deeds, and almsgiving most of all help that soul. If we do not repent in some sin here on earth because of forgetfulness, then through mercy we may avoid the violence of the demonic toll houses. Brethren! Knowing this, let us fear the bitter house of our encounter with the terrible and merciless publicans, an hour in which we will be filled with bewilderment at what to answer those who test us. Today let us repent of all our sins, let us give alms according to our ability, for it can lead us from earth to heaven and deliver us from being held by the demons. Great is their hatred of us, and so great is the terror that awaits us in the air. It is a terrible thing![82]

St Symeon the Stylite, the one who told Patriarch John about the toll houses, was a contemporary of John, though older than him. A short excerpt of this teaching has come down to us, in which he speaks of the fate of the Christian after death. In this teaching, the saint first reveals that the Holy Spirit told him that only a small number of people were being saved during this life. Then he said that a soul without blemish, a righteous soul, was accepted by the angels with love and with singing. The angels fought off the demons and raised such souls above the aerial toll houses. On the contrary, a sinful soul would not be allowed into the land above the air. The devil had reason to detain and accuse it. He would battle with the angels that carried it, accusing it of the sins that prove his lordship over it, insisting that its virtues were insufficient for salvation and for free passage through the aerial region.[83]

St John of Raithu, in a letter to St. John of the Ladder, mentions the aerial toll houses, the princes of this world, the spirits of evil, desiring that the soul-saving teachings of the luminary of Sinai would help monks reach the gates of heaven preserved from the dark powers that guard the way. St John of the Ladder notes that fallen monks who offer propound and constant repentance, among their many words of propound prayer and sorrow, would say the following, "The roiling waters would have gone even go over our soul" (Ps 123:5). They said this because they had not received the assurance that they would, but still they saw from a distance what sorts of things occurred in the aerial region.[84]

St Isaiah the Recluse, in a final instruction to his disciples, commanded that they hold death before their eyes daily and that they care for the manner in which "their soul will pass from the body through the powers of darkness who will encounter them in the air."[85] In his seventeenth homily, he says,

> Think of the joy of the soul that commits itself to the service of God and that accomplishes this service! After leaving this world, his deeds will labor for his sake: the angels, seeing him delivered from the powers of darkness, will rejoice with him. When the soul will leave

the body, angels will accompany it; the dark powers will come against it, desiring to hold it back, and, testing it, they will find nothing in it that belongs to them. Then the angels will not fight against the enemy, but the deeds performed by the soul will protect it and preserve it from the enemies and not allow them to touch it. If the deeds will be victorious, the angels will sing a song of glory and will lead the soul with joy before the face of God. In that hour, it forgets everything that belongs to the earthly life, all the difficulties it endured there. With all care and strength let us try in this short time allotted to us to do good and to preserve good untouched by evil, so that we may have a chance to be saved from the hands of the princes that await us. They are evil and merciless. Blessed is he in whom nothing will be found that belongs to them: his joy, happiness, peace, and crown are beyond all reckoning.

A certain monk who lived in the coenobitic monastery of Abba Serida, where the elder Barsanuphius labored in reclusion, asked that holy man, as he approached death, if he would accompany him on that terrifying road after death. Barsanuphius the great answered, "Brother! I commend you to Christ, who willed to die for us, the Lord of heaven and earth and all that lives, may He lessen in your eyes this fear of death and may He make the passage of your soul unhindered."[86]

Abba Dorotheus, who came from the same monastery of Abba Serida, wrote in one of his letters, "If a soul is hard-hearted, it is good for it to frequently read the Holy Scriptures and the softening words of the God-bearing Fathers, it is good to remember the dread judgment of God, the passage of the soul from the body, of the powers that will encounter it after death, with whose cooperation it performed evil in the short and calamitous earthly life."[87]

St John of Karpathos, in his consoling letter to the monks of India, who were simultaneously subjected to persecutions from visible and invisible enemies, and who were on the verge of despair, wrote the following:

When the soul leaves the body, the enemy advances to attack it, fiercely reviling it and accusing it of its sins in a harsh and terrifying manner.

But if a soul enjoys the love of God and has faith in Him, even though in the past it has often been wounded by sin, it is not frightened by the enemy's attacks and threats. Strengthened by the Lord, winged by joy, filled with courage by the holy angels that guide it, encircled and protected by the light of faith, it answers the malicious devil with great boldness: "Enemy of God, fugitive from heaven, wicked slave, what have I to do with you? You have no authority over me: Christ the Son of God has authority over me and over all things. Against Him have I sinned, before Him shall I stand on trial, having His precious Cross as a sure pledge of His saving love toward me. Flee far from me, destroyer! You have nothing to do with the servants of Christ." When the soul says all this fearlessly, the devil turns his back, howling aloud and unable to withstand the name of Christ. Then the soul swoops down on the devil from above, attacking him like a hawk attacking a crow. After this it is brought rejoicing by the holy angels to the place appointed for it in accordance with its inward state."[88]

St Hesychius wrote,

If the soul has Christ with it, it will not be disgraced by its enemies even at death, when it rises to heaven's entrance; but then, as now, it will boldly confront them. But let it not tire in calling upon the Lord Jesus Christ, the Son of God, day and night until the time of its departure from this moral life, and He will speedily avenge it in accordance with the promise which He Himself made when speaking of the unjust judge (see Luke 18:1–8). Indeed, He will avenge it both in this present life and after its departure from its body .... The hour of death will come upon us, it will come, and we shall not escape it. May the ruler of this world and of "the prince of the air" (John 14:30, Ephesians 2:2) find our misdeeds few and petty when he comes, so that he will not have good grounds for convicting us. Otherwise we shall weep in vain. For that 'servant who knew his master's will, and did not prepare himself or do according to his will, shall be beaten with many stripes' (Luke 12:47) .... Just as a man blind from birth does not see the sun's light, so one who fails to pursue watchfulness does not see the rich radiance of divine grace. He cannot free himself from evil thoughts, words and actions, and because of these thoughts and actions he will not be able freely to pass the lords of hell when he dies.[89]

St Theognostus said,

Unutterable is the sweetness of that soul that separates from the body while in the assurance of salvation. It casts off the body like clothing. In firm assurance to receive that which was already given in part, without sorrow it throws off the body, peacefully comes out of it toward the bright and quiet angel that was sent from on high to take it. Accompanied by this angel, it passes the aerial region without hindrance, in no way bothered by the evil spirits; joyfully and boldly it rises, amid exclamations of gratitude to God, and finally comes to worship its Creator. There is uttered the command that places it among others who are equal in virtue, to remain with them until the general resurrection ... Though you constantly abide in pure prayer that incorporeally unites the material mind with God, and though you have been found worthy to see, as in a mirror, the blessed state that awaits you after the end of this life, you have received this gift as one who accepted the betrothal of the Spirit and who have acquired the kingdom within you through clear and definite sensations of the soul. However, do not seek to leave your body until you have received assurance of your coming death. Pray fervently for this and be hopeful that you will receive this news when your death approaches, if it is beneficial to you. Prepare for death always, casting off all fear, prepare always to be able to pass the aerial regions, to escape the evil spirits, to enter boldly and without fear into the heavenly mansions, to join the ranks of the angels, to add yourself to the host of all the chosen righteous ones, to see God, as much as such vision is given you.[90]

This spiritual sensation of which St Theognostus speaks is called in the writings of the fathers "notification," because of the precise and exact nature of it. It is produced by the descent of divine grace that accepts the repentant and sorrowful sinner into the spiritual embrace of the Father. It frees the soul of the violence of evil spirits and passions, it changes man completely, uniting him with God, leading the whole man into that wondrous prayer that the Spirit of God Himself prays within man. "All the bones" of such a person speak in unutterable spiritual doxology and gratitude: "Lord, O Lord, who is like unto Thee, who deliverest the poor from him that is too strong for him, and the poor man, and the needy, from him that despoileth him?" (Ps 34:10) This spiritual sensation is so powerful that when it fills a person, it takes away from him any sympathy to other realities; in short, it is the enthronement of the kingdom of God in the soul. He who has acquired such a sensation no longer lives for himself, but for God (see 2 Cor 5:15) striving completely toward Him and having Him abiding within himself. However, he who has fallen into delusion and demonic spiritual deception only imagines himself to have such a sensation, and the difference is evident in the fruits that such a state produces.

"Wake up, my soul," said Evagrius the monk to himself, "and think how you will endure the sudden separation of your soul from your body when the stern angels will come for you and will seize you in that hour that you do not expect, in a time that you do not know! What deeds will you send ahead of yourself into the air when enemies will begin to test you about your deeds?"[91]

This is how the holy ones of God thought and spoke. They knew and they studied the depths of man's fall; they knew and they studied the power of the demons over men that arose out of this fall.

St George, Recluse of Zadonsk, told of an event in a more recent time. Archimandrite Barsanuphius of the Zadonsk Monastery was on his death bed for three days. During this time, his soul already traveled the aerial realm of the toll houses, being tested for all the sins that he committed from his youth, but then he heard the voice of God, "Because of the prayers of the Mother of God, St Mocius, and Andrew Stratelates, his sins are forgiven, and he is given more time for repentance."[92]

The teaching concerning toll houses, like the teaching of the physical location of heaven and hell, is a universally known and accepted teaching of the Church, evident on the level of the Church's hymnography. In the canon to the Lord Jesus Christ and the Mother of God, which is read at the death of every Christian, we read the following, "Vouchsafe me as I leave this earth without hindrance to pass by the prince of the air, the torturer, the guard of the terrible ways, the tester of vain words." "Keep far away from me the master of the bitter toll houses, the prince of the world."

In the daily prayers for the church, in the prayers after the kathisma, the church puts the following words into the mouth of the supplicant: "O Lord, my Lord, grant me tears of contrition, O Thou Who alone art good and merciful, that therewith I may entreat Thee, that I be cleansed of every sin before the end. For frightening and terrible is the place to which I shall go when my soul is separated from the body, and a dark and inhuman horde of demons shall meet me" (Prayer after the Fourth Kathisma).

"Perfect me with Thy perfection, and thus lead me up from this present life, that, having passed through the principalities and powers of darkness without hindrance, even I may, through Thy grace, behold the ineffable beauty of Thine unapproachable glory" (Prayer after the Seventeenth Kathisma).[93]

In the prayer before the kontakia and ekoi[94] [in the Russian *Psalter of the Mother of God*], we read, "O Mother of the King of heaven and earth! Ask forgiveness of all my sins and give correction to my life. And at my death, give me a passage through the aerial enemies without hindrance."[95] In the Akathist Hymn to the Mother of God, ode 8, we hear, "Through thee the dead are brought to life, for thou hast borne Him who is Himself the Life; the dumb are made to speak, lepers are cleansed, diseases are driven out; the hosts of the spirits of the air are conquered ... "[96]

In the Octoechos,[97] we find the following prayers to the mother of God: "At the hour of mine end, O Virgin, rescue me from the hands of the demons, from condemnation and retribution, from dreadful trials and the bitter toll-houses, and from the cruel prince and everlasting damnation, O Mother of God"[98]; "O most pure one, in the dread hour [of death] rescue me from the torture ... of the demons ... "[99] "At the hour of my death, O [Virgin], rescue me from the hands of the demons, from condemnation, sentencing, dread trial, the bitter toll-stations, the cruel prince, and everlasting fire"[100]; "O Lady, Mother of the Redeemer, stand before me at the hour of my departure, when I am tested by the spirits of the air concerning those things I committed with an irrational mind"[101]; "When my soul must needs sever its fleshly bond and depart this life, then stand before me, O Lady. Set at nought the counsels of the incorporeal foe, and crush the jaws of those who seek to slaughter me pitilessly, that, unhindered, I may elude the myriad princes of darkness who inhabit the air ... "[102]

In the "Order at the Parting of the Soul from the Body when One hath Suffered for a Long Time" is read: "Now, then, all the time of my life hath passed away as smoke, and Angels sent from God, henceforth are standing about, mercilessly seeking my wretched soul"; "Behold, a multitude of evil spirits are standing about, holding the handwriting of my sins, and they cry out exceedingly, shamelessly seeking my lowly soul"; "Have mercy on me, O all-holy Angels of God Almighty, and deliver me from all the evil toll-collectors ... "[103]

In the canon to the guardian angel: "May the shameful faces of the enemies be covered with shame when my humble soul leaves my body." "I pray you, my guardian, be a guard and protector when I pass the toll houses of the fierce prince of this world." In the second prayer of St Nicholas: "After the separation of my soul from my body, help me, an accursed one. Pray the Lord, the creator of all things, that He deliver me from the aerial toll houses and eternal suffering." There is also a petition to avoid the toll houses in the prayer to St Sergius of Radonezh, as well as prayers to other saints.

St Theodosius of the Kiev Caves, having felt a final weakness on account of his sickness, sat up in his bed and said, "May the will of God be done: as His good will pleases for me, so let it be done. But I pray You, my Master, Jesus Christ, be merciful to my soul, lest the evil spirits steal it away, but instead may Your angels, taking me through the dark toll houses, lead me to the light of Your mercy."[104] St Dimitri of Rostov prayed thus: "When the terrifying hour of the separation of my soul from my body comes, then, my Redeemer, accept my soul into Your hands, and preserve it unharmed from all dangers, and do not let my soul see the dark gaze of the evil demons, but let it be saved, having passed through all the toll houses."[105]

An exact description of the toll houses and the order in which they follow each other in the aerial realm is found in the vision of Theodora. She, having left her body on earth, was led by two holy angels on a path toward heaven through the aerial realm. When she started to rise up, she was met by the dark spirits of the first toll house, in which all human sins of the word are tested, such as idle talk, foul language, ridicule, blasphemy, singing of foul songs, rude exclamations, sinful laughter, etc. For the most part, people do not consider such sins to be sinful, and so do not repent of them before God and do not confess them to their spiritual father. But the Lord clearly said, "But I say to you that for every idle word men may speak, they will give account of it in the day of judgment. For by your words you will be justified, and by your words you will be condemned" (Matt 12:36–37). And the apostle Paul adds, "Let no corrupt word proceed out of your mouth ... neither filthiness, nor foolish talking, nor coarse jesting" (Eph 4:29, 5:4).

The demons cruelly and stubbornly accused the soul there, showing examples of all its sins in word, committed from the earliest youth, and the holy angels argued with them, showing examples of good deeds to counteract the sins. Thus Theodora, redeemed at this toll house, began to travel further upward and approached the toll house of falsehood, which tests every falsehood, broken promise, utterance of the name of God in vain, non-fulfillment of oaths given to God, or hiding of sins from the confessor at confession. Having passed this toll house as well, she went on to the third toll house of slander, where slander, condemnation, demeaning of your neighbor, ridicule of others (coupled with forgetfulness of one's own sinfulness or lack of attentiveness to them) are all tested. Those who commit such sins are tested especially fiercely by the demons for anyone who passes judgment over another in an anti-Christ, considering himself to be greater the Christ in apportioning judgment and punishment to others.

The fourth toll house tests sins of gluttony, where overeating, drunkenness, secret eating, eating without prayer, breaking of fasts, passionate love of food, satiety—in a word, all sins of the stomach. After passing this toll house, Theodora, becoming a bit bolder, began to speak with the holy angels and said, "It seems to me that no one among those living on earth knows what occurs here and what awaits the soul after death." The angels answered, "Does not the word of God explain all this as it is read daily in the churches and is preached by the servants of God? But those who have passionate attachment to earthly vanities don't pay attention to the word of God, consider it a pleasure to daily satiate themselves and drink to abandon, feasting without fear of God, having as their god their own stomach, not thinking of the future life and not paying attention to the Scriptures that say, 'Woe to you who are full for you shall hunger' (Luke 6:25). Such people consider the Scriptures to be fables; they live inattentively and largely, every day enjoying feasting with music and choirs like the rich man in the parable. Moreover, those of them who do give alms and help the poor and the needy do find easy forgiveness of these sins from God, and for the sake of their alms, they pass this toll house without trouble. As the Scriptures say, 'For almsgiving rescues one from death, and will wash away every sin. Those who do almsgiving and are righteous will be full of life. But those who sin are enemies of their own life' (Tob 12:9–10). Those who do not try to purify their sins through almsgiving cannot avoid calamity at this toll house. They are taken by the publicans and cast down in terrible tortures to the deepest prisons of hell where they keep them in bonds until the dread judgment of Christ."

So discussing, they approached the toll house of laziness. There are counted all the days and hours spent idly, in inattentiveness to God's service; there all shirkers of work are judged, all who profit from the work of others and do not want to raise a finger themselves. Also, all hired workers who do their work badly are judged here. After this toll house followed the sixth toll house of thievery, then the seventh toll house of love of money and avarice, then the toll house of unjust gain, then the toll house of injustice, then the toll house of envy, then the toll house of pride, which includes sins such as price, vanity, high opinion of oneself, disdain of others, self-aggrandizement, insufficient honor given to parents, spiritual and civil authorities, or open disobedience of them. After that followed the toll house of anger and wrath, then the toll house of remembrance of evils. After Theodora passed this toll house, Theodora asked the following:

"Tell me how can these terrible rulers of the air know in such detail all the evil deeds of men, and not only the open ones but even those that are secret?" The angels replied: "Every Christian, as soon as he is baptized, receives from God an appointed guardian angel who guards him invisibly and inspires him night and day to every kind of good deed; he also records all his good deeds, for which that man later can hope to receive from the Lord grace and eternal recompense in the heavenly kingdom. The prince of darkness, who desires to draw into his own destruction the whole race of men as well, also appoints one of his evil spirits to walk in the man's steps and record all his evil deeds. It is his duty to inspire man to such deeds by any vile trickery in his power;

and when he succeeds in his designs, he records all the wickedness of which the man has made himself guilty. Such an evil spirit spreads the report of every man's sins to all the stations of torment, and this is how the sins become known to the princes of the air. When the soul parts from its body and desires to go to its Creator in heaven, the evil spirits prevent the soul and show to it its sins. If the soul has done more good deeds than evil, they cannot keep it; but if the sins outweigh the good deeds, they keep the soul for some time, shut it up in the prison where it cannot know God, and torment it as much as God's power allows them, until that soul, by means of prayers of the Church and good deeds done for its sake by those who are still on earth, should be granted forgiveness.

Those who believe in the Holy Trinity and take as frequently as possible the holy communion of the Holy Mysteries of Christ our Savior's Body and Blood—such people can rise to heaven directly, with no hindrances, and the holy angels defend them, and the holy saints of God pray for their salvation, since they have lived righteously. No one, however, takes care of the wicked and depraved heretics, who do nothing useful during their lives, and live in disbelief and heresy. The angels can say nothing in their defense.

When a soul proves to be so sinful and impure before God that it has no hope of salvation, the evil spirits immediately bring it down into the abyss, where their own place of eternal torment is also. There the lost souls are kept until the time of the Lord's second coming. Then they will unite with their bodies and will incur torment in fiery hell together with the devils. Note also,' said the angels, 'that this is the way by which only those who are enlightened by faith and holy baptism can rise and be tested in the stations of torment. The unbelievers do not come here. Their souls belong to hell even before they part from their bodies. When they die the devils take their souls with no need to test them. Such souls are their proper prey, and they take them down to the abyss."[106]

The next toll house was one that tested murder, which also tests violence of any kind. Then came the toll house of black magic, where the devils could find nothing against Theodora. But they said to her, "We will see if you can avoid the toll house of lust."

As we were rising, I dared to question the holy angels once more: "Do all Christians pass these torments? Is there no possibility to pass by the torments and not be tested in any of the stations?" The angels replied, "There is no other way for the souls that rise toward heaven. Every one goes this way, but not everyone is tormented like you; only sinners like you incur the torments, for they have not confessed their sins fully, and moved by a false sense of shame, have kept their really shameful deeds secret from their spiritual fathers. When a man whole-heartedly confesses his evil deeds and repents and regrets them, his sins are invisibly wiped out by God's mercy. When a repentant soul comes here, the tormentors of the air open their books but find nothing written there; [107] the soul, then, joyfully ascends to the throne of God."[108]

As they spoke, they reached the sixteenth toll house of lust, in which all sorts of sins of the flesh are tested, including sexual relations outside of marriage, sins of the imagination, agreement with the will to the doing of lustful sins, and all sins of the eyes and the touch related to lust. When Theodora reached this toll house, the dark spirits were very surprised that she had risen so far, and they accused her fiercely, especially in her not being completely open with her spiritual father about certain sins. However, she passed, and reached the next toll house of adultery, which also includes sexual sins of those who have given an oath of chastity to the Lord. The eighteenth toll house was the one of sodomy, which tests all sexual perversions, including incest. When she passed this toll house, the holy angels said to her:

"You have seen, Theodora, the frightening and disgusting torments of fornication! Know then that few are the souls that pass them without stopping and paying their ransom, for the whole world lies immersed in the evils of seductive foulness, and all mankind is sensuous. Few guard against the impurities of fornication and deaden the desire of their own flesh. And this is the reason why few pass here freely; many come as far as this place but perish here. The rulers of the torments of fornication boast that they, more than any of the others, fill the fiery abyss of hell with the souls of men. But you, Theodora, must thank God that you have already passed the torments of fornication by the prayers of the holy man Basil, your father. Now you will no longer fear."[109]

After this, she came to the nineteenth toll house of heresy, where all incorrect ideas concerning the faith, all doubts in the faith, and all blasphemy and heresy is tested. After passing this toll house, they were in sight of the gates of heaven; however, they were still accosted by the fierce spirits of the last (twentieth) toll house of lack of mercy, where lack of compassion and cruelty are tested. If someone spent an entire life in ascetic labors, fasting, vigils, prostrations, and prayer; if someone preserved virginity and mortified his flesh, but if such a person was not compassionate and closed his heart to his neighbor, then he is cast down from this toll house and is imprisoned for all time in the nether regions of hell.

Finally, with unutterable joy, they approached the gates of heaven. The gates of heaven shone like crystal; from them an unutterable brightness shone forth, and sun-like youths stood there. Seeing the holy one, led by the angels, they were filled with joy that she, protected by the mercy of God, avoided the aerial toll houses, and with great love she was led into the gates. During her passage through the torments, Theodora noted that each of the toll houses as subject to a single ruler, and the publicans in their appearance were similar to the sin that was tested.

The great saints of God, having completely passed from the nature of the old Adam to the nature of the new Adam, our Lord Jesus Christ, in this subtle and holy newness pass with their pure souls through the aerial demonic toll houses with incredible alacrity and great glory. They are led on high by the Holy Spirit Himself, Who during their earthly wandering constantly inspired in them a desire to leave behind their body and be with Christ (see Phil 1:23). Thus, for example, an ascetic named Mark of Trache passed the aerial region like lightning.[110] When the time came for St Macarius the Great to die, a cherub, who was also his guardian angel, accompanied by a great number of the heavenly host, came for his soul. A host of apostles, prophets, martyrs, bishops, monks, and righteous men came down with the host of angels. The demons then stood in their ranks at their toll houses to watch the passage of the soul of the Spirit-led man. It began to rise. They stood afar off, screaming from their toll houses: "O Macarius! What glory have you received!" And the humble-minded soul replied, "No! I am still afraid, for I do not know if I have done any good." All the while, he rose up toward heaven. From other toll houses, demons cried in anger: "You have escaped us, O Macarius!" And he answered,

"Through the power of Christ Who protects me, 1 have avoided your snares."[111]

The reason that the saints pass the torments of the aerial region so freely is that during this life they battled without mercy against these same demons, and having defeated them in this life, they acquired profound freedom from sins, becoming the dwelling place and temple of the Holy Spirit. No fallen angel can approach such a noetic tabernacle of God.

Spiritually Passing the Torments of the Toll Houses during the Earthly Life

Just as the resurrection of the Christian soul from sinful death occurs during the earthly life, so does the passage through the torments of the toll houses also occur mystically here, on earth. During the passage through the toll houses after death, this earthly state of freedom or imprisonment is merely made manifest.

The commandment given to man in heaven forbade eating from the tree of the knowledge of good and evil. This commandment was never canceled.[112] Even today, we are forbidden from seeing evil in our neighbor and condemning him for it, we are forbidden from seeking revenge, being commanded to do good to those who hate us. We are forbidden to look with desire at the beauty of a woman, the beauty that before the fall never inspired lust. We are forbidden not only to utter blasphemous words, but even from any sinful thought:

> The blessed Moses in figurative language expressed that the soul must not follow two principles that have no agreement between each other (i.e. good and evil), but must attach itself only to good. Also, it must not bring forth double fruits (i.e. both beneficial and harmful) but only beneficial fruit, for he said, "You shall not plow with a young bull and a donkey together" (Deuteronomy 22:10). This means that there should not appear, in the field of your heart's activity, both virtue and vice, but let only virtue be active there. Again, Moses said, "You shall not let your cattle mate with a different species" (Leviticus 19:19). All this mystically indicates that we should not sow both virtue and vice in our hearts, but we should cultivate only good fruits, fruits of virtue, so that the soul

would not have any communion with two spirits, that is, the Spirit of God and the spirit of the world.[113]

As he did in Eden, so now also mankind's murderer, the fallen cherub with his fiery sword, stands before man, implacably waging war against him, trying constantly to inspire him to rebellion against the commands of God and into an even greater fall than the fall of Adam and Eve. The fiery sword in the hand of the king of the air, as the fathers explain it, is the ability of the demon to wound the heart and mind of man, arousing in it various fiery passions.[114] The apostle Paul calls this weapon of the enemy "the fiery darts of the wicked one" (Eph 6:16), while the Psalms call the action of that weapon on the heart "a fire among the thorns" (Ps 117:12).

St Symeon the New Theologian wrote, "From the time that the devil arranged for man, through the fall, an exile from Eden and a separation from God, he has received, with his demons, the freedom to assail the thoughts of every person, some more, some less. The mind has no ability to protect itself, other than through a constant remembrance of God. When the power of the Cross impresses a constant remembrance of God into the heart, then such noetic attacks become impossible. This is the purpose of our noetic labors, which is necessary for every Christian to undertake in the battlefield of faith. Without this fruit, all labors are in vain."[115]

The commandment is not only given for our actions and our words, but mainly for their source, that is, our thoughts, and the attacks of the enemy are primarily directed against the mind. If this leader of man's activity does not secretly agree to the sin, then no sinful word or action can ever come into existence. The weapons of the enemy are sinful thoughts and images.[116] Mankind must battle against the powers of the air in the realm of the mind. Here he will either be victorious or be defeated; here his eternal fate is determined; here he freely chooses either eternal life, given him by the Creator, returned by the Redeemer, or eternal death, promised him in Eden by God's justice for any creature that tramples on the goodwill of the Creator.

The apostle Paul calls us to this great and most important battle, when he writes, "Put on the whole armor of God, that you may be able to stand against the wiles of the devil. For we do not wrestle against flesh and blood, but against principalities, against powers, against the rulers of the darkness of this age, against spiritual hosts of wickedness in the heavenly places" (Eph 6:11-12). The apostle describes both the realm of this terrible war and the weapons that we must use to be victorious in it: "For the weapons of our warfare are not carnal but mighty in God for pulling down strongholds, casting down arguments and every high thing that exalts itself against the knowledge of God, bringing every thought into captivity to the obedience of Christ" (2 Cor 10:4-5). The apostle commands us to bring into obedience to Christ not only our sinful thoughts that are clearly abhorrent to Him, but our entire mental activity, because our evil enemy, who is experienced in the destruction of men, does not inspire, in our initial skirmishes, any clearly sinful thoughts.[117] Instead, he tries to offer, in contrast to spiritual wisdom (i.e., the teaching of the God), the natural wisdom of man, though it be fallen, carnal, and sinful, wisdom in name only. Presenting it as healthy, comprehensive, righteous, and great, he tries then to direct us away from obedience to Christ. Here is an example, given by St Macarius the Great: "Someone, when he is fighting with his brother, becomes distressed inside himself, thinking thoughts like this: should I say this or that to him? No, I will not say it ... He is so unkind to me! Should I slander him perhaps? ... No, it is better to remain silent ... But it is true that we have the commands of God, but we must preserve our honor also ... In this way, it is difficult to completely reject oneself."[118] This is why the apostle Paul commands us to completely cast ourselves off and to put on the entire armor of God, and not to arm ourselves with some other weapon. Fasting alone is not enough, nor is prayer alone enough, nor is almsgiving or chastity by itself! The complete armor of God is this: all the commandments of the Gospel. Having transgressed one of them, you have transgressed them all—the entire law: "Whoever therefore breaks one of the least of these commandments, and teaches men so, shall be called least in the kingdom of heaven." "Therefore have I held straight to all Thy commandments; I have hated every wrong way" (Ps 118:128). "Therefore take up the whole armor of God, that you may be able to withstand in the evil day, and having done all, to stand" (Eph 6:13). Only he who has fulfilled, without exception, all the commandments, can stand in the face of the enemy. "The evil day" is the time of the worst temptations and attacks of the devil, such as the courageous warriors of Christ all encounter during their earthly life, and after they overcome them, they pass from eternal death to a resurrection of their soul.[119] For all other Christians, the evil day is the day of the soul's separation from its body, a time when they will have to cross the toll houses of the air.

The holy ones of God put on the whole armor of God. They took the Gospel as the rule of their life, and their words—the words of their mind, heart, and lips—were the words of God (see Eph 6:17), that is, the name of the Lord Jesus Christ. With this spiritual sword they felled and defeated the fiery sword of the enemy. The words uttered by the devil, and the images that he inspired could not pierce into their souls, being uselessly cast aside. Illumined by divine grace, even from a distance they could sense the approach of the noetic thieves and murderers, and saw in their attentiveness, as in a mirror, the dark faces of the demons.[120] Having rejected their communion here, they deprived them of any authority over their souls after death, and so they passed without hindrance past the toll houses, for they defeated them in their own good time:

> Only he who has truly rejected the world, who labors, having cast off the yoke of the world, who has freed himself and has sincerely separated himself for vain desires, carnal passions, authority and glory of man, who has received mystically in secret asceticism help from the Lord himself, who abides firmly in His service, who totally abandons himself with his soul and body to the Lord, only such a person, I say, can find the opposition, secret passions, invisible nets, hidden battles, and inner warfare. Being in the midst of this warfare and constantly praying to God, he will accept from heaven a spiritual weapon that the blessed apostle described: the breastplate of righteousness, the helmet of salvation, the shield of faith, and the sword of the spirit. Having put these on, he can oppose the secret attacks of the enemies directed at him. Having acquired these weapons through prayer, patience, petitions, fasting, faith, he can courageously wage war against the principalities, powers, and princes of this world, and having defeated the enemy powers through the help of the Spirit and his own virtues, he becomes worthy of eternal life.[121]

Mortal Sin

Earlier we wrote that any mortal sin that is not healed with the necessary repentance will subject the Orthodox Christian to eternal suffering. We also said that pagans and heretics belong, as it were, to hell, and have no hope of salvation, being deprived of Christ, Who is the only means to acquire salvation. Mortal sins for a Christian include the following: heresy, schism, blasphemy against God, black magic, suicide, unlawful sexual intercourse, adultery, sexual perversions, incest, drunkenness, sacrilege, murder, thievery, and any cruel, inhuman violence. Only one of these sins—suicide—is outside the pale of repentance, but each of these other ones does kill the soul, and makes it incapable of eternal blessedness, at least until it heals itself through the necessary repentance. If any person falls at least once to any of these sins, he dies in his soul: "For whoever shall keep the whole law, and yet stumble in one point, he is guilty of all. For He who said, 'Do not commit adultery,' also said, 'Do not murder.' Now if you do not commit adultery, but you do murder, you have become a transgressor of the law" (Jas 2:10–11).

However, if you have fallen into mortal sin, do not despair! Run to the medicine of repentance, to which the Saviour called us until the very last minute of His earthly life, as we read in the Gospel: "He who believes in Me, though he may die, he shall live" (John 11:25). However, it is dangerous to remain in mortal sin, and it is calamitous when mortal sin becomes habitual. No good deeds can buy a soul out of hell if it has not first purified its body of mortal sin before death.

During the reign of Emperor Leo, a famous and very rich man lived in Constantinople. He was known for his great feats of almsgiving to the poor. Unfortunately, he was an adulterer, and he remained an adulterer until old age. Though he constantly gave alms, he kept falling to the sin of adultery. Then, he suddenly died. Patriarch Gennadius and the other bishops spoke for a long time, wondering about his future fate. Some said that he was saved, because of these words from the Scriptures: "The ransom of a man's soul is his own wealth" (Prov 13:8). Others insisted this could not be the case, because a servant of God must be pure and without blemish, since the Scriptures also say, "whoever shall keep the whole law, and yet stumble in one point, he is guilty of all" (Jas 2:10). God also said, "I will judge every one of you according to his ways" (Ezek 33:20). The patriarch commanded all the monasteries and all the recluses to ask God that He would reveal the fate of the dead man, and God did so to a certain recluse.

He invited the patriarch and told him the following: "Last night, I was standing at prayer and saw a certain place where at the right hand stood Eden, filled with unutterable good things, but to the left stood a fiery lake whose flames reached the clouds. Between blessed Eden and the terrible fire stood the dead man, tied up completely, groaning horribly. He often looked at paradise and wept bitterly. And I saw a light-bearing angel approaching him, who said, 'Man! Why do you groan? Here, for the sake of your almsgiving, you have avoided torment; however, for not abandoning adultery, you are also deprived of Eden.'"

The patriarch and those who were with him, having heard this, were filled with terror and said, "Truly did the apostle says, 'Flee sexual immorality. Every sin that a man does is outside the body, but he who commits sexual immorality sins against his own body'" (1 Cor 6:18). Where are they who say, if we commit sexual immorality, we will be saved by alms? A merciful man, if he is truly merciful, first must have mercy on himself and acquire bodily purity, without which no one will see God. Silver given by an impure hand and an unrepentant heart brings no benefit whatsoever.[122]

Passions

Also deprived of hope of salvation are those Christians who have acquired sinful passions and through them have entered communion with Satan, having rejected communion with God. Passions are those sinful habits of the soul that have after frequent repetition become, as it were, a natural quality of the person. These include overeating, drunkenness, sensuality, a scattered life, forgetfulness of God, remembrance of evils, cruelty, love of money, miserliness, despair, laziness, hypocrisy, falsehood, thievery, vanity, pride, and so on. Each of these passions, if they become a natural part of a person's character and as such a kind of rule of life, makes him incapable of spiritual consolation either on earth or heaven, even if the person never fell to mortal sin. "Do not you know that the unrighteous will not inherit the kingdom of God? Do not be deceived. Neither fornicators, nor idolaters, nor adulterers, nor homosexuals, nor sodomites, nor thieves, nor covetous, nor drunkards, nor revilers, nor extortioners will inherit the kingdom of God" (1 Cor 6:9-10). "Now the works of the flesh are evident, which are: adultery, fornication, uncleanness, lewdness, idolatry, sorcery, hatred, contentions, jealousies, outbursts of wrath, selfish ambitions, dissensions, heresies, envy, murders, drunkenness, revelries, and the like; of which I tell you beforehand, just as I also told you in time past, that those who practice such things will not inherit the kingdom of God. But the fruit of the Spirit is love, joy, peace, longsuffering, kindness, goodness, faithfulness, gentleness, self-control. Against such there is no law. And those who are Christ's have crucified the flesh with its passions and desires" (Gal 5:19-24).

The passions require the assiduous application of the medicines of repentance and a timely rooting of the virtue opposed to the passion. Passion is not always expressed in action; it can secretly live in the heart of a person, ruling over his feelings and thoughts. A passion is known when a person cannot stop imagining the sin and finding pleasure in that imagining, when the one in bondage to the sin has no power to fight against the inclination to sin both in thought and in imagination, which in its sweetness completely swallow up his wisdom and strength. The passionate one does not stop sinning in imagination and in the thoughts of his heart, and through this, he persists in his communion with the dark spirits, confirming their lordship over him, and, consequently, his eternal damnation. The Lord said to his prophet: "Cry aloud with strength and spare not; lift up your voice like a trumpet, and declare to My people their sins, and to the house of Jacob their lawlessness. They seek Me day by day, and desire to know My ways. As a people who did righteousness, and did not forsake the judgment of their God, they now ask Me about righteous judgement, and desire to draw near to God, saying 'Why have we fasted, but You did not see it? Why have we humbled our souls, but you did not know it?' Because in the days of your fasts you seek your own wills, and mistreat those under your authority" (Isa 58:1-3).

Or, in the words of St Isaac the Syrian, "O your evil thoughts! You offer them sacrifices as to idols! You have confessed your evil thoughts to be your gods, and you offer them the highest sacrifice: your freedom, which you should have dedicated to Me in your good will and pure conscience."[123]

Man can only feel a hope of salvation when he will see himself a constant victor in the invisible warfare. This is the thought expressed by David: "By this 1 know Thou favorest me, that mine enemy doth not triumph against me" (Ps 40:12). He prayed to be given this blessed state when he said, "O cleanse Thou me from my secret faults, and from strangers spare they servant";[124] "if they get not the dominion over me, then shall 1 be undefiled, and 1 shall be cleansed of great sin" (Ps 18:13–14). "O give me the comfort of Thy salvation, and stablish me with Thy governing Spirit." "And the words of my mouth, and the meditation of my heart shall be always acceptable before Thee, O Lord, my helper, and my deliverer" (Ps 50:14, 18:15). Evidently, what David calls the secret and great sin is what we call passions. He associated this great sin with "strangers," because it is formed from the pleasant thoughts inspired by the demons that have become habitual, though they are foreign to the soul's natural state, and they make the soul sick, since they are unnatural to it.

Purity worthy of heaven appears after passions are rooted out of the heart. Only the Holy Spirit can fully purify man of passions and return his authority over himself, which the devil stole. In a state of dispassion, man can acquire pure love, and his thoughts begin to constantly remain with God and in God. The soul that has sensed the presence of the Spirit, that has seen itself defeated by sinful thoughts and images, begins to sense an inexplicable joy of salvation. This joy is nothing like normal human joy, which is born solely of vanity, which is formed of self-satisfaction, when man deludes himself and when others delude him, or when his earthly success deludes him. Spiritual joy that announces salvation is filled with humble-mindedness, filled with gratitude to God, accompanied with abundant and constant tears, constant prayers; it is not ever satiated with self-condemnation and self-humiliation; it pours out into confession to God, into glorification of God, and it leads to a deadening toward the world. It is a foretaste of the eternal life. It is a living knowledge of God, crying out mystically:

> The voice of joy and salvation is in the dwellings of the righteous;
> the right hand of the Lord hath brought mighty things to pass. The
> right hand of the Lord lifted me up; the right hand of the Lord hath
> brought mighty things to pass. I shall not die, but live, and declare the

works of the Lord. With chastening hath the Lord chastened me, but He hath not given me over unto death. Open unto me the gates of righteousness, that, having gone into them, I may give thanks unto the Lord. This is the gate of the Lord, the righteous shall enter into it. I will thank Thee, for Thou hast heard me, and art become my salvation. (Ps 117:15–21)

The gates of the Lord are grace-filled humility.[125] When these gates of Divine Righteousness open before the mind, man ceases to condemn his brother, to remember evil things done to him, to accuse him; he ceases justifying himself, and he comes to recognize the ineffable hand of God in all that occurs; therefore, he rejects his own righteousness as foulness. Man enters these gates through the confession of the countless benefits of God and his own countless sins, washed away by tears of repentance and compunction, through pure prayer and spiritual vision approaching even the face of God. Let us flee, let us flee from our murderer—sin! Let us flee from not only mortal sin, but even forgivable sin, lest such small sins turn, because of our inattentiveness, into a passion that in hell will be weighed the same as mortal sin.

Yes, there are forgivable sins. If someone were to become enamored of gluttony, of looking with lust at someone and enjoying lustful thoughts; if someone were to speak foul words, lie, steal some small thing, become vain or proud of oneself, become angry, become upset with someone for a short time—if repentance follows these sins, we quickly receive forgiveness from God. A forgivable sin does not sever a Christian from divine grace; it does not kill his soul, as mortal sin does. However, even forgivable sins are pernicious if one does not repent of them, but only increases their burden by frequent repetition. As an example, according to the Fathers, a man can be equally drowned by a single large rock tied to his neck or a bag filled with sand. Thus, one can go to hell because of either a mortal sin or an accumulation of many small, forgivable sins. After all, what did the rich man in the parable do that was so terrible, if he daily feasted using money that was his to dispose of? And yet, the Gospel makes clear that the reason he perished was precisely this frivolous lifestyle, since it led him to completely forget his eternal future and virtue. Frivolity had become his passions; he knew no other life outside of it.

It is a terrible calamity to be wounded in the heart by a passion! This wound sometimes is inflicted by the most insignificant events: a single, seemingly innocent glance, one frivolous work, a single careless touch can infect a person with an incurable illness. What sort of sin could a recluse possibly fall to, since he never left his cell, never tempted anyone, and instead served as edification for those who knew him? And yet, he perished because of his invisible converse with Satan, for which reason he did not spend even a single hour in the consolation of communion with the Holy Spirit.

An abbess's niece lived in the same convent as her aunt. This niece was physically very beautiful, and she had a beautiful character as well. All the sisters admired her and were edified by her angelic appearance and her unusual modesty. She died and was buried triumphantly, in the first assurance that her pure soul had ascended into the mansions of heaven. Upset by being separated from her, her aunt the abbess prayed constantly, adding fasting and vigils, and asked the Lord to reveal the degree of spiritual glory that her niece had received among the host of blessed virgins in heaven. One time, when the abbess, prayed in the silence of her cell at midnight, the earth suddenly opened up before her feet and bubbling lava poured out. Beside herself in terror, she looked into the pit yawning at her feet, and she was shocked to see her niece among those in the flames.

"My God!" she cried out in despair, "Is that you that I see?"

"Yes," answered the dead woman with a terrible groan.

"Why?" her aunt asked with pain in her heart. "I had hoped to see you in heavenly glory, among the hosts of angels, among the pure lambs of Christ, but you ... Why?"

"Woe is me, an accursed one!" answered her niece. "I am at fault for coming down into this flame that constantly eats at me but never destroys me. You wanted to see me, and God revealed to you the secret of my situation."

"But for what reason?" once again the abbess asked with tears.

"For this reason," answered the tortured one, "that I only seemed to be virginal to your eyes, but in fact I was not. Although I never defiled my flesh with sexual sin, but my thoughts and my secret desires and the movements of my heart were dedicated to sexual immortality. Though my virginal body was pure, I was not able to preserve the purity of my soul, my thoughts, and the movements of my heart. For this reason, I suffer. Because of my carelessness, I fed inside myself a sense of attachment to a certain young man, finding sweetness in my thoughts and imagination with images of his beautiful body and carnal union with him, and knowing that this was a sin, I was ashamed to reveal this to my spiritual father during confession. Because of this sinful pleasure at impure thoughts and imagination, the angels disdained me after death, and left me in the hands of the demons. And now I burn in the fire of Gehenna, and I will burn forever, and there will never come a time when my tortures will end, for those who are rejected by heaven will suffer eternally."

Saying this, the unfortunate woman groaned, gnashed her teeth, then, carried away by a wave of fiery lava, was hid from the gaze of the abbess.[126]

"We must preserve the soul and keep it pure by any means possible," said St Macarius, "lest it be united to impure and evil thoughts. Just as the body, when it united with another body, becomes infected with impurity, so also the soul becomes corrupted when it is united with impure and evil thoughts and agrees with them. This is true not only concerning one or two kinds of thoughts that lead to sin, but all evil thoughts in general, such as thoughts of doubt, flattery, vanity, anger, envy, and excessive ardor. To reject all such thoughts is to follow the words of the apostle: 'Beloved, let us cleanse ourselves from all filthiness of the flesh and spirit, perfecting holiness in the fear of God' (2 Corinthians 7:1). Know that even the secret parts of the soul are corrupted by the activity of sinful thoughts, according to the words of the great apostle: 'If anyone defiles the temple of God, God will destroy him. For the temple of God is holy, which temple you are' (1 Corinthians 3:17). Thus the one who destroys the soul and the mind by uniting and coupling with evil, is worthy of death. Just as we must preserve the body from visible sin, so also we must preserve the soul, that bridegroom of Christ, from impure thoughts. 'I have betrothed you to one husband ... Christ' (2 Corinthians 11:2). As another passage from Scriptures says, 'Keep your heart with all watchfullness, for from these words are the issues of life' (Proverbs 4:22 LXX). And again: learn from the Scriptures that 'dishonest reasoning separates people from God' (Wisdom of Solomon 1:3)."[127]

St Nilus of Sora says this concerning passions:

> Passions result either in proportionate repentance or future suffering.
> One must repent of passions and pray for deliverance from it; it will
> lead to future suffering for lack of repentance, but not if there is inter-
> nal war against it. If the battle itself were a cause for future sufferings,
> then no one but the completely dispassionate would ever receive for-
> giveness of sins, while Peter of Damascus makes it clear that many do
> receive it. He who is attacked by any passion whatsoever must assidu-
> ously battle against it, as the Fathers say. Let us offer the example of the
> passion of lust. He who is attacked by the passion of lust toward some
> person must avoid any converse with this person or even being in the
> same place at the same time, or even any touch of that person's cloth-
> ing or any smell of that person's presence. Whoever does not preserve
> himself in all these ways is subject to passion, and he will fall into lust
> in his thoughts and his heart, as the Fathers say. Such a person lights
> the oven of passions himself, and opens the door for evil thoughts like
> wild beasts.[128]

Preparation for Death

Let us prepare ourselves for eternity and for the passage into eternity
that we call death, even in this earthly life, in this threshold of eternity.
Our earthly life does not belong to us, but it is a constant battle between
life and death. From time to time we lean in one direction, then in another,
vacillating between them, being fought over by both. If we correctly assess
that short moment during which we have our earthly life, comparing
it with the incalculable majesty of eternity, then we can only find one
possible use for this earthly life. As the Word of God Himself spoke of
this earthly life:

> "Do not fear, little flock, for it is your Father's good pleasure to give
> you the kingdom. Sell what you have and give alms; provide yourselves
> money bags which do not grow old, a treasure in the heavens that does
> not fail, where no thief approaches nor moth destroys. For where your
> treasure is, there your heart will be also. Let your waist be girded and
> your lamps burning; and you yourselves be like men who wait for their

master, when he will return from the wedding, that when he comes and knocks they may open to him immediately. Blessed are those servants whom the master, when he comes, will find watching. Assuredly, I say to you that he will gird himself and have them sit down to eat, and will come and serve them. And if he should come in the second watch, or come in the third watch, and find them so, blessed are those servants. But know this, that if the master of the house had known what hour the thief would come, he would have watched and not allowed his house to be broken into. Therefore you also be ready, for the Son of Man is coming at an hour you do not expect." ... And the Lord said, "Who then is that faithful and wise steward, whom his master will make ruler over his household, to give them their portion of food in due season? Blessed is that servant whom his master will find so doing when he comes. Truly, I say to you that he will make him ruler over all that he has. But if that servant says in his heart, 'My master is delaying his coming,' and begins to beat the male and female servants, and to eat and drink and be drunk, the master of that servant will come on a day when he is not looking for him, and at an hour when he is not aware, and will cut him in two and appoint him his portion with the unbelievers." (Luke 12:32–46)

Small and lowly is the noetic flock of true Christians. It is held in contempt, persecuted by the proud sons of this world. However, the Lord commanded us not to weaken in sorrows or be afraid, He commands us not to pay any attention to our sorrows, instead striving with our entire attention to the heavenly kingdom promised by the good will of God the Father. He commands us to transform our earthly money, through alms, into heavenly money, so that the very treasure of man, being in heaven, might lead him toward heaven. He commands us to so arrange our circumstances and lead such a life that we will constantly be ready for death. Calling this earthly life a dark night, He tells us that it is unknown in which hour of this night our death will come. It may come during childhood, during youth, in adulthood, or in old age. The Lord threatens all who believe their deaths to be far from them, allowing themselves to abuse their earthly life and the gifts of God, with sudden death.

The true disciples of Christ have fulfilled this command of God to the letter. The apostle Paul says concerning himself that he died daily (see 1 Cor

15:31). Truly, whoever is prepared for death every day dies daily. Whoever has trampled all sins and sinful desires, whose thoughts have ascended from here to the heavens and remain there, such a person dies daily. Whoever dies daily already lives with an eternal, true life.[129]

Very few Christians attain such a life of keeping their mind and heart in heaven while living on earth, a life that is a daily passage into eternity, so to speak. Even those who live in monasteries rarely attain such a life; naturally, those who live in the world have even greater difficulty in attaining such a spiritual state. Earthly cares constantly weigh down the mind to the earth, yoking it to temporary and perishable realities, stealing the memory of eternity from the mind. However, this should not lead Christians to despair. If a Christian cannot constantly abide mentally in the realm of the eternal and spiritual, he may turn to it often and prepare himself properly for death. Such preparation consists of daily or at least frequent confession of sins, both before one's spiritual father and in one's own spiritual cell before the one Knower of hearts—God. We must prepare ourselves for death through abstaining from excessive food and drink, through abstinence from idle talk, jokes, laughter, frivolity, and games. We should limit the luxuries that the world requires in its vanity and avoid all excesses that banish the remembrance of death from the mind, deluding it into thinking that earthly life is eternal. We must prepare ourselves by praying from a humble and contrite heart, with tears, sighs, and weeping. We must prepare ourselves with abundant almsgiving, forgiveness of offences, love and goodwill toward enemies, patience in the face of all earthly sorrows and temptations, because all these redeem us from eternal sufferings in hell. If death catches a Christian amid such labors, then, of course, he will be as though girt about the loins, that is, prepared for the completion of the long journey from earth to heaven, with a lit torch in his hand, that is, led by reasonings and actions that have been illumined by Divine truth.

Remembrance of Death

One of the most effective means of preparing for death is the remembrance and memory of death. Evidently, from the aforementioned words of the Saviour, this is commanded by God Himself. Even the Old Testament says, "Remember the time that you will die, and you will never sin"

(Wisdom of Sirach 7:36). Holy monks especially exercised this part of their spiritual labors. In them, the remembrance of death, augmented by grace, turned into a living vision of the mystery of death, and such vision was accompanied with fiery prayer, abundant tears, and profound groaning of the heart. Without constant remembrance of death and the coming judgment of God, they admitted that any exalted spiritual labors are profoundly dangerous, as they can lead to spiritual delusion.

St Anthony the Great, in his instructions to his disciples, recommends remembrance of death:

> For if we too live as though dying daily, we shall not sin. And the meaning of that saying is, that as we rise day by day we should think that we shall not abide till evening; and again, when about to lie down to sleep, we should think that we shall not rise up. For our life is naturally uncertain, and Providence allots it to us daily. But thus ordering our daily life, we shall neither fall into sin, nor have a lust for anything, nor cherish wrath against any, nor shall we heap up treasure upon earth. But, as though under the daily expectation of death, we shall be without wealth, and shall forgive all things to all men, nor shall we retain at all the desire of women or of any other foul pleasure. But we shall turn from it as past and gone, ever striving and looking forward to the day of Judgment. For the greater dread and danger of torment ever destroys the ease of pleasure, and sets up the soul if it is like to fall.[130]

St Isaac the Syrian says,

> Who is worth to be called wise? He who actively has come to know that there is a limit to this life; such a one can put a limit to his sins.[131] The first thought sent by God's love for man and that accompanies his soul into eternal life, is the thought of one's death. This thought naturally leads to a disdain of the world. It also begins in man all good activity, instructing him unto life. Divine power that cooperates with man, when it wants to reveal life within him, places this thought at his foundation, as we have already said. If man does not put out this light through earthly cares and idle talk, but will grow in silence, going deep into himself and practicing stillness, then it will lead him to profound vision that is unutterable in words. This thought is extremely

hateful to Satan, who uses all his powers to steal it from man. If it would be possible, he would give man all the kingdoms of the entire world, if only through this to remove that thought form the mind of man. He would do it eagerly if he could. The cunning one! He knows that if the remembrance of death is rooted out of man, then his mind will no longer remain in the land of delusion, and all demonic cunning will fail to approach him. Do not think that we are thinking of the first thought that awakens in us after we remember death; we area speaking of the complete thought, when this remembrance constantly comes to man, always confirming him and leading him to wonder. The first thought is carnal, while the second state is spiritual vision and wondrous grace. This vision is clothed in radiant thoughts. He who has it no longer pays attention to the world and does not care for his own body.[132]

When you approach your bed, say to it: "O my bed! Will you become today my coffin? I do not know what will happen to me tonight. Perhaps, instead of a temporary sleep, I will encounter eternal sleep tonight. While you have feet, run to act until your feet are tied by unbreakable bonds. While you have fingers, crucify them for prayer before death comes. While you have eyes, fill them with tears until they are covered with dust and ashes. As a rose fades as soon as wind touches it, so you also die if any of the elements shake your internal composition. O man! Root inside your heart the thought of your own death and remind yourself constantly: Look! Here is the summoner who comes for me. He is at the gates already. Why are you sitting? This journey is for all time, and from it you will not return."[133]

As of all foods bread is the most essential, so the thought of death is the most necessary of all works. The remembrance of death amongst those in the midst of society gives birth to distress and frivolity, and even more—to despondency. But amongst those who are free from noise it produces the putting aside of cares, and constant prayer and guarding of the mind. But these same virtues both produce the remembrance of death and are also produced by it. He who wishes ever to retain within him the remembrance of death and judgment and God, and at the same time yields to material cares and distractions, is like a man who is swimming and wants to clap his hands. A vivid remembrance of death cuts down food; and when in humility food is cut, the passions are cut out too. Just as the Fathers lay down that perfect love knows no sin, so I for my part declare that a perfect sense of death is free from fear. Just as some declare that the abyss is infinite, for they call it a bottomless place, so the thought of death brings chastity and activity to a state of incorruption. It is impossible, someone says, impossible to spend the present day devoutly unless we regard it as the last of our whole life. Let us rest assured that the remembrance of death, like all other blessings, is a gift of God; since how is it that often when we are at the very tombs we are left tearless and hard; and frequently when we have no such sight, we are full of compunction?[134]

Barsanuphius the Great insists that a person who cuts of his will in all this, who has a humble heart and always keeps his death before his eyes can be saved by the grace of God, and no matter where he might be, no fear will touch him. Such a one forgets those things which are behind and reaches forward to those things which are ahead (see Phil 3:13). As he writes to one of his monks: "Let your thoughts be strengthened by the remembrance of your coming death, for no one knows the hour of its coming. Let us strive to do good before we pass from this life. We do not know what day we will be called, and so let us not be among those outside the bridal chamber, standing with the five foolish virgins who took their lamps, but did not bring enough oil."[135]

To another monk he wrote, "Know that time waits for no man, and when the hour comes, the summoner of death is implacable. Who has ever begged him and been heard? He is a true slave of the true Master, exactly fulfilling His commands. Let us fear that terrifying day and hour in which neither brother, nor relative, nor master, nor authority, nor riches, nor glory will save us. All that will remain is man and his deeds."[136]

"It is good for man to remember his death, so that he may make a habit of the knowledge that he is mortal. A mortal man is not eternal; a moral man will leave this age not according to his own will. Through constant memory of death, man begins to willfully to do."[137]

St Philotheus of Sinai recommends that each monk dedicate every morning to sober and prolonged prayer, and after eating some food, to dedicate some time to the remembrance and thoughts of death.[138] Quoting the witness of this ancient Father, our own St Nilus of Sora advises monks to dedicate some time after meals to thoughts of death and the judgment.[139] Anyone who wishes to learn remembrance of death and become freed of the delusive and false mental state in which man imagines he is immortal (and that death is only a reality for other people) should follow these instructions of the Fathers, for they are the result of blessed experience. After forcing yourself to think of death, the merciful Lord will send you a vivid foretaste of it, and such a state will help any ascetic of Christ during his prayer. It has the effect of taking the monk in good time to the dread judgment of Christ; and at this judgment the man may beg the man-loving Lord concerning the forgiveness of his sins, and he will receive it. Therefore, St John of the Ladder called the prayer of those who truly pray a judgement before the throne of the Lord, a judgment preceding the general coming judgment.[140]

St Philotheus of Sinai wrote that the remembrance of death purifies the mind and body:

> Having once experienced the beauty of this mindfulness of death, I was so wounded and delighted by it—in Spirit, not through the eye— that I wanted to make it my life's companion, for I was enraptured by its loveliness and majesty, its humility and contrite joy, by how full of reflection it is, how apprehensive of the judgment to come, and how aware of life's anxieties. It makes life-giving, healing tears flow from our bodily eyes, while from our noetic eyes rises a fount of wisdom that delights the mind. This daughter of Adam—this mindfulness of death—I always longed, as I said, to have as my, companion, to sleep with, to talk with, and to enquire from her what will happen after the body has been discarded. But unclean forgetfulness, the devil's murky daughter, has frequently prevented this.[141]
>
> Perpetual and vivid mindfulness of death has the same effect: it gives birth to grief accompanied by a certain sweetness and joy, and to watchfulness of intellect.[142]
>
> He who really redeems his life, always dwelling on the thought and remembrance of death, and wisely withholding the intellect from the passions, is in a far better position to discern the continual presence of

demonic provocations than the man who chooses to live without being mindful of death. The latter, by purifying the heart through spiritual knowledge alone, but not keeping in mind any thought of grief, may sometimes appear to control all the destructive passions by his skill; yet he is unwittingly fettered by one of them, the worst all—pride, into which, abandoned by God, he sometimes falls. Such a person mast be very vigilant lest, deluded by conceit, he becomes deranged. For, as St Paul says (cf. 1 Cor 4:6, 18, 19; 8:1), souls that gather knowledge from here and there tend to become haughty and disdainful towards their inferiors, as they regard them; they lack the spark of the love which builds up. But he who all the day long is mindful of death discerns the assaults of the demons more keenly; and he counterattacks and repels them.[143]

Vivid mindfulness of death embraces many virtues. It begets grief; it promotes the exercise of self-control in all things; it is a reminder of hell; it is the mother of prayer and tears; it induces guarding of the heart and detachment from material things; it is a source of attentiveness and discrimination. These in their turn produce the twofold fear of God. In addition, the purging of impassioned thoughts from the heart embraces many of the Lord's commandments.[144]

St Hesychius of Jerusalem includes in his list of examples of temperance the constant remembrance of death, contained in the heart. He compares remembrance of death to a guard standing at the gates of the soul and forbidding entrance to all evil thoughts. "Let us, as much as possible, remember death constantly. From such remembrance is born within us the casting aside of all cares and vanities, the preservation of the mind, and constant prayer."[145]

The constant remembrance of death is a wondrous grace, the exclusive recourse of the saints, especially those who dedicated themselves to intense repentance in unbreakable silence. Only in silence do the most exalted virtues blossom and bear fruit, like rare flowers in a greenhouse. As for us, weak and passionate ones, it is necessary to force ourselves to remember death, to assimilate to the heart the habit of thinking about death, even if such thoughts are extremely abhorrent to a sin-loving and world-loving heart. To make such training more secure, according to the teachings of the Fathers already mentioned, it is very useful to set aside

a certain hour every day, free from all cares, during which one may dedicate one's thoughts to the salvific remembrance of our terrifying, implacable death. At first, even the most dispassionate thoughts about death will
be difficult to force on our minds, and this is only further proof (among
many others sources of proof) of the fallenness of our nature. The constant
diversion of our thoughts, a distraction that has become natural to use,
and the accompanying dark forgetfulness, constantly steal the thought
of death from those who begin to work at frequently remembering it.
Then other hindrances begin to appear: unexpectedly, extremely urgent
work appears precisely at the time dedicated to this salvific training. Later,
to completely stop this activity, even the remembrance of the existence
of this important work—the remembrance of death—disappears from our
memory. When, having recognized this as the snare of the devil, we keep
stubbornly at our labor, then we will see in ourselves a new kind of warfare—thoughts of doubt about the worth and effectiveness of this labor,
as well as blasphemous thoughts and thoughts of ridicule, which diminish
the remembrance of death as foolish and ridiculous, or as manifestations of false humility, and so the demons use false virtue to separate us
from this saving work.

If, by God's great mercy, we are victorious in this attack, then horrifying fear will appear, produced by a vivid remembrance and visualization
of death, even a kind of foretaste of it, which at first is incredibly painful
for our aging self. Our imagination is seized with terror; cold shivering
covers our bodies, weakening them physically. The heart is crushed by
unbearable sorrow, often connected with hopelessness.

We should not reject this state; nor should be fear its apparently
pernicious consequences. "The fear of sufferings and the physical illness
that comes from it is beneficial to anyone who begins to live in God," says
Symeon the New Theologian. "He who imagines beginning the life in
God without this physical illness and the accompanying difficulties not
only lays a foundation of his future activity on sand, but he is like someone who plans to build a house in the air without any foundation at all,
which is impossible. This illness soon gives birth to all joys; these difficulties tear apart all the bonds of sins and passion; this torturer is the
source not of death, but eternal life. Whoever does not seek to avoid this

illness that comes from the fear of eternal suffering, and who does not jump away from it, but instead, by the goodwill of his heart, leans into it and lays on his own shoulders its bonds, such a one will begin walking more quickly, and this illness will then present him to the King of kings."

"When this occurs, and the ascetic partially sees the glory of God, then the bonds will immediately be loosed, the terrifying fear will flee, the illness of his heart will transform into joy, and a source of tears will open up like an ever-flowing river. In the mind will appear quietude, tranquility, meekness, unutterable sweetness, courage, helping the ascetic strive freely and without hindrance to complete obedience to the commandments of God."[146]

It is clear: such a transformation occurs because of the grace-filled appearance of the hope of salvation in the heart. Then remembrance of death will make sorrow melt into joy, and bitter tears will turn into tears of joy. The person who begins by weeping at the remembrance of death as a remembrance of his coming execution, suddenly begins to weep at this remembrance as at the remembrance of a return to a long-lost and priceless fatherland. This is the fruit of remembrance of death. Since this fruit is so important, we must be courageous in cultivating it and in overcoming all rational objections through labor and constancy. We must believe that the fruit will be acquired by us in its own good time, according to the mercy and grace of God. The remembrance of death, and the fears that will accompany it, this remembrance, when accompanied by sincere prayer and tears for oneself, can replace all other ascetic labors lasting throughout the course of a person's entire life. It can give a person purity of heart, and it can attract the grace of the Holy Spirit, giving him a free ascension to heaven past the aerial powers.

A Call to Remember and Think of Death

Before we acquire this blessed state of prayer during which the mind immediately sees one's imminent death and fears that death (as a creature must fear the threatening of the Creator, uttered together with the commandment) it is useful to arouse within oneself the remembrance of death through frequently visiting cemeteries, visiting the sick in hospitals, being present at their death and burial, and by frequent calling to mind our contemporaries' recent deaths. How many of our acquaintances who loved the earthly life and enjoyed good things during their life, who hoped to live a long life and were not in any sense old, were still seized by death unexpectedly! None of them could say to impending death, "Wait! Go away! I do not want to die yet!"

Others did not have the time to make any sort of will or preparation. Still others were taken right in the middle of a festive meal, at a luxurious banquet. Others died on the road. Others drowned; others committed suicide or were murdered. Others were attacked by wild beasts. Others lay down to sleep, hoping to comfort the body with a short, temporary sleep, but fell asleep eternally. Look around you: what a multitude of relatives, friends, and acquaintances, seized by death, have been taken from our society! Among them, the glorious left their glory behind, along with their power and their honors. The rich left behind their riches, gathered with great care and difficulty, kept with extreme miserliness. Death separated parents from large families, husbands from wives, friends from friends. It has struck the genius in the middle of his great deeds. It took from human society its most important members at the most inopportune moments. No one could stop death or counteract it. No one could demand an account of it, especially when it acts so contrary to human reason. What is not vain on this earth? What is not passing? What has any kind of constancy? Truly, it is only the life in Christ, which extends beyond the limits of the coffin and only grows and develops in all its beauty and brilliance after the death of the body. Everything else is more passing than a shadow, more delusive than a dream ... The long labors of man for the sake of passing things are destroyed by death in a single moment.[147]

Having come to understand the brevity of our earthly life and the vanity of all earthly gain and advantages, having come to know the horrifying future awaiting those who disdain the Redeemer and His redemption, instead offering themselves as a whole burnt offering to sin and corruption, let us turn aside the eyes of our mind from the delusive and seductive beauty of this world, which easily ensnares weak human hearts into slavery. Instead, let us gaze at the terrifying, but salvific vision of our imminent death. Let us cry for ourselves in good time; let us wash and purify ourselves with tears and the confession of our sins, written int the books of the prince of this world. Let us acquire the grace of the Holy Spirit, which is the proof of being chosen for salvation. This grace is necessary for our swift passage through the aerial region and to be granted access through the gates of heaven into those heavenly mansions.

The "unrighteous mammon" (Luke 16:11) is what the Gospel calls all earthly gain that we receive because of our fallenness. Let us use it, according to the advice of the Gospel, to acquire heavenly treasures by abundant almsgiving. Let us use our earthly life, this great gift of God, as it should be used, as God intends it to be used, to come to know God and our own selves, and to arrange our eternal fate properly. Let us not lose any time; let us use our time wisely. It will not be given to us twice; its loss is irrevocable.

O exiles from Eden! We are not on earth for the sake of parties or banquets or games, but we are here to kill the death that killed us, using faith, repentance, and the cross. If we do this, we will find our lost Eden.

May the merciful Lord give the readers of this word, and the one who wrote it, the remembrance of death during this earthly life. Through this remembrance of death, and by destroying all striving toward all earthly vanity, and by living for eternity, we will remove from ourselves the terror of death when it approaches, and we will pass into the blessed, eternal, true life. Amen.

CHAPTER 3

Theological Teaching on Death

"Homily on Death" was written only with an ascetic aim. However, readers have asked for more exactness in a theological sense concerning some issues in the text. Therefore, I have written this addition, which was published in later editions of this work. Several objections were made concerning several dogmatic teachings of the Orthodox Church that I included in my work "On Death." Unfortunately, these objections come from teachings written in Western, Catholic sources. For this reason, I do not find it excessive to inform the children of the Orthodox Church of certain opinions of Western Catholic writers concerning spirits, heaven, and hell, in order to show their unfoundedness and imprecision. I used as my exemplar of the Western position the Theological Encyclopedia of Abbe Bergier.[1]

This is a summary of the Catholic position offered by Abbe Bergier. The West, having accepted in recent years many teachings that are foreign, even abhorrent, to the Orthodox Church, have also recently accepted a foreign and abhorrent teaching concerning the total immateriality of created spirits. Thereby, Western theologians ascribe to created spirits the same kind of immateriality as God. They have placed God, the Creator all things, in the same row as the created spirit, believing them to be independent of space completely, rejecting that they have any kind of bodies capable of movement. In a word, they ascribe to created beings the same qualities as God has, even though they still insist on these creatures being created and limited. There is an obvious contradiction in this teaching; it destroys itself. Western writers thought to establish their opinions on the holy Scriptures, on the Fathers of the Church, and on science. In three specific ways, we find it necessary to offer a definite rebuttal that will serve simultaneously as proof of the truth and holiness of the teaching offered by the Orthodox Church.

God is perfect Being, having nothing in common with created beings. He alone is Existence itself. "I AM the Existing One," He said of Himself (Exod 3:14). "I am the way, the truth, and the life" (John 14:6), "I am Life" said the Lord concerning Himself. "For as the Father has life in Himself, so He has granted the Son to have life in Himself" (John 5:26). The existence of created beings and their life differs from the Life of God just as light that is a reflection of the sun differs from the sun itself. Existence and life in created things is a weak reflection of the existence and life that comprise God's essence. St John of Damascus wrote the following:

> God Who is good and altogether good and more than good, Who is goodness throughout, by reason of the exceeding riches of His goodness did not suffer Himself, that is His nature, only to be good, with no other to participate therein, but because of this He made first the spiritual and heavenly powers: next the visible and sensible universe: next man with his spiritual and sentient nature. All things, therefore, which he made, share in His goodness in respect of their existence. For He Himself is existence to all, since all things that are, are in Him, not only because it was He that brought them out of nothing into being, but because His energy preserves and maintains all that He made: and in especial the living creatures. For both in that they exist and in that they enjoy life they share in His goodness. But in truth those of them that have reason have a still greater share in that, both because of what has been already said and also because of the very reason which they possess. For they are somehow more dearly akin to Him, even though He is incomparably higher than they.[2]

Other Fathers write very similar things. For example, St Athanasius the Great wrote, "It would be foolish to consider different essences to be equal. What possible similarity can exist between the Creator and those objects He creates?"[3] St Basil the Great: "In the creation there is nothing similar to the Creator: on the contrary, the creation in all ways is not similar to the Creator."[4] St Dimitri of Rostov offered the words of Sylvester, Pope of Rome: "There is no image and likeness between angels and God, nor is their nature and power the same, but there is one essence of God, and another essence of angels."[5] Blessed Theophylact of Bulgaria: "All created essences, when compared to God, are bestial; therefore, even the hosts in heaven can be called sheep."[6] St Macarius the Great, when describing the way the human soul relates to God, to the essence of God, wrote, "He is God; the human soul is not God. He is the Lord; it is the creature. There is nothing in common with God in man's essence, but only by His endless, unutterable, and unthinkable mercy did He will to enter into His own reasonable creation."[7]

> "The essence of God," says St John Chrysostom, beyond measure super-sedes the essence of men, angels, archangels, and all reasoning crea-tures. His essence cannot be conceived by them.[8] "Not that anyone has seen the Father, except He who is from God; He has seen the Father" (John 6:46). The Lord here indicates "vision" to be knowledge, and he did not simply say, "No one has seen the Father," then went silent, lest someone think that He spoke only of man, but instead desiring to show that no angel, archangel, or any member of the highest hosts can see Him, and he make this clear with the following addition: for he said "Not that anyone has seen the Father," and He added "except He who is from God, He has seen the Father," "He who is the blessed and only Potentate, the King of kings and Lord of lords, who alone has immor-tality, dwelling in unapproachable light" (1 Timothy 6:15-16). Stop here for a moment and ask the heretic what "dwelling in unapproachable light" means. I want you to notice how exact Paul the apostle is. He did not say that the light is unapproachable, but that the He lives in unapproachable light, so that you may know that if the house itself is unapproachable, all the more so is God Himself, who lives in this house. He did not say that He abides in inconceivable light, but in unapproach-able light, which is much greater than inconceivable. What is inconceiv-able cannot be understood through the study and learning; however, the unapproachable is that which, in its essence, cannot even be sub-ject to the idea of learning. What will you say to this? Of course, you will say that that which is inconceivable is only so for men, but not for angels and the higher powers. So that you may know that He is unap-proachable not only for men, but for angels as well, hear that Isaiah

says through the inspiration of the Holy Spirit: "In the year King Uzziah died, I saw the Lord sitting on a throne, high and lifted up. The house was full of His glory. Around Him stood seraphim; each one had six wings: with two he covered his face, with two he covered his feet, and with two he flew" (Isaish 6:1-2) Tell me, why do they cover their faces with wings? Why, I ask, if not that they cannot bear the brightness of the rays that shine from the throne? Thought they saw not the light itself without lessening, nor the pure Essence, but all that they saw was adapted for their needs. What is this adaptation? God appears not as He is, but He lessens Himself in accordance with the abilities of him Who must see Him, and He adapts Himself to the weakness of the one who sees. As for the fact that this vision was a lessening is clear from Scripture itself. The prophet says, "I saw the Lord sitting on a throne high and lifted up." God does not sit on a throne, because such a posture only applies to one who has a body; God cannot be placed on a throne, for the divinity is not defined by a specific place. But even in such a lessened form, the seraphim who stand near Him cannot look at Him. They could not see precisely because they were close to Him. Near, that is, not in terms of space: by these words, the Holy Spirit revealed that the Powers are nearer than we are to that Being, but they cannot see the Essence. And so, though you may hear that the prophet says, "I saw the Lord," do not think that he saw the Essence of God. He sees an image adapted to his limitations, and he saw it not as clearly as the angels see Him. He could not even see as much as the Cherubim.[9]

St Athanasius the Great, in answer to a question from Antiochus, wrote,

In what form did the prophets often see God present Himself to them? After all the prophets, after the coming of Christ, the apostle, evangelist, and Theologian John said, "No one has seen God at any time" (John 1:18). In order to give these words the utmost veracity, since they are extremely important and essential, he added, "The only begotten Son, who is in the bosom of the Father, He has declared Him." (John 1:18) The holy apostle Paul also says, "no man has seen or can see [Him]" (1 Timothy 6:16). Thus, no human being could ever see the essence of God as it is. However, God, adapting Himself to the limitation of man, took on an appropriate image and appeared to the prophets. It is known that He, being bodiless, often appeared in the form of a man in flesh. From this, it becomes clear that they saw not the essence of God, but His glory.[10]

St Macarius the Great very clearly described this adaptation of God when He appears to the souls of holy people:

He, who is as He will and what He will, through His unspeakable kindness and inconceivable goodness change and diminish and assimilate Himself, embodying Himself according to their capacity in holy and worthy faithful souls, that He, the invisible, might be seen by them, He, the impalpable, be felt, after the subtilty of the soul's nature—and that they might feel His sweetness, and enjoy in real experience the goodness of the light of that ineffable enjoyment? When He pleases, he becomes fire, which burns up every base passion that has been introduced into the soul; for our God is a consuming fire. When He pleases, He is rest unspeakable, unutterable, that the soul may rest in the Godhead's own rest.[11]

To each of the holy fathers He appeared in the manner that pleased Him and was best for them in one way to Abraham, in another to Isaac, another to Jacob, another to Noah, to Daniel, to David, to Solomon, to Isaiah, and each of the holy prophets in one way to Elijah, in another to Moses. To each of the saints He appeared as He pleased, to give them rest and salvation and lead them to the knowledge of God. Everything is easy to Him that He chooses. As He pleases, He diminishes Himself by some embodiment, and transforms Himself to come under the eyes of those who love Him, manifesting Himself to those who are worthy in an inaccessible glory of light, according to His great and unspeakable love, and by His own power.[12]

Such adaptation for communion with His reasoning creatures is necessary not only for human souls, but for angelic ones as well, according to the teaching of John Chrysostom and Macarius the Great, because God, being different from all creatures through a limitless difference and superseding them with an infinite superiority, cannot be by his own essence either seen or understood or approached, not in any possible way. Explaining this fact, Macarius the Great further elucidates: The infinite, inaccessible, uncreated God, through His infinite and inconceivable kindness, embodied Himself, and, if I may say so, diminished Himself from His inaccessible glory, to make it possible for Him to be united with His visible creatures, such as the souls of saints and angels, that they might be enabled to partake of the life of God-head. For each of these, after its kind, is a body, be it angel, or soul, or devil. Subtle though they are, still in substance, character, and image according to the subtilty of their respective natures they are subtle bodies, even as this body of ours is in substance a gross body.[13]

This summary is self-evident. There are created, limited spirits, and their essence and qualities are consequently also limited. If their essence and their qualities are limited, their spirituality must also be limited. If their spirituality is limited, then they must by necessity have a certain level of materiality, appropriate to their nature. On the contrary, if we ascribe to them complete immateriality, that is, unlimited spirituality, then we must logically also ascribe to them completely limitless essence, because only unlimited essence can have, and must have, unlimited qualities. The creation of the reasoning creatures in different forms, in different levels, the giving to them of various qualities are ascribed by St Macarius, completely correctly, to the omnipotence of God and His will, for which there is nothing difficult or impossible: "He willed, and easily made, of things that were not, substances solid and hard, like earth, mountains, trees—you see what hardness of nature is—and again waters intermediate, and commanded that birds should be produced from them— and again more subtle objects, fire, and winds, and things too subtle to be seen by the bodily eye."[14]

Modern science in no way contradicts this teaching; on the contrary, it agrees with it in wondrous ways. It is only obsolete ideas, universally admitted to be false, that contradict it.

From these quotes of the Holy Fathers, which belong not exclusively to the Eastern Church but to the entire world, it is evident what great difference, what an infinite difference that Holy Fathers believed and confessed to exist between the essence of God and the essence of angels, demons, and the soul, even if the Holy Scripture and the Holy Fathers in general call God a spirit, as well as angels and demons and human souls. This expresses, however, only that God, like angels and demons and human souls, is invisible to human eyes. They are called bodiless, immaterial for the reason that they do not have bodies like ours, our crude materiality. They are not subject to our physical senses, which separate them from all the objects that act upon our senses. They are called reasoning, noetic, or intellectual because of their unique quality, that is, their mind or spirit. They have the ability not only to think but also to sense spiritually. For this last reason, mankind is also called a reasoning creature. He is called reasoning because he can reason and speak, a quality that comes from the spirit of his soul, something the animals do not have, and so they are called irrational, even if they also have the power of life, instinct, and a kind of sensory apparatus, which even the Scriptures call a "soul." This is how it was always understood by mankind from ancient times. This is how it is still acceptable to speak about these matters in our time as well.

Even in common parlance, scientists outside their laboratories are accustomed to call things that are subject to our senses as material, while those that are not as spiritual or immaterial. The same kind of *lingua franca* is used by the Scriptures and the Holy Fathers, since it is universally understandable. Neither the Fathers nor the Scripture use scientifically technical language that would be understandable only to a narrow group of specialists, not for the masses. However, both the Father and the Scriptures still preserve an exactness of meaning that can always be demonstrated.

The way ancient Christians understood the nature of spirits and even the word "spirit" is definitively explained by St Cyril of Jerusalem in his catechetical lectures, and his explanation is entirely based on Scripture:

> But since concerning spirit in general many diverse things are written in the divine Scriptures, and there is fear lest some out of ignorance fall into confusion, not knowing to what sort of spirit the writing refers; it will be well now to certify you, of what kind the Scripture declares the Holy Spirit to be. For as Aaron is called Christ, and David and Saul and others are called Christs, but there is only one true Christ, so likewise since the name of spirit is given to different things, it is right to see what is that which is distinctively called the Holy Spirit. For many things are called spirits. Thus an Angel is called spirit, our soul is called

spirit, and this wind which is blowing is called spirit; great virtue also is spoken of as spirit; and impure practice is called spirit; and a devil our adversary is called spirit. Beware therefore when you hearest these things, lest from their having a common name thou mistake one for another. For concerning our soul the Scripture says, *His spirit shall go forth, and he shall return to his earth* [Psalm 146:4] and of the same soul it says again, *Which formeth the spirit of man within him* [Zechariah 12:1]. And of the Angels it is said in the Psalms, *Who makes His Angels spirits, and His ministers a flame of fire* [Psalm 29:7]. And of the wind it saith, *Thou shalt break the ships of Tarshish with a violent spirit* [Psalm 48:7]; and, *As the tree in the wood is shaken by the spirit* [Isaiah 7:2]; and, *Fire, hail, snow, ice, spirit of storm* [Psalm 148:8]. And of good doctrine the Lord Himself says, *The words that I have spoken unto you, they are spirit, and they are life*; *spirit* [John 6:63], instead of, "are spiritual." ... But sin also is called spirit, as I have already said; only in another and opposite sense, as when it is said, *The spirit of whoredom caused them to err.* [Hosea 4:12]. The name "spirit" is given also to the *unclean spirit*, the devil; but with the addition of, "the unclean;" for to each is joined its distinguishing name, to mark its proper nature. If the Scripture speak of the soul of man, it says *the spirit* with the addition, *of the man*; if it mean the wind, it says, *spirit of storm*; if sin, it says, *spirit of whoredom*; if the devil, it says, *an unclean spirit*: that we may know which particular thing is spoken of, and thou mayest not suppose that it means the Holy Ghost; God forbid! For this name of spirit is common to many things; and every thing which has not a solid body is in a general way called spirit [Origen, *de Principiis*.i§2]. Since, therefore, the devils have not such bodies, they are called spirits ...[15]

Having so defined the meaning in which the word "spirit" is used in the Scriptures and generally among Christian people, and having said that there is nothing similar between the created spirits and God the Spirit, Cyril calls the spirits bodiless and fleshless, but only in the generally accepted sense. In his homily on the Meeting of the Lord, he says, "He is God the Word, having brought into being all from nothing with a single word. He is the Morning Star, having created before the morning star all the bodiless powers of heaven, the fleshless, invisible hosts and

ranks." As for the essence of the devil, St Cyril says that "he was created good, but by his free will he was made the devil, having received a
name (*diabolos*) from his manner of activity. Having first been an archangel, he received the name devil from his falsehood. Having been a good
servant of God, he became and was called Satan, because Satan means
'opponent.'"[16]

In a similar way St Macarius the Great, in his fourth homily, only mentioned in passing that angels, demons, and the human soul, in spite of
their subtlety compared to the crude fleshly bodies of human, have as a
quality a degree of materiality. In other homilies, like other Fathers, He
calls spirits immaterial creatures. For example, he begins homily 16 in the
following way: "All spiritual substances, that is to say, of angels, and human
souls, and devils, were made by the Creator innocent and perfectly simple." All other Fathers (Basil the Great, Athanasius the Great, etc.) express
themselves in a similar way, speaking of the spirits as having subtle, ethereal bodies. They call spirits, in the same general way as do the Scriptures,
simple creatures, invisible, without bodies. Those of the Holy Fathers who
did not directly say that their spirits have a degree of materiality (such
as John Chrysostom) still describe spirits in such a way that it becomes
clear that he assumed spirits have ethereal bodies. This materiality is
what all the anciently called "simple" spirit.

The idea that spirits have complete immateriality and are subject to
neither time nor space, in effect ascribe the same essence to spirits as
God's, first appeared in the seventeenth century. It was taken up by Descartes for the most part from the writings of ancient pagan philosophers.
So how could the Fathers be proponents of an idea that appeared his-
torically centuries after they lived? Even if it had appeared during their
time, how could they have agreed with this idea when it blasphemously
ascribes an equality of essence between created spirits and God the Spirit,
when all the Fathers always preached the infinite and immeasurable
difference between God's essence and the essence of spirits, especially
when they openly rejected a similar teaching offered by the Platonists.

The mistake of Western thinking in this area is found in that they try
to match the Fathers' teaching with the philosophy of Descartes concerning the immateriality and bodilessness of spirits, and in turn hide
the Fathers' original understanding concerning this immateriality and

lack of bodies, which was completely founded on Scriptures, not secular philosophy. By cunningly associating Descartes's hypothesis with the teaching of the Fathers, the Western thinkers try to force apparent contradiction between the teachings of individual fathers, laying open to criticism the idea of the consensus of the Fathers. However, it is clear that the Fathers always preached the immateriality of spirits in the Scriptural sense, which only speaks of their immateriality in comparison with human bodies.

Some of the Fathers, as we have already said, called the spirits bodiless, but they also mentioned that they had bodies appropriate to their essence. Some Fathers, calling the angels bodiless, did not mention that they had any bodies at all, but described them in ways that make it clear that spirits have a materiality appropriate to them. Western thinkers try to pit these latter Fathers against the former, slandering these fathers by suggesting that they supported Descartes's hypothesis (which they could not have known about) or the universally rejected postulates of Plato. Again, even if the Fathers had known Descartes's ideas, they would not have supported them. They would have committed these teachings to anathema as blasphemous teachings that place God on the same level as His creation. Such an idea would simply nullify the most important events reported in the Scriptures.

Thus, for example, how could Archangel Gabriel, when he appeared to Zechariah, have stood to the right of the altar if he had no reference point to matter whatsoever? How could the Archangel have first entered to visit the Mother of God, tell her the good news, and then leave her, if he had no means of movement nor any reference point to time or space? And how could the angels first appear to the shepherds in Bethlehem, then sing the doxology to the incarnate God, and finally go back to heaven, as the Gospel recounts, if they had no reference point to space, time, or matter? Descartes's ideas lead to a rejection of the Scriptures, to lack of faith. Descartes's rationalism did in fact have this effect: his ideas led to widespread atheism, having fooled many frivolous thinkers by the external brilliance of his thought. Now he has fallen, since his ideas have no sense, and one can only believe in him if one is foolish. Only dated thinking that is ignorant of recent scientific developments can believe something that rejects and contradicts the Scriptures and tradition of the Orthodox Church.

Descartes's teaching of the immateriality of spirits, of their independence of time and space, being verified by science, ends up as nothing more than a rejection of the existence of spirits. Having placed them on an equal rank with God, it makes their existence impossible. There can, logically, only be one infinite Being. If we were even to consider the existence of two such beings, not even a multitude, these two beings could only be expressed numerically as having limits with reference to each other, and so they would cease to be infinite. That which is unlimited in quality must always be unlimited in essence. This is the general conclusion of mathematics, against which there can be no objection. There are two dimensions that are not subject to space: infinity and a point. To be independent of space, you must be one or the other. So, what are infinity and a point? They are ideas.

Infinity is an idea that appears in the mind of man because of the gradual increase of numbers. It is an idea expressing a magnitude that is greater than all numbers. For this reason, infinity is a magnitude without definition, inconceivable for man, both in what it is (essence) and in its qualities. But the very law of numbers gave us many true, noteworthy insights concerning the nature of infinity. We were not left with a fruitless idea. We have come to know, for example, that infinity, if it is to remain infinite, must not be subject to any change when numbers are added to it or when numbers are subtracted from it. The difference between infinity and all numbers is infinite. For this reason, all numbers are equal to each other when compared with infinity.

If numbers are added and subtracted without reference to infinity, they have a certain difference among themselves. Again, what does magnitude mean? It is an idea that appears in our mind when we compare objects with ourselves. It is entirely a relative concept, not a material one. According to the laws of mathematics (which, having not found human language sufficient to express the process of science, use the symbolic language of numbers), God with exactness is expressed as infinite. Thus, based on mathematical thinking, God must be admitted to be a Being that is greater than any definition, having nothing in common with creatures that could and must be expressed using numbers, including spirits. Even according to this wonderful law, if God is an essence, then without exception all creatures who are given life are no longer essences, but something else. If they are essences, the God is something else, something infinitely greater than that we which call essence.

This is the distinction between God and the rational creation. These are the ideas, which are given by science in its present development. Mathematics, using symbols, expresses both objects and their qualities through these symbols, and by doing so uses the most correct way to attain knowledge, knowledge that sometimes cannot be expressed in words. In order to explain this with an example that will be universally understandable, we will point at the custom in schools to rate students by numbers based on their aptitudes. Why is this done? Because number express these abstract concepts with exactness and certainty that words generally lack.

In contrast to the idea of infinity, the idea of the point or of zero was reached through the gradual subtraction of numbers. A point is a magnitude that takes up no space either in length, width, height, or depth. Evidently, there is in nature neither a point nor a trace of a point, that is, a line. Only bodies exist in nature, that is, only objects that exist in three dimensions. Everything that exists in space, that is limited by space or place, is a body. The geometric point and line are bodies that approximately depict an abstract point or line. They are sufficient for the mechanism of science, but they do not express the exact meaning of the ideas. This is proven quite conclusively. If you remove space from any object, you, not having any ability of raising the limited to the infinite, must inevitably reduce it to a point or to zero, that is, reject the existence of this object. In this way, we can see the complete foolishness of a totally abstract understanding of spirits, which many people have imagined for themselves, naturally, since they have not studied this matter with the diligence possible only for a Christian ascetic. Abstract ideas concerning spirits are nothing other than a complete rejection of spirits.

Descartes, through his erudition, amazed many of his contemporaries. It is true that he moved the progress of science forward significantly; however, this progress is insignificant compared with recent advances in chemistry. Chemistry has significantly changed man's understanding of matter, and many ideas that before were considered sacrosanct for thousands of years have now been archived as curiosities in the history of science, after being proven to be completely false. Descartes's contemporaries loved to repeat his assertion: give me motion, and I will become a creator. He could only boast thus because of the limited understanding concerning matter available to him during his time, because of lapsed ideas of the four elements, of simplicity and complexity, and so on. Creation ex nihilo is a quality only of the infinite. Only the infinite can produce numbers and transform it into zero by infinite action.[17]

However, let us assume that movement was given to Descartes. How would he then begin to create when the sources of human nature are unknown and cannot be known? What can one do with movement alone? Creation depends on what is known, which can only be derived from what is already known. The creation of an unknown from an unknown is impossible. Let us take water, for example. During Descartes's time, it was considered to be simple, not a complex, substance. However, in more recent times, it has been divided into two different gases—hydrogen and oxygen. Depending on the caloric state of a substance, water can appear as a solid, a liquid, or a gas. Under a microscope, you can see many microscopic microorganisms inhabiting water. When science makes such a discovery, it correctly calls this knowledge a degree of knowing, not complete knowledge. This is made obvious by the nature of the knowledge itself. For, by dividing water into its constituent parts, we do not know what happens to the microorganisms, even though their existence is a clear fact. Consequently, we admit that this division of water is not complete, and a further subdivision of the elements impossible, which we have not yet discovered.

Because of his paucity of knowledge, Descartes might have uttered a complete idiocy, and his contemporaries might have trumpeted this idiocy as an incredible manifestation of genius. It is very useful to find proofs for faith from science. The truth of faith is found in oneness with the history of science. But why must we accept nonsense from that history when later on everyone agrees that it was one of many inevitable missteps along the way? Any mathematician or chemist must by necessity reject Descartes's silly teaching about spirits, which the Western heretics trumpet as a teaching of faith, thereby equating faith with foolishness that deserves neither respect nor attention. This is exactly what happened. Most mathematicians and chemists in the West came to doubt Christianity and became deists. They could not become atheists, since they discovered many wondrous rules in nature that only confirmed in them the reality of the infinite mind of the Maker, and of His limitless qualities. These people became deists only because the faith was slandered and perverted before their eyes.

When we carefully read the Holy Fathers, it becomes clear that all the Fathers spoke of the simplicity, immateriality, and bodilessness of spirits in the Scriptural sense, which was also the sense in universal use by the science of that time. But this is not enough. The Holy Fathers used the word "spirit" in the sense that the Scriptures used it. They could not have given the word "spirit" any other meaning, and they did not. Otherwise, they would have separated themselves from Scriptures and would have preferred their own human reasoning before the reasoning of Scriptures, which is a way of thinking that the Holy Spirit Himself gave to people. Completely basing their writings on the Scriptures and their own experiences that accorded with the Scriptures, the Fathers, like the Scriptures, spoke of spirits only with the intention of guarding people from the evil activity of the demons and of helping them assimilate them to the good spirits. The Fathers inform us of the nature of spirits only as much as is necessary for our salvation. They do not expend energy to exactly describe that which can only be partially known. Not only spirits, but even our bodies and the bodies of animals, as well as all objects in the plant kingdom remain only known to us partially. Anyone who ascribes to himself full knowledge of this or that object only proves his own stupidity. We know something; we hardly know everything.

What is the leaf on a tree? What is the grass under our feet? What is a flower in the field? Why are plants, which take nourishment from the same source underground, appear with such different qualities? How do roots soak up nourishment from the soil and then transform it into a fruiting body? Why various fragrances, colors, tastes, and other countless qualities form because of this process? One can ask an endless number of such questions; to answer all of them is impossible for our limited human minds. The creation is produced by an unlimited Mind. Thus, only the

Creator can fully and completely know it. Man is given to know only a small part of the laws that govern the massive cosmos. Such knowledge is like a door that opens to further knowledge and confession of the unlimited greatness of God. Orthodox theology leads one to this door. So does modern science, which separates the Creator from His creatures with an infinite separation.

St John of Damascus writes:

> An angel, then, is an intelligent essence, in perpetual motion, with free-will, incorporeal, ministering to God, having obtained by grace an immortal nature: and the Creator alone knows the form and limitation of its essence. But all that we can understand is, that it is incorporeal and immaterial. For all that is compared with God Who alone is incomparable, we find to be dense and material. For in reality only the Deity is immaterial and incorporeal .... They are circumscribed: for when they are in the Heaven they are not on the earth: and when they are sent by God down to the earth they do not remain in the Heaven. They are not hemmed in by walls and doors, and bars and seals, for they are quite unlimited. Unlimited, I repeat, for it is not as they really are that they reveal themselves to the worthy men to whom God wishes them to appear, but in a changed form which the beholders are capable of seeing. For that alone is naturally and strictly unlimited which is un-created. For every created thing is limited by God Who created it.[18]

Furthermore, they are immortal not by nature, but by grace. Only God is immortal by nature, as we can read clearly in the Holy Scriptures (see 1 Tim 6:16). "God," says St Macarius the Great, "is indescribable and inconceivable, everywhere present, on the mountains and in the sea and in the abyss. However, this is not a change of place, as the angels descending from heaven to earth. He is at the same time in heaven and on earth."[19] The same is said by other Fathers, in contrast to this new teaching of the West.

This is the teaching of the Orthodox Church concerning created spirits. We see in both the theology of the Orthodox Church and in the writings of the Holy Fathers a special care to speak truth, as well as many frequently repeated warnings lest someone, because of a misunderstanding, ascribe the same essence to created spirits and God. Why do they do this? Because to ascribe any quality of God to created beings is blasphemy. The holy angels do not desire any incorrect or unnecessary veneration on our part. They rejoice incomparably more when we offer the necessary honor and glory to God. They inspire us in this veneration; they help us worship God. As St John wrote in his Revelation, "I, John, saw and heard these things. And when I heard and saw, I fell down to worship before the feet of the angel who showed me these things. Then he said to me, 'See that you do not do that. For I am your fellow servant, and of your brethren the proph-ets, and of those who keep the words of this book. Worship God" (Rev 22:8–9).

The officially sanctioned textbook *Orthodox Dogmatic Theology*,[20] when expounding on the Orthodox teaching concerning angels, references all the Fathers in general, but makes a special note of mentioning John of Damascus by name, as well as his *Exact Exposition of the Orthodox Faith.* St John of Damascus, one of the ancient Fathers, systematized the teach-ings of the Orthodox Church. Living in the eighth century, he studied the Fathers who preceded him both by reading their works carefully and by coming closer to them in spirit by living a profoundly righteous life. He collected the teachings of these Fathers, found in different places in their various homilies and epistles, into a single work that systematized the teachings of Christianity. His teaching is the teaching of the Fathers who came before him. In the introduction of this dogmatics textbook, you would find the following:

St John of Damascus is one of the great teachers of the Church, whose works and labors were dedicated to the benefit of his contemporar-ies and were salvific for all future children of the Church of Christ. St John's books on the Orthodox Faith give us the right to call him a teacher of the faith of Christ. In this work, this teacher of the Church summarized the truths of the faith of Christ so clearly, so exactly, and furthermore in such perfect subsequence of thought and fulness that no other book before him compares. The truths of the word of God he explained using the same word of God, but he also calls upon sober reason, illumined by the light of revelation, and more often than not, he repeats the thoughts of Fathers who came before him. This book on the Orthodox Church is a treasure trove of the Fathers' thoughts concerning the faith. St John united them all into a single book, all the Fathers' writings and the Councils' determinations concerning the faith. Not only did he collect the sayings of the fathers but having pierced with his vision into the spirit of these teachers of the faith, he revealed the spiritual depths of the many teachers of faith who lived in different times.

St John based his teachings concerning angels on previous writings of Athanasius the Great, Gregory the Theologian, Theodoret, Maximus the Confession, and Nemesius, as we can see from his citations.

The Holy Scriptures do not offer a separate, specific teaching concerning spirits, as it does concerning other subjects. However, the teaching of the Holy Scriptures concerning spirits is still quite clear and sufficient. It is given with the exactness and fullness that are necessary for our salvation. The requirements of empty curiosity or vain inquisitiveness are constantly disdained and decried by the Scriptures (see Mark 8:11–12).

From reading the Scriptures, we can distill the following teachings concerning spirits. Created spirits are limited creatures, gas-like in their composition, endowed with the power of speech. Spirits are so called because all gaseous matter is called "spirit" in the Scriptures (see John 3:8). This word indicates the subtlety of the nature of spirits, which is an essential difference between their essence and our crude materiality.[21] Moreover, this difference is only a difference of degree; it comes from the limitation of man's knowledge, which accepted the human body as normal, even in its fallen state. The soul of man, like the created spirits, is called a spirit in the Scriptures (see John 19:30), but it is enveloped in a crude body. This is the only difference between human beings and created spirits. Spirits, not having human bodies or flesh, are called bodiless or fleshless. They are called invisible because we cannot see them with our physical eyes.

God created all spirits, and he created them as good, subtle essences. Some of them, according to their own free will, remained good, united to God through the communion of His grace. Others, also according to their own free will, separated themselves from God, becoming the sources of evil. The good spirits are called angels; they are divided into ranks; they live in heaven; they descend to earth and act on it. The evil spirits are called demons, devils; Satan, or the Devil, is the greatest of them. They live in the aerial region, the surface of the earth, and the abysses under the earth. In all these places, they act according to the laws of limited beings, as do the angels. Spirits can affect matter, and matter can affect spirits. They can touch people, and people can feel their touch. When God opens a person's spiritual eyes, he becomes capable of seeing the spirits in their proper form. This ability can extend to animals as well.

When angels appear to men, they always appear in the form of people, illumined by God's grace. The Scriptures mention specifically that they have eyes, fingers, hands, feet, clothing; they can walk, fly, sit, speak, and listen. The Scriptures also ascribe senses to them: sight, hearing, touch, and smell. The saints, after the resurrection, will be together with the angels in their sanctified, spiritual bodies. Sinful people, together with the demons, will be imprisoned in hell. Men and angels will share their dwellings, sufferings, and blessedness; the separation between spirits and people, which occurred because of the fallen body subject to corruption, will be destroyed. Essence will approach essence until likeness ["like angels" see Matt 22:30, Mark 12:26] or even equality ["equal to angels" see Luke 20:3]. The natural and inevitable consequence of the teachings of Scriptures concerning spirits is the idea of the materiality of spirits, at least according to the most recent understandings concerning materiality. This idea of the materiality and limitation of spiritual essences is closely tied with an understanding of the dependence of spirits on both place and time. Any action of a limited being in space with a change of place is defined as movement. A limited being, acting in space and having movement, must also have a form. This is the universal law of matter.

Many of the Fathers, when describing the essence of spirits, focus on this passage of the Scriptures: for He "maketh His angels spirits, His ministers a flaming fire" (Ps 103:4). If we are to accept these words literally and describe them according to the latest determinations of science, then we can say that angels are beings with gaseous, ethereal qualities, since Scripture generally calls any moving gaseous substance "spirit." The Fathers expressed themselves in nearly the same way. If we are to understand this expression in a more exalted sense, understanding that only God is spirit, then God, by illumining the angels with His grace, makes them spirit and fire, leading them into that exalted dignity that they could not have by nature. In this case, angels are still material, since they commune of divine spirituality only as a gift and to a certain, limited degree, since they do not have it by nature. Like angels, spiritual people, according to the activity of divine grace, receive certain qualities and abilities that are not natural to mankind when he abides in his natural, fallen state.

The following accounts from the Scriptures clearly show us these qualities of spirits. Two angels came in the evening to Sodom in the form of human beings. Lot invited them to his house, because he thought they were wanderers. He had no idea that these were angels. When the Sodomites learned that wanderers had come to stay at Lot's house, they surrounded Lot's house, intending to rape the visitors. Lot came outside to speak to the mob, and they mocked him mercilessly. Then the angels, "reached out their hands, pulled Lot into the house with them and shut the door. Then they struck the men at the doorway of the house with blindness, both small and great, and they became weary trying to find the door" (Gens 19:10–11). When the morning came, when Lot did not hurry to escape Sodom, "the angels seized his hand, and the hands of his wife and two daughters and brought them outside the city" (Gen 19:16–17).

Here it is very clear that the angels are subject to time, space, and matter. We see them move; we see how they act in ways similar to men, as well as certain actions that human beings are not capable of, for example, the blinding of the Sodomites. We also see another ability of the angels that supersedes human abilities: their cooperation in the burning of Sodom and Gomorrah: "Then the Lord rained brimstone and fire on Sodom and Gomorrah from the Lord out of the heaven" (Gen 19:24). However, this is what the angel said to Lot about this event: "Hurry to escape there, for I cannot do anything until you arrive there" (Gen 19:22). In other words, the doer was God, but the tool of that action was an angel. The angels performed a terrifying transformation of matter in the air, leading to fire and brimstone. In order to act on material reality in this way, one needs material means and material power.

Furthermore, David mentions that the punishments of Egypt during the Exodus were performed by evil angels (see Ps 77:49). The magicians of Egypt, as we read in Exodus, were able to perform similar miracles to Moses through their magic, that is, by the power of the demons (see Exod 7:11). The demons, like the angels, have the ability (which we do not have or understand) to effect wondrous transformations of material, natural reality.[22] They know the laws of nature much better than we do; in their nature, they have more power to affect created nature, and in their activity, they are much freer than we are. The devil caused fire to appear to fall from heaven, which burned up Job's flocks as well as the shepherds pastoring them (see Job 1:16). By the power of the devil, "a great wind came from the desert and struck the four corners of the house; and it fell on the the children, and they died" (Job 1:19). When St John the Theologian described the devil as a serpent, and the Antichrist as the beast, he said, "The dragon gave him his power, his throne, and great authority" (Rev 13:2). He also wrote that through this power, the Antichrist "performs great signs, so that he even makes fire come down from heaven on the earth in the sight of men" (Rev 13:13).

These abilities that the angels have to affect matter through material means that we do not understand (as well as other qualities of spirits) are vividly shown in this account from the Scriptures. An angel appeared to Gideon, who would later become a judge of Israel, and commanded him to deliver the people from the Midianites. This angel sat at first under an oak tree, then stood before Gideon, looking at him and announcing the calling of God. Gideon at first expressed his doubt in the messenger's words, evidently thinking him to be a simple man, and he asked for a sign. The angel, who held a staff in his hands, commanded that a burnt offering be prepared. When the sacrificial table and the sacrifice were ready, the angel "stretched out the end of the staff that was in his hand and touched the meat and the unleavened bread; and fire rose out of the rock and consumed the meat and the unleavened bread. And the angel of the Lord departed out of his sight" (Judg 6:21). Seeing the miracle, Gideon understood that this was no man, but an angel of the Lord. After the angel departed, Gideon said, "I have seen the angel of the Lord face to face" (Judg 6:22).

Thus, the angel had not only a hand, but a face, just as Gideon had a face. In his physical appearance, the angel looked like a human being. The action of his staff was a material action that we do not understand. With the discovery of electricity, we have come to understand that matter can act in powerful and subtle ways, in ways that may have seemed impossible or magical to ancient man.

Angels can touch people, and people can sense that touch: "Then Jacob was left alone; and a Man wrestled with him until the breaking of day" (Gen 32:24). The "man" in question is called a man because he appeared in a form like a man. "He touched the socket of his hip, and the socket of Jacob's hip was dislocated as He wrestled with him .... and he limped on his hip" (Gen 32:25, 31). During Elijah's flight from the wrath of Jezebel, he asked for God to give him death in the desert. From his exhaustion and sorrow, he fell asleep under the shadow of a tree. Unexpectedly an ⌈angel touched him and said to him, "'Arise and eat.' Then Elijah looked, and there by his head was a cake made of wheat and a jar of water. So he ate and drank, and lay down again. Again the ⌈angel of the Lord came back the second time, touched him, and said, 'Arise and eat, because the journey is a great many days for you.' So he arose, ate and drank; and he went with the strength of that food forty days and forty nights, as far as Mount Horeb" (3 Kgdms 19:5–8 LXX).

In the Acts of the Apostles, we read that Herod decided to ingratiate himself with the Jews, and executed James, the son of Zebedee, and imprisoned Peter, intending to do the same with him. The night before the planned execution, the apostle slept between two soldiers, bound by two chains. There were also guards at the doors of his cell. All this was done to prevent any possibility of escape:

Now behold, an angel of the Lord stood by him, and a light shone in the prison; and he struck Peter on the side and raised him up, saying, "Arise quickly!" And his chains fell off his hands. Then the angel said to him, "Gird yourself and tie on your sandals"; and so he did. And he said to him, "Put on your garment and follow me." So he went out and followed him, and did not know that what was done by the angel was real, but thought he was seeing a vision. When they were past the first and the second guard posts, they came to the iron gate that leads to the city, which opened to them of its own accord; and they went out and went down one street, and immediately the angel departed from him. And when Peter had come to himself, he said, "Now I know for certain that the Lord has sent His angel, and has delivered me from

the hand of Herod and from all the expectation of the Jewish people."
(Acts 12:7-11)

We read another wonderful example of angelic interference in the book
of Acts. After the apostle Philip baptized the eunuch of Candace in the
source of water by the road leading from Jerusalem to Gaza, "the Spirit[23]
of the Lord caught Philip away, so that the eunuch saw him no more ...
But Philip was found at Azotus" (Acts 8:39-40).

A similar event is described in the prophecy of Daniel. When Daniel
was cast into the lion's den in Babylon, he remained among these lions
(who had been purposely famished in an advance) for six days without
food or water. During that time, Prophet Habbakuk, who lived in Judea,
had prepared a pottage for workers in his field, and he went to the field to
give them the food. Suddenly, an angel appeared and said:

> "Go carry the dinner you have into Babylon to Daniel who is in the
> lions' den." Habakkuk said, "O Lord, I have never seen Babylon, nor do
> I know the den." Then the angel of the Lord took him by the crown,
> and carried him by the hair of his head, and with the speed of the wind
> set him in Babylon over the den. Then Habakkuk cried out saying,
> "O Daniel, Daniel, take the meal God has sent you." Daniel said, "You
> have remembered me, O God, and You have not forsaken those who
> love You." So Daniel arose and ate; and the angel of Lord immediately
> set Habakkuk down in his own place once more. (Dan 12:33-39 LXX)

The rushing sound of wind is ascribed by the Scripture to the essence
of the spirit. In a similar way, the angel who descended into the fiery
furnace in Babylon to protect the three youths, "made the inside of the
furnace to be as though a dew-laden breeze [wind] were blowing through
it" (Dan 3:50 LXX). Evidently, the word "wind" (or "spirit") indicates a subtle material, because an abstract spirit cannot produce any kind of noise
whatsoever.

Similarly, the noise that accompanied the descent of the Holy Spirit
on the apostles was ascribed to the great multitude of heavenly hosts
that descended to be present at this great act of God: "And suddenly there
came a sound from heaven, as of a rushing mighty wind, and it filled
the whole house where they were sitting" (Acts 2:2). For the Holy Spirit,

Who is everywhere present and fillest all things, there is no need for movement to reveal His activity in any place. As St Cyril of Jerusalem says, the Holy Spirit "is one and the same; living and subsisting, and always present together with the Father and the Son; not uttered or breathed from the mouth and lips of the Father or the Son, nor dispersed into the air, but having a real substance, Himself speaking, and working, and dispensing, and sanctifying."[24] Everything that the Holy Church says of God the Word can also be said of God the Spirit: "His descent was divine, not a material passing." ["For this was a divine condescension and not a change of place."][25] The quick movement of the created spirits produced a noise in the air like a strong wind. Natural spirits can naturally make such a noise, not only holy spirits, but also demons. Their natures are one and the same, as are their qualities. The moral difference occurs because the former are holy and the latter have been completely perverted by evil.

The ability of angels to move from place to place and to occupy space (which may even mean that angels have degrees of magnitude or size) is especially clearly demonstrated in the following places of the Holy Scriptures. Archangel Gabriel, as we read in the Gospel according to Luke, appeared in the temple during a festal service to Zechariah and told him of the coming birth of the forerunner of the Lord. When he did, he stood to the right side of the altar of incense. The same Archangel Gabriel was sent later by God to the Galilean town of Nazareth to the most pure Virgin Mary to tell her that she would become the Mother of God. He entered her home, and, having delivered his message, left the home. According to the account of Mark, the myrrh-bearing women, as they approached the tomb of Christ, saw a young man dressed in white clothing, sitting on the right side of the tomb. This was an angel. Matthew reports concerning this angel that he, having come down from heaven, cast the stone aside from the entrance to the tomb, and sat on that stone. "His countenance was like lightning, and his clothing as white as snow" (Matt 28:3).

Mary Magdalene approached the open tomb, leaned in to look inside, and she saw two angels in white clothing; the angels sat inside the narrow opening of the tomb; one sat at the head, the other at the feet of the place where Jesus's body had lain. The ability to move from place to place and to wander in different regions belongs to the demons as well. The

Lord said the following concerning the wandering demon that could not find a place after he was cast out of a man: "When an unclean spirit goes out of a man, he goes through dry places, seeking rest, and finds none. Then he says, 'I will return to my house from which I came.' And when he comes, he finds it empty, swept, and put in order. Then he goes and takes with him seven other spirits more wicked than himself, and they enter and dwell there; and the last state of that man is worse than the first. So shall it also be with this wicked generation" (Matt 12:43–45).

Satan, upon arriving in the midst of the angels, answered the Lord's question about where he came from thus: "I came here after going about the earth, and walking around under heaven" (Job 1:7). When the devil tempted Jesus, he took Him to the holy city, placed him at the pinnacle of the temple, then took him to the summit of a very tall mountain. These quick journeys across space are similar to how the angel moved Philip from the road to Gaza to Azotus. After the Lord defeated the devil's temptations, He said, "'Away with you, Satan.' ... Then the devil left Him, and behold, angels came and ministered to Him" (Matt 4:10–11).

In the account concerning the false prophet Balaam, who acted against the people of Israel, it is said that an angel was sent to hinder the false prophet in his work. Balaam rode on a donkey, accompanied by two slaves. This event was witnessed, in other words. The donkey, according to the Scripture, saw the angel of the Lord standing in his way with a drawn sword in his hand, and he turned aside from the road into a field. Then the angel, changing his place, stood in a vineyard that was fenced from both sides. The donkey again saw the angel and stopped next to the fence, pressing Balaam's leg against the fence. Balaam began to beat the donkey. Then the angel of God moved from that place and stood in a narrow pass from which it was not possible to move either to the right or to the left. The donkey this time dropped to his knees under Balaam, and the irate false prophet beat his donkey again. But God then opened Balaam's eyes, "and he saw the Angel of the Lord standing in the way with His drawn sword in His hand; and he bowed and worshipped. The Angel of the God then said to him, 'Why did you strike your donkey a third time? Behold, I have come out as your adversary, because your way was not acceptable before Me. So when the donkey saw Me. she turned aside from Me this third time. If she had not turned aside from Me, surely I would have killed you by now, and let her live" (Num 22:31-33).

The donkey saw the angel according to the will of God in the same way Balaam did: by the opening of her eyes through God's omnipotence. Irrational animals can only see material reality, just like men can only see material reality with their physical eyes.

In the invisible world we cannot see there are phenomena, which are still material, that can act in extremely powerful ways on the objects of the visible world. This in no way contradicts science; on the contrary, it harmonizes with the most recent findings. We know, for example, only part of the matter that pertains to this earth; there is a far greater amount of material reality beyond the atmosphere that remains unknown to us. However, this material reality exists, because everything in space and everything that is limited by space is matter.[26]

The Scriptures, in agreement with science, reveal invisible reality for us much more clearly than science does, which can only limit itself to asserting that invisible creation exist and is material. The Scriptures tell us as much as we need concerning heaven, hell, the matter of heaven and hell, the nature of created reasoning creatures, for whom heaven is a blessed home and hell is a prison. The very concept of the earth, in connection with these ideas, receives its proper orientation and leads to true conclusions, leading one away from delusion and teaching us to relate to this earth as though it were a roadside hotel, not a place worthy of offering the entire sacrifice of our soul and body.

In the account of Balaam we have already offered, we hear that the angel had a sword in his hand; in the account of Gideon, we heard of an angel who had a staff in his hand, and that the touch of this staff burned the sacrifice on the altar. These events indicate that there is a tangible relationship between visible and invisible matter. Church tradition tells us that the separation of the soul from the body at death occurs through the mediation of angels. The Scriptures tell that angels are used as weapons of God's justice. Herod was stuck by an angel with disease when he ascribed divine glory to himself. He died while being eaten alive by worms (see Acts 12:23). Naturally, the king's associates and his doctors did not know the source of his sickness; it is the Scripture that reveals it to us.

When God sent plague on the people of Israel when they trusted in their own strength over God's, in the shortest possible time, seventy thousand people died. The angel even extended his hand over Jerusalem to strike it down with plague. But the Lord had mercy, and said to the angel who was destroying the people, "It is enough; now restrain your hand." And the angel of the Lord was by the threshing floor of Orna the Jebusite. Then David spoke to the Lord when he saw the angel who was striking the people, and said, "I am the shepherd and I have done wickedly, but these sheep—what have they done? Let Your hand, I pray, be against me and against my father's house." (2 Kgdms 24:16-17 LXX).

In a single night, the angel of the Lord, having descended into the camp of the Assyrian army, killed one hundred eighty-six thousand warriors (see 4 Kgdms 19:35 LXX). Demons are also capable of striking people with disease. The devil struck Job with open wounds from his head to his feet. He would have struck the righteous man, so hateful to him, with death, except that God forbade it. The Lord Himself said that the woman bent over double had been in bondage to Satan (see Luke 13:16). The demon Asmodeus killed seven men, all of whom were married to Sarah, the daughter of Raguel (see Tob 3:8).

Just as spirits have a tangible effect on matter, so also matter can influence spirits directly. The rejected spirits will suffer eternally in the fires of hell, but those fires are material, while the holy spirits will eternally live in blessedness in the mansions of heaven. The resurrected bodies of the righteous will partake of the pleasures of heaven and Eden together with the angels; the resurrected iniquitous will share the eternal sufferings with the demons. This makes it clear that spirits have their own materiality like the spiritual bodies of resurrected humanity. And how can the heavenly reality not have materiality if its king, the God-Man Himself, has a human body? We confess that the body of the God-Man is incomparably greater in a spiritual sense that angelic nature, and we glorify the Mother of God in these words: "More honorable than the Cherubim, and beyond compare more glorious than the Seraphim." This hymn, which was first proclaimed by the angels themselves, would have no place if the holy ones in heaven were not similar or even equal to the angels, as the Saviour Himself said (see Matt 22:30, Luke 20:36). That the angels are capable of singing, and that they utter words during this singing is clear from the Gospels and the books of the prophets (see Luke 2:8–15, Ps 6:3).

The effect that earthly matter can have on angelic nature is especially made clear in the book of Tobit. Archangel Raphael accompanied, in the form of a man, Tobias, the son of Tobit, in his journey from Assyria to Midia. During this journey, Tobias caught a fish in the Tigris River, and the Archangel commanded that he preserve the heart and liver of the fish. When Tobit asked why these organs were needed, the angel answered, "As for the heart and the liver, if a demon or evil spirit gives trouble to anyone, you make a smoke from these before the man or woman, and that person will never be troubled again." In other words, some material objects have objective influence over the evil spirits. Later, the archangel Raphael expressed his wish that Tobias marry Sarah, the only daughter of Raguel, a relative of Tobias. Tobias answered, "I have heard that the girl has been given to seven husbands and that each died in the bridal chamber." But the angel said to him, "Do not worry about the demon … When you enter the bridal chamber, you shall take the live ashes of incense and lay upon them some of the heart and liver of the fish so as to make a smoke. Then the demon will smell it and flee away and will never again return." After the marriage, Tobias did as the angel said, "and he took the live ashes of incense and put the heart and liver of the fish upon them and made a smoke. And when the demon smelled the odor he fled to the remotest parts of Egypt, and the angel bound him" (see Tobit chapters 6, 7, and 8).

When angels appear to people, they always appear in the form of people. The Scriptures do not tell of the appearance of angels in any other form; moreover, in recounting these events, The Scriptures nowhere qualify this reality, which it certainly would have if angels had no form or did not appear as people. We have no right to otherwise imagine angels than how the Scriptures depict them. When the angels appeared to Lot, they are first called angels, then the rest of the time they are simply called men. These same angels, before they came to Sodom, appeared to Abraham at the Oak of Mamre and are also called simply "men" by the Scriptures (see Gen 18:1–2).

The Commander of the Army of God appeared to Joshua. When speaking of this event, the Scripture says the following: Joshua "looked up and saw a man standing before him with a sword drawn in his hand. So Joshua came near and said to him, 'Are you for us or for our adversaries?'" (Josh 5:13–15) An angel also appeared to the wife of Manoah, the mother of Sampson, announcing her pregnancy to her. After the appearance, this is how the woman spoke of it to Manoah:

So the woman went in and told her husband, saying, "A Man of God came to me, and His appearance was like the appearance of an Angel of God, very frightening. But I did not ask Him where He was from, and He did not tell me His name. And He said to me, 'Behold, you are pregnant and shall bear a son. Now drink no wine or strong drink, and do not eat anything unclean, for the child shall be holy to God from the womb to the day of his death.'" Then Manoah prayed to the Lord and said, "Lord Adonai, please let the Man of God whom You sent come to us again and teach us what we shall do for the child who will be born." And God listened to the voice of Manoah, and the Angel of God came to the woman again as she was sitting in the field, but Manoah her husband was not with her. Then the woman ran in haste and told her husband, and said to him, "Look, the Man who came to me the other day has just now appeared to me!" So Manoah arose and followed his wife. When he came to the Man, he said to Him, "Are You the Man who spoke to my wife?" And the Angel said, "I am." Manoah said, "Now let Your words come *to pass!* What is to be the decision regarding the boy and his activities?" So the Angel of the Lord said to Manoah, "The woman will guard herself from everything I have told her. She may not eat anything that comes from the vine, or similar strong drink, nor eat anything unclean. All that I command her let her observe." Then Manoah said to the Angel of the Lord, "Let us delay You here, and we will prepare a young goat for You." And the Angel of the Lord said to Manoah, "Though you delay Me, I will not eat your bread. But if you offer a burnt offering, you must offer it to the Lord." For Manoah did not know He was the Angel of the Lord. Then Manoah said to the Angel of the Lord, "What is Your name, so when Your words come to pass we may honor You?" And the Angel of the Lord said to him, "Why do you ask My name, is it extraordinary?" So Manoah took the young goat with the sacrifice and offered it upon the rock to the Lord. And the Angel wrought a distinct work, while Manoah and his wife were looking on. And so it happened as the flame went up above the altar toward heaven, that the Angel of the Lord ascended in the flame of the altar. When Manoah and his wife saw this, they fell on their faces to the ground. (Judg 13:13–20)

This is how the husband and wife realized that they were dealing with an angel.

When the Lord ascended in the presence of his apostles, and when their eyes were intent on the sky, two men in white clothing appeared and said to them: "Men of Galilee, why do you stand gazing up into heaven? This same Jesus, who was taken up from you into heaven, will so come in like manner as you saw Him go into heaven" (Acts 1:11). Clearly, these were two angels.

An angel appeared to the centurion Cornelius. He saw an angel of God descending to him. When recounting this vision to the apostle Peter, Cornelius said, "Four days ago I was fasting until this hour; and at the ninth hour I prayed in my house, and behold, a man stood before me in bright clothing" (Acts 10:30).

When Nebuchadnezzar, the king of Babylon, cast the three youths into the fiery furnace, an angel descended together with them into the furnace and took the power of the flame away. The young men began to sing a song of praise and glory to God within the furnace. Nebuchadnezzar, hearing them singing, was amazed and asked: "'Did we not cast three men bound into the midst of the fire?' They replied to the king, 'Truely, O king.' Then the king said: 'Behold I see four men untied and walking in the midst of the fire, yet they are not destroyed; and the vision of the fourth is like the Son of God .... Blessed be the God of Sadrach, Meshach, and Abednego, who sent his Angel, and saved His servants who trusted in in him: for they altered the word of the king and handed over their bodies to be burned, so as not to serve and worship any god other than their God" (Dan 3:91–95).

The holy Prophet Daniel called Archangel Gabriel a man. "While I was speaking in prayer, then the man Gabriel, whom I saw in my vision at the beginning, flew and touched me about the time of the evening offering" (Dan 9:21). In another vision, an angel appeared to the prophet, and Daniel again calls him a man. This man was dressed in a linen robe, and his girth encircled with gold: "Then I heard from the man clothed in fine linen who was above the water of the river, as he held up his right hand and his left hand to heaven" (Dan 12:7).

When the protomartyr Stephen, who was greatly filled with the grace of the Holy Spirit, stood before the gathering of the Jewish elders who had killed Jesus, "And all who sat in the council, looking steadfastly at him, saw his face as the face of an angel" (Acts 6:15).

All these references from the Holy Scriptures prove that angels not only have the form of a human body, but they have all the same members as the human body has. According to the Scriptures, they have a face, eyes, fingers, hands, and feet. And even this is not enough! The Scriptures indicate that the spirits have the same senses as do people: vision, hearing, smell, and touch, and we can see that they speak with their mouths. The fallen spirits are ascribed the same limitations that fallen humanity has, including deafness and the inability speak. The Lord Himself called one of the demons a "deaf and dumb spirit" (Mark 9:25). It is natural for the spirits to have senses, for the soul of man has them as well, and the soul is by nature similar to the created spirits. The senses of man belong to his soul, not his body, even though the human being acts in this earthly life through the members of the body. The entire soul, even its reasoning capacity, acts through the members of the body. The senses abandon the body together with the soul; or rather, the soul, as it exits the body, takes away with it all the senses that belong to it. If the senses belonged to the body, then they would remain with the body after the soul left or would leave the body at a different time, not the moment of separation of soul and body.

Demons have the same physical appearance as angels, that is, the appearance of a human body. Because of this similarity, the Lord called the devil a man (see Mark 5). The demons have perverted themselves through the destruction of all good things inside themselves, and through the cultivation and development of evil. For this reason, the Scripture calls them beasts, and the chief of them a dragon. "O deliver not the soul that confesseth Thee unto the wild beasts" (Ps 73:19). "Now the serpent was more cunning than all the wild animals the Lord God made on the earth" (Gen 3:1). The hatred and fall of the demons is reflected in their external appearance. Having preserved their natural form, they perverted it with bestial qualities and horrible ugliness. Job saw the devil as a horrifying monster and expressed what he saw with very vivid language (see Job chapters 29–41).

All spirits have their place, their proper home, which accords to their nature and their willingly assimilated characteristics, for which reason some have entered the most intimate union with God, while others have been rejected by God and have been infected with insane hatred for Him. The place the angels inhabit is heaven. This was revealed to us by the Lord Himself. "In heaven, [the] angels always see the face of My Father who is in heaven" (Matt 18:10). "in the resurrection they neither marry nor are given in marriage, but are like the angels of God in heaven" (Matt 22:30). Many other passages of the Scripture show that heaven is the home of the angels. Being in heaven, they are sent by God to earth to enact His various commands, as we have already seen in the passages quoted. They are also sent to help those who strive to be saved, as the apostle Paul wrote, "Are they not all ministering spirits sent forth to minister for those who will inherit salvation?" (Heb 1:14) At the glorious and terrible Second Coming, the Lord "will send His angels with a great sound of a trumpet, and they will gather together His elect from the four winds, from one end of heaven to the other" (Matt 24:31).

While the devil was a bright and holy angel, he also inhabited heaven. It was in heaven that the unfortunate change occurred, and many angels separated themselves from the hosts of the Heavenly army, becoming a host of dark demons, led by the fallen cherub himself. Many of the higher ranks, the principalities, powers, and rulers, fell away with the devil (see Eph 6:12). Because of this event, "war broke out in heaven: Michael and his angels fought with the dragon; and the dragon and his angels fought, but they did not prevail, nor was a place found for them in heaven any longer. So the great dragon was cast out, that serpent of old, called the Devil and

Satan, who deceives the whole world; he was cast to the earth, and his angels were cast out with him" (Rev 12:7–9).

The new home of the fallen angels became the aerial region, which all the ancients called the air. They also inhabit the earth itself and hell. This is also made clear in the Scriptures, as we have already shown. The existence of the fallen angels in the aerial region, according to the Fathers, is indicated by these words of St Paul: "For we do not wrestle against flesh and blood, but against principalities, against powers, against the rulers of the darkness of this age, against spiritual hosts of wickedness in the heavenly places" (Eph 6:12). Leading this host is "the prince of the power of the air, the spirit who now works in the sons of disobedience" (Eph 2:2).

The fact that the demons also inhabit the earth is clearly seen from the passages in the Scripture that tell of the various actions of demons on earth, their many evil deeds. Demons not only inhabit the surface of the earth, but sometimes entire human bodies or the bodies of animals with their entire gaseous substance (see Luke 8:33). They enter the body in a way similar to how a person breathes in air, similar to how other gases enter. The demon, as it enters a person, does not intermix with that person's soul, but remains in the body, possessing violently that person's body and soul. Gases by their nature have the ability of filling out the entirety of the space they find themselves in; evidently, demons have the same quality, because many of them can fit into a single person, as the Gospel says (Mark 5:8–10).

At this time, the devil, the head of the fallen angels, lives in hell, Tartarus, the abyss, the depths of the earth. Isaiah prophesied that this would be the home of the fallen archangel: "Yet you shall be brought down to Sheol, to the lowest depths of the Pit" (Isa 14:15). This prophecy came true through the power and authority of the Saviour of mankind, the God-Man. The Saviour is that Angel of Great Counsel who has the keys to the abyss, Who descended from heaven and having become man used his human body (that great rope), crucified on the Cross, for the binding of the devil, the ancient serpent, the devil, Satan. The Lord bound Satan for the entirety of the time between his first and second comings, and he imprisoned him in the abyss, locking the gates and sealing them in. Being imprisoned in a material prison, the devil must have a material essence; otherwise, no material prison could ever hold him. Before the Second Coming of Christ, "Satan will be released from his prison and will go out to deceive the nations which are in the four corners of the earth" (Rev 20:7–8).

The created spirits are called fleshless both in the writings of the Fathers and in common parlance. This is founded in the Scriptures. "A spirit does not have flesh and bones as you see I have" (Luke 24:39), said the Lord, appearing to His disciples after the resurrection in His glorified body. The comparison "as you see I have" is a comparison with the human body of the God-Man. St Basil the great sees the same comparison between angelic essence and human bodies in the words of the apostle: "We do not wrestle against flesh and blood" (Eph 6:12). This Holy Father speaks more definitively than others about the ethereal essence of spirits; however, based on the passage from Ephesians, he also insists that the essence of the devil is bodiless, meaning that he does not have the same body as human beings.[27] In this sense, the soul of man, when it leaves the body, becomes a bodiless substance.

The Scriptures only mention the form and essence of human souls in passing. But from the few references, it becomes clear that the human soul has the same form as the human body, in the same way as all other created spirits do. The apostle John the Theologian reveals that he saw "the souls of those who hand been slain for the word of God ... Then a white robe was given to each of them" (Rev 6:9, 11). This vision was repeated: "I looked, and behold, a great multitude which no one could number, of all nations, tribes, peoples, and tongues, standing before the throne and before the Lamb, clothed with white robes, with palm branches in their hands" (Rev 7:9). The Scripture describes these souls in the same language as it describes appearances of angels. When the Theologian says that he saw souls in "a great multitude," that means that he sees them in human form. Their clothing and the palms in their hands also confirm their materiality.

When the witch of Endor called up the soul of Samuel from Hades, he appeared to her, and she saw "A man is coming up, standing upright, and he is covered with a mantle" (1 Kgdms 28:14). The soul appeared in the form of a man, in the clothing of a man, and with clear indications of gender. The soul is expressed here in the same way as John the Theologian described the souls in heaven.

During the Transfiguration, the face of the Lord was illumined like the sun, and His clothing became white as snow. The Lord showed the primal glory of created man, demonstrating how much the body in that state differs from the body that was corrupted by the fall. Moses and Elijah stood next to Him on Tabor, and they spoke with Him concerning the sufferings and the death on the Cross, which He was intending to willingly undergo in Jerusalem for the sake of healing the human race. Elijah stood there in a body that was changed after his ascension into Eden; Moses stood in his soul, which, evidently, looked like a body. Otherwise, how could the apostles have seen him? How could the apostle Peter have said anything about preparing a tent for Moses? The apostles saw Moses, as they saw Elijah, after their eyes were opened. Moses was present in his soul: the Fathers[28] make it clear that the Lord, descending into hell, raised Moses from hell with the other Old Testament righteous, a fact that in no way contradicts the Gospel, while also according with the resurrection of many saints after the resurrection of the Lord (see Matt 27:52). In part, the Scripture does speak of the burial of Moses, but remains silent about his resurrection.

The apostle Paul, when speaking of his being exalted to Eden and heaven, said that he did not know if it occurred in body or outside the body (see 2 Cor 12:3). If the soul had been different in form from the body, the apostle could have easily determined in what form he was exalted, in the body or in the soul. We can conclusively say, however, that Paul was exalted in soul, not body. Similarly, the soul of St Andrew the Fool for Christ was exalted, and he, like Paul, said that he did not know whether he was exalted in body or soul, although he saw himself with all his bodily members intact, and his bodily senses fully functional. We can definitively say this because of the teachings of the Fathers concerning this issue (see a more detailed explanation of this in "On Death" earlier in this volume).

The holy martyr Maura said concerning herself, "When I was nailed to the cross, a certain wondrous man appeared, whose face shone like the sun. He took me by the hand and raised me to heaven. There I was shown the blessedness prepared for myself and for my husband, who was to be martyred with me. After this, the light-bearing man returned me to the body hanging on the cross, and said to me, 'Return now to your body. Tomorrow, at the sixth hour, angels will come for your soul.'"[29]

Examining these passages from Scripture, we are naturally led to the conclusion that created spirits and human souls have a materiality appropriate to them. They have an external form similar to the form of a human body. Like men, spirits are subject to space and time. They can move. The essence of spirits is much more subtle than human bodies. For this reason, spirits in their activity are much freer, and in their powers are much more developed than men. This is a general property to matter. In its more subtle state, matter acts much more powerfully and expansively than in its solid state. In its subtle state, it acquires new characteristics that it did not have in its solid state. To make this more understandable for everyone, let us simply point out how water differs in its three states: solid, liquid, and gas.

The Scripture teaches us that there are earthly bodies and heavenly bodies, that there are spiritual and ethereal bodies, and that the nature and characteristics of these bodies are different (see 1 Cor 15:39-46). The Scripture calls our bodies, which we inhabit during our earthly lives, "soul-bodies."[30] It also calls these same bodies "spiritual bodies," referring to when they will resurrect with the qualities of immortality and other qualities that are necessary for our immortality to be immortal. The saints will abide in their spiritual bodies eternally with the holy angels, receiving with them a single blessedness and a common spiritual growth, a common referenced point to space and time. In this sense, science accords with the Scriptures. It admits that matter is present wherever there is space. The concept of materiality is contiguous and inseparable from the concept of space. Science has determined that gases that belong on earth and are known to us layer themselves in the atmosphere depending on their density. This also means that beyond our atmosphere are more subtle gases, called ether, that layer themselves in a similar way. These ethereal gases must exist because no space can exist without an accompanying presence of matter. The space that we call heaven must naturally have its own proper materiality.

What is man? He is the same kind of created spirit as angels, but covered in a body. Other created spirits differ from people in that they do not have a fleshly body. For this reason, they are called bodiless, fleshless, immaterial. They are called invisible because we, being perverted and terribly damaged by our fall, cannot see them in our natural state. Our body is not at all the same as it was at our creation. It was made into a prison for man; it was deprived of many natural characteristics. It is tied down by many weaknesses. However, it will resurrect in a different form, and man, without ceasing to be man, will enter the ranks of the created spirits, will join their ranks, will find himself in communion and communication with them. Then, human nature will relate to the world in the same way as angels do.

Scriptures definitively contradict Descartes's teaching, which has become the universally accepted teaching in the West. There is not a single passage in the Scriptures that would in any way confirm the Western teaching. On the contrary, to accept this teaching is to reject all the most important teachings of the Scriptures concerning the spirits. For example, the Lord, when telling of His glorious Second Coming, said, "When the Son of Man comes in His glory, and all the holy angels with Him, then He will sit on the throne of His glory" (Matt 25:31). The resurrected people will see the Son of God (see Matt 26:64), invisible in His divinity, but visible in His divine human body, and they will see the angels in their proper form. If the angels did not have form, then the resurrected people would not be able to see them, and the Son of God would stand at judgment in a strange solitude. If the angels could not move, then they could not come with the Lord Who in His humanity naturally has the ability to move.

Here the Lord expressed the movement of the angels as like His own movement. It is expressed as a single action. Moreover, we believe that the movement of God's body, by the divinity of that body, is incomparable with the movement that the angels are capable of: that is how much his movement supersedes theirs. Some saints have already seen in visions the image of the Second Coming. St Dionysius the Areopagite, in a letter to Monk Demophilus, tells of a certain disciple of the apostle Paul named Carpus, a man great in virtue, capable of divine vision because of the purity of his mind. Carpus was so spiritually advanced that he never started to serve Divine Liturgy until he saw a vision of the Holy Spirit. Once he was given to see the heavens opened, like Protomartyr Stephen, and the Lord Jesus standing amid the multitudes of angels. Carpus saw these angels in the form of men. This is also how they will appear at the Final Judgment.

All appearances of angels to the saints of the New Testament Church have the same character as the appearances of angels in the Scriptures. These visions prove that spirits are material, that they have the external appearance of people, that they have all the same members of the human body, the ability to speak, cry, and laugh. They prove that the invisible world in which spirits live has its own proper materiality and that the spirits are dependent on matter, space, and time, and that they have motive force. We will provide several examples to help the reader acquire more knowledge from the lives of the saints.

The holy martyr Parasceve, torn apart and half-dead, was cast into prison. The torturers thought that she would die very soon. At midnight, an angel appeared in her cell; he was encircled with a golden belt around his shoulders and chest, and in his hands he held the instruments of Christ's crucifixion. The angel commanded that the virgin stand, announcing that Christ would heal her. The martyr, who was lying insensate on the ground, stood up as though waking up from sleep. The angel approached her, washed her wounds with a sponge, which had the effect of wiping away her wounds, and her face became even more beautiful than it was before she began the labor of martyrdom. The angel then became invisible.[31] The manner of the healing, the means by which she was healed, and the speed with which her wounds were wiped away are inconceivable for us, but the account still makes it clear that they were material.

St Titus, a hieromonk [a priest and a monk] of the Kiev Caves Lavra, was on his death bed. The brotherhood, anticipating his imminent death, led a certain Hierodeacon [a deacon and a monk] Evagrius to his bed. These two monks had quarreled, and the monks wished them to be reconciled before Titus's death. The sick man, while in his bed, with great difficulty made a prostration to the hierodeacon, asking him for forgiveness and desiring reconciliation. But Evagrius uttered the following horrifying words: "I will never be reconciled with him; neither in this age, nor in the one to come." No sooner did he say these words than he suddenly fell down, dead. Titus, on the other hand, stood up immediately, completely healthy, as though he had never been sick. Titus then explained to the astounded brothers that, being on his death bed, he saw both angels and demons near his bed. The former cried that Titus was dying while still not reconciled with his brother, while the latter rejoiced at his impending perdition. When Titus bowed to Evagrius, while Evagrius refused to be reconciled, one of the angels, who was holding a fiery spear in his hands, struck the unrepentant man with it, and Evagrius immediately died. The same angel then reached out a hand to Titus and raised him from his bed of death, after which Titus was immediately healed.[32]

A material object was used to strike down Evagrius, though it was invisible and its qualities unknown to man. Death can also be dealt by demons. St Euthymius the Great told an account of a certain monk who was tortured and eventually killed by a demon, who used a fiery trident for his foul work.[33] Demons can weep as well. They wept that Macarius the Great had avoided their hands and entered heaven.[34]

St Amphilochius, Bishop of Iconium, a friend of Basil the Great, was consecrated a bishop by angels. He was a monk and labored in reclusion, having lived for forty years in a deserted cave. At that time, the bishop of Iconium died. An angel of the Lord appeared to Amphilochius and said, "Amphilochius! Go to the city to pastor your spiritual sheep." Amphilochius did not listen to the angel, being afraid of demonic lies. The next night, the vision happened again, but Amphilochius again did not leave his cave. The third night, the angel came to him while he was lying in his bed and said, "Get up from your bed." Amphilochius did, but he said to the angel, "If you are an angel, then pray with me." And he began to pray. The angel, having prayed with him, took Amphilochius by the right hand and led him to the nearest church. The doors of the church opened before him, as the doors of the prison opened before Peter in the book of Acts. They entered the church, which was illumined with a great light and filled with a multitude of men in white clothing. These men took Amphilochius, led him to the altar, and gave him the Holy Gospel, saying, "The Lord is with you."

One of them, surpassing the others in his brightness and nobility of appearance, said loudly, "Let us all pray." Then he began to say, "Holy grace places our brother Amphilochius as bishop of the city of Iconium; let us pray for him, that the grace of God may work within him." After the prayer, they gave him the peace of Christ and became invisible.[35]

St Pœmen the Much-suffering, a monk of the Kiev Caves Lavra, was tonsured into the monastic habit by angels. This holy man was sick from his childhood to his old age. Having come to a youthful age, Pœmen begged his parents to let him become a monk; but they would not agree. Once, the disease of the young man became extremely serious. His parents, who now despaired of his life, against their own will brought him to the Kiev Caves monastery, asking the monks to pray for the sick man. The fathers prayed a great deal for the health of Pœmen, but their prayers were not heard. God prepared a different path for His chosen one. Both father and mother remained with him constantly, fearing that he would be secretly tonsured in their absence, while the future saint kept praying God that He would find him worthy of becoming a monk. One night, when his parents and servant slept near him, angels entered the room, some in the form of beautiful young men, others in the form of the abbot of the Lavra and the other monks, bearing candles, the Gospel, a hair shirt, a robe, and everything else necessary for tonsure. They asked the sick man, "Do you want us to tonsure you?" he answered, "Truly, I do. The Lord has sent you to fulfill the desire of my heart ... "

They immediately began to perform the rite of monastic tonsure. Having tonsured him into the Great Schema,[36] they called him Pœmen (his name at baptism is not given in the life) and put a lit candle into his hands. Then they said that the candle would burn for forty days and forty nights, and he would continue to suffer from his disease for his entire life. He would be miraculously healed before the end, but that event would be a sign of his impending death. Having finished the rite, they greeted Pœmen according to the monastic custom, and left, putting his shorn hair in a towel and placing it on the tomb of St Theodosius.

The monks who lived in nearby cells, having heard the voices of singing monks, and thinking that the abbot was tonsuring the sick man or that he had already died, came into the cell to see. Everyone was sleeping deeply there, and the cell was filled with fragrance. The monks saw the sick man rejoicing and dressed in monastic clothing. They asked him, "Who tonsured you? What was the singing we heard that your parents did not?" He answered, "The abbot and the brethren tonsured me, and they sang the hymns that you heard. They also gave me this candle that you see, and they said that it would burn for forty days and nights, and they took my shorn hair, wrapped it in a towel, and carried it into the church." The brethren came to the church, but it was locked. They called the ecclesiarch who had the keys, and he swore that the church had remained closed after compline and that no one had entered into it. The monks then told the abbot of the miracle. The church was opened, and they found the hair on the tomb of St Theodosius. After examining all the events carefully, they understood that the tonsure was performed by angels. Their conclusion was proven by the fact that the candle, which should have run out in a few hours, burned for forty days. Saint Pœmen did remain in his serious illness for his entire life, never getting up from bed. Before his death, he was miraculously healed, and, revealing in himself the presence of the grace of God, died a blessed death.[37] Once again, the miraculous effect of the candle is a material reality that we do not understand.

In the same Kiev Caves monastery, St Alypius, an iconographer, had a vision of an angel. A certain pious individual ordered an icon of the Dormition to be painted in time for the feast of the Dormition. Alypius promised to finish the icon in time, but when he prepared the board and all the tools for the job, he fell deathly ill. The one who had ordered the icon came often to the monastery to find out about the icon, and he grew very sorrowful that the icon had not even been started. However, St Alypius advised him to hope in God's providence. Finally, the man came on the eve of the feast itself after Vespers, and, having reproached the saint for not giving the job to another iconographer, he left the monastery in great distress. After he left, an unknown young man entered Alypius's cell and began to paint the icon. Alypius at first thought that this was a man, another iconographer sent by the man who ordered the icon. However, the incredible speed and beauty of the process showed him that this must be an angel. The icon was finished after only three hours. After he finished, both the iconographer and the icon disappeared.

During this time, the man who had ordered the icon did not sleep all night in his distress; early in the morning, he went to the church for which he had ordered the new icon in order to pour out his grief to God. Having entered the church, he saw that an icon of wondrous beauty stood at its place. He hurried to the abbot of the Lavra and told him the miracle. Together with the abbot, they came to Alypius and found him already on his deathbed. However, the abbot still asked him how he had managed to finish the icon. Alypius told them of his vision and added, "An angel painted this icon, and look! Here he is, ready to take me." Saying this, the holy man died.[38]

St Andrew the Fool for Christ was especially sensitive to vision of the invisible world:

A vision of St. Andrew: Walking one day along the streets of Constantinople, St. Andrew saw a large, splendid procession. A rich man had just died, and his funeral procession was majestic. However, when Andrew looked more closely, he saw many black figures capering around the corpse with joy: some laughing like prostitutes, others barking like dogs, others grunting like swine, and others pouring a foul liquid over the body of the deceased. They all mocked the processional chanters, saying: "You are chanting over a dog!" Astonished, Andrew wondered what this man had done in his life. Glancing around, he saw a handsome youth standing by a wall and weeping. "For the sake of the God of heaven and earth, tell me the reason for your weeping!" he said, and the youth replied that he was the guardian angel of the deceased. The dead man had grievously offended God by his sins and had rejected the counsels of his angel. He had completely given himself over to the black devils. The angel said that that man had been a great and unrepentant sinner: he had been a liar, a despiser of men, a miser, a perjurer and a libertine, who had defiled three hundred souls by his debauchery. He had been honored by the emperor and respected by men, but all in vain. The great funeral retinue was also in vain. Death had caught up with the rich man in his unrepentant state, and the harvest had come to him suddenly.[39]

Here is another vision of St Andrew. In the early days of his assumed lunacy, St Andrew was thought to have become possessed by a demon, and so he was bound with chains and put in the church of St Anastasia the Deliverer from Potions:

All of that day, bound as he was, [the Blessed Andrew] did not eat anything. That night, at midnight, as he was praying mystically to God and to the Martyr [St. Anastasia], the devil appeared to him visibly, appearing as a [dark being]. Together with him was a multitude of demons. Some were carrying pickaxes, others knives, others sticks and clubs, swords and spears, and others ropes. That dragon was the general. Because of this, many demons had come with him, in order to darken the blessed one. The [dark being], therefore, was foaming at the mouth. In this manner, the demons charged against him. Then, the blessed Andrew lifted up his hands and cried out with tears to God: "Lord, do not cast to the beasts the soul that confesses You!" And immediately, he added: "O St. John, Apostle and Evangelist, Beloved Theologian, help me." At that instant, from on high was heard the roaring of thunder. And an Elder with large eyes appeared, whose face shown like the sun! Many were following him. He made the sign of the Cross in the air and told those with him: "Lock the doors, so that none might escape!" Those with him [i.e., the Angels] speedily seized all the demons. As they were all locked within the church, the demons cried to each other: "How dark is the hour that we are experiencing! John is strict and will torture us terribly." That precious Elder gave a command to his attendants to take the chain from the neck of the blessed Andrew. He took it and stood outside the door and cried out: "Bring each of them to me." And they brought him the first one. "Lay him down," he said. Then, he folded the chain of the blessed one in three, and gave around 100 strikes to the demon, who cried out like a man: "Mercy, mercy, have mercy on me!" Later they laid out and terribly flogged the second, followed by each of the demons. When the blessed Andrew heard the word "mercy," he began to laugh. It appeared to him that the demons were bound and flogged perceptibly just like men. In reality, however, God was flogging them. And he was flogging them with such an astonishing beating, such that human nature couldn't bear it. He who was flogging them cried out: "Go now to your father, to Satan, and show him the predicament that you are in and see if it pleases him ... " When

all of the [dark beings] disappeared, that precious Elder approached
the servant of God, and put the chain back on his neck, telling him:
"Do you see how quickly I came to help you? I greatly care about you,
because God commanded me to care for your salvation. Have patience,
so that you might everywhere appear to be worthy. Soon, your master
will remove you from your bonds, so that you might go free where you
will." "Tell me, O Lord," the blessed Andrew asked, "who are you? I don't
recognize you." "I am John," he replied, "I reclined upon the spotless and
life-giving bosom of our Lord, God and Savior Jesus Christ." As he said
this, he disappeared like lightning from before his eyes. He remained
ecstatic, and glorified God, because He helped him and delivered him
from those evil demons that had surrounded him.[40]

Thus, from these lives of saints it is clear, in accordance with the book
of Revelation, that the head of the fallen angels, Satan, remains bound
in hell, while on the earth various demons are active, under the lordship
of other princes of the air of higher ranks. Demons go back down to hell
to receive instructions from Satan, reporting to him concerning their
activities on the surface of the earth.

One time, a demon appeared to St Andrew and spoke a prophecy concerning the future spiritual and moral dissipation of Christians in the end
times: "'In those days', the demon said, 'men will be more evil than I, and
small children will surpass old men in cunning. Then I will rest! Then I
will not need to teach men anything! They will do my will without my
asking it!'" St. Andrew asked the demon, "How can you know this? Demons
cannot know the future." The demon answered, "our most wise father,
Satan, being in hell, guesses at the future with all sorts of black magic and
he tell us when he finds. We know nothing on our own."[41]

St Nephon, of whom it was said that he conversed with angels as though
they were his friend and saw demons openly, told that one time a prince
of the demons named Alazion sent a coin to Satan in hell with a few of
his underling demons. This coin came from the hand of Christian who
paid a gleeman.[42]

Church tradition tells us that the Holy Apostles, who were scattered
around the world preaching the Gospel, were taken up by angels and
brought to Jerusalem for the day of the dormition of the Mother of God.

This event is sung about extensively in the hymnography to the feast, as well as the Akathist to the Dormition.

St Nikon the Withered, a monk of the Kiev Caves monastery, was taken prisoner by the Cuman (Polovtsian) nomads when they attacked Kiev. Taking Nikon back with them to their country, the Cumans tortured him in various ways, including depriving him of food and other necessities. Nikon lived for three years under such conditions. Then he received a divine revelation that he would soon be delivered from captivity. He told his torturers this. The Cumans, thinking that he was planning an escape, sliced the ligaments in his legs and put him in irons, guarding him at all hours of the day and night. Three days after his vision, before the clock struck noon, when the armed Cumans sat around Nikon, he suddenly became invisible, and his guards heard an invisible choir singing "Praise the Lord from the heavens." Nikon was deposited in the church of the Caves Lavra during the singing of the communion hymn at the liturgy. The brothers ran to him and asked how he had returned. Nikon wanted to hide the manner of his return from them, but it was impossible. The irons, his body covered in festering wounds, the blood still pouring from his recently severed ligaments—they were vivid witnesses to a miraculous event. Nikon then told what happened, and glorified God.

In the meantime, peace was proclaimed with the Cumans. The Cuman who had kept Nikon imprisoned came to Kiev and visited the monastery. There, to his great shock, he saw his former prisoner, and he told the abbot and the monks how Nikon acted during his imprisonment and how he escaped. The Cuman was so amazed that he ended up becoming a Christian and a monk at the monastery. Many other Cumans followed his example, for the miracle had many witnesses, and it ended up having very positive, far-reaching results.[43]

The ability to cross great distances quickly, which all people consider to be a great miracle, belongs not only to angels, but to demons as well. Demons can carry both physical objects and people over great distances.[44] St John, Archbishop of Novgorod, once stood at prayer in his cell at night, as was his custom. At midnight, a demon came with the intention of somehow frightening the holy man and distracting him from prayer. For this reason, the demon entered the bathroom and started to agitate the water held in a vessel. The saint tied the demon up and bound him in the vessel with the sign of the cross. The demon began to cry out in a human voice and beg the saint to let him out of the vessel. St John answered, "As payment for your brazenness, I command you to carry me to Jerusalem tonight to the church at the tomb of Christ and bring me back to my cell immediately afterwards." The demon promised to do as the saint asked.

Then the saint, in the name of the Lord, freed the demon and commanded him, "Be prepared in front of my cell in the form of a horse." The demon left the vessel in the form of a dark mist, and then turned into a horse at the door of the saint's cell. The saint sat on him and was carried in a moment to Jerusalem. The doors of the temple of the Lord opened of their own accord before him, and the candles and oil lamps lit themselves up for him. John glorified God and prayed to Him intensely for a time and venerated all the holy places and icons. When he left, the doors again closed behind him, and the demon still stood there in the form of a horse. The saint sat on the demon, and before dawn was back in Novgorod. This event gives us some appreciation for the speed with which the spirits are able to travel, for if it is evident that Prophet Habbakuk's travels from Judea to Babylon and back occurred quickly, the Scripture says nothing specific about the time taken. Here, the time is clear: everything happened during the second half of the night, meaning the whole event took two or three hours.[45]

A certain priest named Adam lived with his small son Michael in the monastery of St Nilus of Sora. Once, the father sent his son on some business to the sexton. When the child left their room, he encountered a wild man who took him and carried him like a wind to impenetrable swamps, where some tiny hut stood. The wild man carried the child into the hut and put him down. In this hut sat a man with an imperious air. He told a woman who was sitting there, "Feed the child." Many vegetables were brought, and they tried to force him to eat, but Michael stood in place and bitterly cried. His father, seeing that his son was not returning, began to look for him. When he did not find him, he called together all the monks and together they went to a chapel not far from the monastery. There was an icon of the mother of God there, and the monks began to serve a molieben before that icon, shedding tears and asking St Nilus to help them. At that moment, the child saw that St Nilus himself walked up to the hut, and standing at the window, struck it with an iron rod, and the hut shook, casting all the demons inside onto the ground. Michael stood and wept, looking at St Nilus. The saint then said, "You accursed ones! How dare you attack my monastery and take this child! Immediately take him back from where you took him." The wild man immediately took the boy up and brought him in a wind back to the mill of the monastery and put him on a haystack. Michael began to cry out from there. At this moment, the priest and the monks were returning from the chapel and heard his screaming. They came to the haystack, and seeing him at the top, glorified God and His saint Nilus. Taking Michael down, they asked him how he had ended up there. Michael told them what had happened to him. From that moment, Michael became much quieter, but the effects of the encounter remained with the boy for some time. Father Adam and his son ended up moving away from the monastery.[46]

In many divine revelations given to the saints of the New Testament Church, the souls of departed people appeared in the same form as the angels are described in the Scriptures. Two of Emperor Maximian's highest-ranked soldiers, Sergius and Bacchus, entered the arena of martyrdom for the sake of Christ. Bacchus was beaten to death with sticks. Sergius, during this time, was in prison. Having heard of the martyrdom of his friend, he began to weep that he did not die together with him, and he prayed God for the gift of the martyr's crown. Midnight struck. Sergius continued his vigil with prayer and tears. Suddenly, Bacchus appeared to him, surrounded by heavenly light. His face was that of an angel; he was dressed in shining armor. He comforted and strengthened his friend, telling him that his time to suffer for Christ would come soon.[47]

Of especial interest is how St Peter the Athonite was freed from prison by St Symeon the God-receiver and St Nicholas of Myra. This event is very similar to how the apostle Peter was freed from prison by an angel, and it vividly illustrates the life of the saints after death. St Peter of Athos was a military commander in the world. Several times, he contemplated monasticism, and several times he even swore an oath to God that he would become a monk, but he was constantly distracted by the world, and kept putting off his intention and his oath. At that time, the Byzantine

Empire was feeling the first thrust of the Moslem threat; war between the Orthodox and the Moslems was nearly constant. Once, the Byzantine army was sent to Syria. Peter was part of this army. The Moslems defeated the Byzantine army and took a great number of prisoners. Among them was Peter. Bound with heavy chains, he was taken to the city of Samarra on the [Tigris] River, and there cast into a dark prison.

Lying in that dark prison, Peter remembered his oath, and he understood that his dilatory fulfillment of that oath was the reason he was now imprisoned. So, he began to pray to St Nicholas to free him, renewing with ardor his oath, and adding a labor of intense fasting to his prayer. Twice, St Nicholas appeared to him in a dream, and the third time he appeared to him while awake, accompanied by St Symeon the God-receiver. The great Symeon was an astounding sight, beautiful in his form, shining with heavenly light. He was dressed in the linen ephod of the Old Testament priesthood, and he held a gold staff in his hand. Peter, seeing the two saints before him, was shaken with fear. St Symeon said to Peter, "You asked my brother Nicholas to free you from this prison?" Peter could barely open his mouth, so terrified was he. "Yes," was all that he could manage. St Symeon then said, "Will you fulfill your obligation and enter a monastery, and swear to live a life of virtue?" Peter answered, "Truly, my master, with the help of God, I will." Symeon: "If you promise to do this, then walk out of here and go wherever you wish." Peter pointed at his feet, which were bound with chains. St Symeon touched the chains with his golden staff, and the chains melted as though they wax before a flame. Peter stood and saw that the door of the prison was open. He walked out, following Saints Nicholas and Symeon, and suddenly found himself outside the city walls.

When this occurred, Peter thought that perhaps all this was simply a vision, and not real? Immediately, St Symeon turned to him and said, "Why do you doubt this mercy of God to you? Can you not see with your own eyes where you are and whom you follow?" After this, St Symeon became invisible. Peter continued, following St Nicholas. It grew light. St Nicholas asked Peter if he had any food for the journey. Peter answered, "Master! I have nothing to take with me, so I have nothing now." The saint told him to enter a garden nearby. "There you will find a man who will give you vegetables, as many as you need. Take them and follow me." Peter did as he was told and continued to follow St Nicholas, and soon afterward he found himself at the border of the Byzantine Empire. Then St Nicholas said to Peter: "Brother! You are in your fatherland now, and you have all the freedom you need to fulfill your oath. Do so without delay, lest you find yourself in Samarra in chains once again." Saying this, St Nicholas disappeared.[48]

More recent appearances of spirits within the Orthodox Church also share many similarities with the appearances in the Lives of the Saints and the Scriptures. We bring to your attention especially the vision of Schemamonk Cyriacus from Valaam Monastery. He was granted a vision while he was still a layman, after his conversion from the Old Believer schism, as he stood in the altar of the church of St Lazarus in the St Alexander Nevsky Lavra in St Petersburg during the early liturgy. At first, Cyriacus smelled an incredible fragrance. Then, when the priest began to invoke the Holy Spirit to transform the gifts, he saw cherubim surrounding the holy altar and the priest. Soon the whole altar was filled with cherubim. The serving priest was covered in fire. When he did a full prostration before the holy altar, a white dove, smaller than most doves, flew from above and began to hover over the discos, then flew to the chalice, and folding its wings, flew into the cup, while the powers of Heaven, falling on their faces, bowed before the holy altar. When the priest said, "Especially the most holy Virgin ... " the powers of Heaven once again fell to the ground. When the choir sang, "It is truly meet," they bowed a third time, then surrounded the priest, covered his head with a wondrous shroud, and became invisible. Cyriacus, when he was in schism, lived a strict monastic life and was an instructor of the schismatics. For this reason, he was subjected to tortures, as was the political reality of that time. Having joined the Orthodox Church in 1783, he died the death of a saint in 1798.[49]

The ancient Fathers of the Church also had similar visions of the powers of heaven during the Eucharist. St Niphon was given such a vision. Once he concelebrated with a bishop in one of the churches of Constantinople. The spiritual eyes of Niphon were open, as it is written in his life, and he saw that fire descended from heaven, covering the altar and the bishop. During the singing of the Trisagion,[50] four angels appeared and began to sing with the choir. During the reading of the Epistle, the apostle

Paul himself appeared, standing behind the reader, observing his reading. When the reading of the Gospel began, the words flew upward to heaven in fiery glory. When the time came for the Anaphora [the calling down of the Holy Spirit on the Gifts (bread and wine)], the ceiling of the church opened up, heaven revealed itself, and a great fragrance filled the space as the angels came down, singing, "Glory to Christ God!" They carried a child of incredible beauty, and placing him on the discos, surrounded the altar, while two Seraphim and Cherubim, hovering over the head of the child, covered it with their wings. During the sanctification of the gifts, one of the brightest angels approached, and taking a knife, pierced the Child, and poured His blood into the cup, then placed the Child back on the discos, after which he joined the ranks of the other angels. After the end of liturgy, Niphon saw the Child whole and unwounded, in the hands of the angels as they ascended into heaven.[51] Similar visions were described by other saints.[52]

Even in our time, angels appear in the form of winged, beautiful youths. Even today, the souls of holy people appear in the form of human beings surrounded by heavenly glory, and demons appear in their foul, horrifying form that, though monstrous, still bear the shape of a human body. This is how they appear when they appear in their own form; they can also assume the shapes of beasts and vipers, especially their favorite form of a serpent. Here we will add an account of a recent event that was told to us personally by a person whom we trust absolutely.

In a village by the name of Tosno, located on the road between St Petersburg and Moscow, a certain driver named Theodore Kazakin lived. He was married, without children, no longer young. Although illiterate, he was a simple and meek man of generally good behavior. His hobby was smithing, and for this reason he often burned coal in the forest about three *versts* from the village, downstream on the Tosna River, on the right bank. Once, Kazakin was smithing at his makeshift coal pit. Suddenly, though it was the middle of the day, he saw a host of demons in human form of both sexes, in various kinds of clothing, all wearing hats. The demons were sitting on the trees and playing various musical instruments, singing, "These are our years! Our will be done!" They sang other words that Kazakin did not hear. Neither crossing himself nor praying had any effect on the demons.

Kazakin ran home in terror. The way home hugged the riverbank, and on this shore grew tall birch trees. As he approached the river, he saw the demons in the birches playing their instruments and singing, "These are our years! Our will be done!" Kazakin ran in terror. About one *verst* away from his place of work, he saw the demons a third time in the trees playing instruments and singing the same thing. The demons did not speak to Kazakin and did not hinder him in any way. In horror, he ran back toward his village, being on the other side of the river from it. Seeing no barge or boat on this bank, he sat down to rest. During this time, some villagers saw him and began to push a barge toward him. As he sat there, a huge snake appeared at his feet, preparing to bite him. But Kazakin jumped away.

Soon word of this event spread like wildfire. The reader of the church in the village, John Andreev (who later became a monk in the St Sergius Hermitage and later became the abbot of the Ostrov [Island] Monastery of the Entrance of the Mother of God and still later the abbot of the [Nativity of the Mother of God] Konevets Monastery) heard from Kazakin personally about this adventure and believed the account to be truthful, since Kazakin was not the kind of person to invent such a tale. The singing of the demons soon made sense: soon afterward (1817), the village of Tosno had a serious fire. The church burned down, as well as three houses belonging to clergy and eighteen other homes. Soon after this, the schismatic preacher Peter Antropov, who was a great orator, came to the village, and more than half of the inhabitants of this large village ended up leaving the Church.

Western writers insist that Saints Basil, Athanasius, John Chrysostom, Cyril of Jerusalem, Gregory of Nyssa, and other Eastern Fathers believed created spirits to be purely intellectual creations, that is, they subscribed to Descartes's teaching that spirits have no form, no movement, no materiality. But is this true? In his Homily on the Holy Spirit, St Basil the Great writes the following:

> Thus too in the case of the heavenly powers; their substance is, peradventure, an aerial spirit, or an immaterial fire, as it is written, "Who makes his angels spirits and his ministers a flame of fire" [Psalm 104:4]; wherefore they exist in space and become visible, and appear in their proper bodily form to them that are worthy. But their sanctification, being external to their substance, superinduces their perfection

through the communion of the Spirit. They keep their rank by their abiding in the good and true, and while they retain their freedom of will, never fall away from their patient attendance on Him who is truly good. It results that, if by your argument you do away with the Spirit, the hosts of the angels are disbanded, the dominions of archangels are destroyed, all is thrown into confusion, and their life loses law, order, and distinctness. For how are angels to cry "Glory to God in the highest" [Luke 2:14] without being empowered by the Spirit? For "No man can say that Jesus is the Lord but by the Holy Ghost, and no man speaking by the Spirit of God calls Jesus accursed"; [1 Corinthians 12:3] as might be said by wicked and hostile spirits, whose fall establishes our statement of the freedom of the will of the invisible powers; being, as they are, in a condition of equipoise between virtue and vice, and on this account needing the succor of the Spirit.[53]

Now of the rest of the Powers each is believed to be in a circumscribed place. The angel who stood by Cornelius [Acts 10:3] was not at one and the same moment with Philip; [Acts 8:26] nor yet did the angel who spoke with Zacharias from the altar at the same time occupy his own post in heaven. But the Spirit is believed to have been operating at the same time in Habakkuk and in Daniel at Babylon, and to have been at the prison with Jeremiah, and with Ezekiel at the Chebar. [Ezekiel 1:1] For the Spirit of the Lord fills the world, [Wisdom 1:7] and "whither shall I go from your spirit? Or whither shall I flee from your presence?" And, in the words of the Prophet, "For I am with you, says the Lord ... and my spirit remains among you." [Haggai 2:4–5] But what nature is it becoming to assign to Him who is omnipresent, and exists together with God? The nature which is all-embracing, or one which is confined to particular places, like that which our argument shews the nature of angels to be? No one would so say.[54]

In his Homily on Psalm 33, he writes the following:

The fear, however, which is salutary and the fear which is productive of holiness, fear which springs up in the soul through devotion and not through passion, what kind would you have me say it is? Whenever you are about to rush headlong into sin, consider that fearful and intolerable tribunal of Christ, in which the Judge is seated upon a certain high and sublime throne, and every creature stands trembling beside His glorious presence, [Psalm 33:10] and we are about to be led forth, one by one, for the examination of the actions of our life. And beside him who has done many wicked deeds throughout his life certain horrible and dark angels stand, flashing fire from their eyes and breathing fire because of the bitterness of their wills, and with a countenance like the night because of their dejection and their hatred of man. Then, there is the deep pit and the darkness[see Matt 8:12] that has no outlet and the light without brightness, which has the power of burning in the darkness but is deprived of its splendor. Next is the poisonous and flesh-devouring class of worms [see Isaiah 66:24], which eat greedily and are never satiated and cause unbearable pains by their voracity; and lastly, the severest punishment of all, that eternal reproach and shame. Fear these things, and being taught by this fear, check your soul, as with a bit, from its desire for wickedness.

The father promised to teach us this fear of the Lord, and not to teach indiscriminately, but to teach those who wish to heed him; not those who have long fallen away, but those who run to him through a desire of being saved; not 'strangers to the covenants' [Eph 2:12], but those who are reconciled through baptism by the word of the adoption of sons. Therefore, he says, 'Come'— that is, 'because of your good deeds approach me, children'—since you are considered worthy because of your regeneration to become sons of light. You, who have the ears of your heart open, hear; I shall teach you fear of the Lord, that fear which a little while ago our sermon described.[55]

In another place, St Basil writes that the armies of the demons, subject to their prince, abide in the aerial region, and that this word (air) assumes the entire space between heaven and earth.[56]

The demons, as those dedicated to sensuality and the passions, find significant pleasure and sustenance in sacrifices. While sacrifices are burnt, the blood of animals is converted into gasses, and having been broken down in this way into subtle parts, it passes into a substance that corresponds to the essence of demons. They of course all sustain themselves with ethers, not in the sense that they eat them or fill their stomach with them but like unto certain beasts such as oysters and others of this kind, which absorb their food through their entire body. For this reason, the demons hungrily swallow up gasses that rise up from the burning of sacrifices, and pull into themselves the smoke of incense, as essences that are appropriate for them as food. Perhaps among the animals we may find some naturally occurring similarity to the bodies of demons.[57]

"Wail [Howl] O carved images in Jerusalem and in Samaria! For as I did to Samaria and the things made by human hands, so shall I do also to Jerusalem and her idols" (Isa 10:10).

"How will the *graven images howl,* they that are made of wood, stone, or some other material, when it is art that shapes them into the images of men, or dumb quadruped animals, or birds, or even reptiles, such as the fetishes of the Egyptians?" "Howl" (Ὀλολυγμός) is a grieving voice expressing the pain of the heart with some inarticulate sound. So how will the *graven images howl?* They will *howl* because near these objects (pieces of wood, or stone, or in some places even gold and silver, or ivory shaped by human hands, or whatever else the idols of precious or non-precious material that are worshiped by the Gentiles are made of), near them I say there are present demons which invisibly fly to them and enjoy the pleasure of impure fumes of sacrifices. For just as ravenous dogs rub their shoulders around the places of meat markets where there is blood and ichor, so also the ravenous demons longing for enjoyment from the blood and steam of sacrifices flit around pagan altars and statues which are devoted to them. Perhaps their bodies—which are aerial, or indeed fiery, or made of both elements mixed—are also fed in this way. The history of *Kings* also shows that demonic power is present near statues dedicated to them. For it says, "The aliens took the ark of God and brought in into [the house] where Dagon was. And the men of Azot rose up in the morning, and behold, Dagon had fallen on its front on the ground" (1 Sam 5:2–3). Accordingly, Dagon was the visible statue, whereas he who had fallen upon his face was a demon conquered by the glory which was about the ark of God. He fell upon his face, and also threw down the hand-made effigy along with himself. That is why those who eat *meat offered to idols* are called *sharers* in the *table of demons*. Since from an offering which is brought to an idol something is apportioned to the demon which is present near it, so the demon takes some part of the evaporating blood, and the fat melting into smoke, and other whole burnt-offerings. And he who drinks from the cup from which a libation is made, *drinks the cup of demons*. Because of this the *graven images* shall howl, that is the demons with the same name as the *graven images*. And when it is said that "the Lord shall come to Egypt, and the hand-made [effigies] of Egypt shall be shaken and their hearts shall faint" (Isa 19:1), we infer the same meaning. For at the time of the advent of the Lord, the demons that occupy the space above the earth *shall be shaken*, being put to flight, and in their proper place in the abyss shall be completely forgotten. Therefore "cursed is every man who shall make a graven or molten image, the work of the hands of craftsman, and shall put it in a secret place" (Deut 27:15); because through the graven image he has procured for himself an evil treasure—a demon that follows after it, and with the demon, he has drawn into his house a curse as a cohabitant.[58]

It would not be excessive to note that Basil the Great explains the way demons interact with gases that come up as a result of the burning of sacrifices in a way that accords fully with the book of Tobit. Also, in concert with the Scriptures, he sees a commonality between the essence of demons and certain material qualities of animals. This is how low the demons have fallen! Having lost without the possibility of recall all the striving for which they were created by God, they instead strive to acquire the desires of beasts and animals. Having preserved their reason, the demons have used their reasoning capacity to develop their animalistic desires to a frightful level, for which reason the Scripture calls the devil "more cunning than all the wild animals the Lord God made on earth" (Gens 3:1).

Certain Western thinkers, when examining the Fathers through the lens of their self-delusion, because of their literalistic approach to the texts, their blindness, their distance from the Fathers' true way of reasoning, have been confused by these opinions of St Basil concerning spirits. They have even dared suggest that these passages are not authentic to St Basil, ascribing them, with a wild smile of foolish irony, to the imagination of a pagan poet! But other writers have proven that such delusions have no foundation, that these passages are indeed authentic, since similar ideas are found in the writings of St Gregory the Theologian.[59]

St Gregory, in his oration on Pascha, writes the following:

> But since this movement of Self-contemplation alone could not satisfy Goodness, but Good must be poured out and go forth beyond Itself, to multiply the objects of Its beneficence (for this was essential to the highest Goodness), He first conceived the Angelic and Heavenly Powers. And this conception was a work fulfilled by His Word and perfected by His Spirit. And so, the Secondary Splendours came into being, as the ministers of the Primary Splendour (whether we are to conceive of them as intelligent Spirits, or as Fire of an immaterial and incorporeal kind, or as some other nature approaching this as near as may be).[60]

We give our minds, the thoughts and the emotions of the soul the name "spirit"; however, St Gregory understands the words "spirit" and "fire" as the ancients did, that is, matter in gaseous state, not in solid state, which alone is called bodily and material. This thought is also expressed in other passages of his work. Using the same expressions that Basil the Great used, Gregory bases his thought on the same passage of scripture as Basil:

> The angelic nature, then, is called "wind" and "fire"—wind, to signify that part of their nature that is pure intelligence, and fire, to signify that part of their nature that purifies; for I know that the same names are appropriate to the First Nature. But we must reckon the angelic nature incorporeal, at least in comparison with our nature, or as nearly so as possible ... ever circling in chorus round the First Cause—else, how could we sing their praises, these beings who shine with brilliance drawn from the purest Splendour, or one in one degree and one in another, according to their nature and rank? ... They are servants of God's will, powerful by their innate strength and by that which was imparted to them, traversing the universe, readily present to all at any place through their zeal for service and the agility of their nature.[61]

Here we see a definition of spirits that is taken from the Scripture, which equates spirits with gaseous substance; here we also see how spirits have reference not only to place, but also to time, and we see their ability to move from place to place within allotted time. Finally, here we also see the quickness of angelic movement that is ascribed to their essential "agility," that is, lightness, which is a material quality. In another oration on Theophany, St Gregory repeats the same teaching about the angels. He calls them reasoning spirits or immaterial and bodiless fire, or some essence close to it.[62]

It is obvious that he speaks of the gaseous state, which to the ancients was simply unknown. Why are the angels called spirits with reasoning ability? Because the ancients called wind, air, and all substances that did not have solid bodies or were invisible by the general name "spirit." Why does Gregory say that the nature of angels, if not fiery or spiritual, is close to these? Because the existence of gases was not known at the time, and there was no better way of expressing this reality.

In our limited knowledge, we know of no animal that exists in a gaseous state. Knowing the gases that exist on earth and limiting our discussion to the existence of ether or combinations of gases, we can only say that the angels have an ethereal or gaseous nature. We have no better way of explaining it. Furthermore, we know that gases and ether are material; the ancients believed them to be spirits. In order to better explain this usage of the term "spirit" by St Gregory, we add the following passage, where he described how Julian the apostate openly communed with demons:

He had descended into one of those sanctuaries, inaccessible to the multitude, and feared by all (as would that he had feared the way leading unto hell before proceeding to such extremities), in company with the man that was as bad as many sanctuaries put together, the wise in such things, or sophist more rightly to be called; for this is a kind of divination amongst them to confer with darkness, as it were, and the subterranean demons concerning future events: whether that they delight more in darkness, because they *are* darkness, and makers of the darkness of wickedness, or that they shun the contact of pious persons above ground, because through such they lose their power. But when, as my fine fellow proceeded in the rites, the frightful things assailed him, unearthly noises, as they say, and unpleasant odours, and fiery apparitions, and other fables and nonsense of the sort, being terror-struck at the novelty (for he was yet a novice in these matters), he flies for help to the Cross, his old remedy, and makes the sign thereof against his terrors, and makes an ally of Him whom he persecuted. And what follows is yet more horrible. The *Seal* prevailed: the demons are worsted; the terrors are allayed. And then what follows? The wickedness revives, he takes courage again; the attempt is repeated, the same terrors return; again, the sign of the Cross, and the vanishing demons; the neophyte in despair. The celebrant is at hand, explaining away the truth: "We have made ourselves abominable, we have not terrified them;" the worse side conquers, for these were his words: and by dint of talking he persuades, and by persuading he leads his disciple into the pit of perdition And no wonder at it, for a vicious disposition is more ready to follow what is better than to be checked by what is better. Now what he said, did, or was deceived in, before he was sent up again, those may know who initiate and are initiated into these rites: at any rate he reascends full of the demon both in mind and in his actions, and indicating by the frenzy of his eyes whom he had been worshipping; if indeed he was not possessed with a demon from the very day on which he first took up with such bad ideas; but then, it became more conspicuous, in order that he might not have gone down there in vain, and become partaker with demons: a thing which those people call "enthusiasm," putting a handsome name upon it.[63]

In his praise of St Cyprian, the Theologian says, "Why is it strange if he (the devil) through the mediation of Cyprian, attacked her holy soul and body? Cyprian himself acted upon her and used as his tool not some old woman capable of such work, but a certain demon, a lover of bodies and carnal desires. The enemy powers eagerly hurry to fulfill such service, seeking to increase the number of people who share in their fall. The reward for this work was sacrifices and oblations offered in an ethereal fashion, in the exhalations from the blood of sacrifices, which the demons can subsume."[64]

To properly understand and interpret the fathers, who wrote with the aid of divine grace and through the mediation of their ascetic labors, we also need the mediation of our own experience and grace. Illumined by grace, the Fathers turned away from many ideas, especially concerning essential things, that the science of their time offered to them. They sometimes made assertion that only the science of modern times has confirmed, as we see in nearly every page of St Basil's Hexaemeron. St Callistus Angelicudes, who was illumined by the work of the prayer of the mind and heart, did not even stop to say that only God is simple essence by nature.[65] Those who make assertions about the nature of matter when they have no firm knowledge about the matter are often led by incorrect thinking to incorrect conclusions. Such great minds announce all sorts of things with great conviction about the visible and invisible words, thinking that their ideas are already incontrovertible axioms, and not understanding that the distinction between the visible and invisible world is relative, that in fact, there is no essential difference between them at all.

What is the visible world? It is the world that we see. What is the invisible world? It is the one that we do not see. Christianity, which is correctly studied only through the Christ-commanded path of lifelong asceticism, leads to the knowledge that our senses are perverted by the fall, damaged by changeability, and so can in no way be considered an objective source for the acquisition of knowledge. Thus, the division between the visible and the invisible is a function of our damaged senses, not an objective aspect of reality. Science in fact confirms this, because it has expanded in many ways our ability to see through mechanical means, making the invisible visible through telescopes and microscopes. If we then accept this understanding about the nature of the visible and invisible worlds, we must also alter our understanding about the nature of matter. We already have done so partially because of recent advances in chemistry: much that used to seem immaterial to us is now confirmed to have matter. Evidently, matter extends beyond the realm of our senses to an infinite degree, subject to laws that are unknown to us. Science in fact leads us to this great idea, to this wonderful truth, through which a much wider, more holy contemplation may open before our mind, helping us gaze with clarity into the mystical spectacle of the visible world, confirming the insignificance of man and the majesty of God the Creator.

St Athanasius the Great follows the same teaching expressed by St Basil. Like St Basil, he says that spirits have subtle and light bodies, and that, having these bodies, they are capable of traveling quickly from place to place, and that the place of the demons' residence is the aerial region, that

the demons have fearsome appearance, while the holy angels are beautiful. St Athanasius wrote the life of St Anthony the Great, with whom he
was personally acquainted and whom he considered a friend in the Lord.
In this life of St Anthony, St Athanasius gives a very expansive teaching concerning the spirits and the various kinds of temptations that he
suffered from them.[66]

The thoughts belong to Anthony, the writing to Athanasius. However,
Athanasius assimilated much of his thinking from Anthony and repeats
much of his insights in his expansive corpus. St Athanasius calls the angels
bodiless, but only in comparison with human beings.[67] Only God is good in
Himself; the angels are good because of the divine grace acting in them.[68]
They are living beings, reasoning, without flesh (*avlos*), capable of singing,
deathless.[69] The essence of demons in no way differs from angelic nature;
they are only different in their willing use of that nature, just as a sinner
has one disposition of spirit, while a saint has another.[70]

When speaking of the book of Tobit and insisting on its inclusion in
the canon of Scripture, St Athanasius mentions the demon Asmodius, who
loved Sarah, the daughter Raguel, and killed all her husbands. He also cites
the words of the archangel Raphael concerning the smoke from the burning fish heart and liver that would drive the demon away.[71]

And once more, if the devil, the enemy of our race, having fallen from
heaven, wanders about our lower atmosphere, and there bearing rule
over his fellow-spirits, as his peers in disobedience, not only works
illusions by their means in them that are deceived, but tries to hinder
them that are going up (and about this the Apostle says: "According to
the prince of the power of the air, of the spirit that now works in the
sons of disobedience"); while the Lord came to cast down the devil,
and clear the air and prepare the way for us up into heaven, as said the
Apostle: "Through the veil, that is to say, His flesh"(Hebrews 10:20)—
and this must needs be by death—well, by what other kind of death
could this have come to pass, than by one which took place in the air,
I mean the cross? for only he that is perfected on the cross dies in the
air. Whence it was quite fitting that the Lord suffered this death. For
thus being lifted up He cleared the air of the malignity both of the devil
and of demons of all kinds, as He says: "I beheld Satan as lightning fall

from heaven" (Luke 10:18); and made a new opening of the way up into heaven as He says once more: "Lift up your gates, O you princes, and be lifted up, you everlasting doors" (Psalm 14:7) ....[72]

Or when have the oracles among the Greeks, and everywhere, ceased and become empty, save when the Saviour has manifested Himself upon earth? Or when did those who are called gods and heroes in the poets begin to be convicted of being merely mortal men, save since the Lord effected His conquest of death, and preserved incorruptible the body he had taken, raising it from the dead? Or when did the deceitfulness and madness of demons fall into contempt, save when the power of God, the Word, the Master of all these as well, condescending because of man's weakness, appeared on earth? Or when did the art and the schools of magic begin to be trodden down, save when the divine manifestation of the Word took place among men?[73] ...

And whereas formerly every place was full of the deceit of the oracles, and the oracles at Delphi and Dodona, and in Bœotia and Lycia and Libya and Egypt and those of the Cabiri, and the Pythoness, were held in repute by men's imagination, now, since Christ has begun to be preached everywhere, their madness also has ceased and there is none among them to divine any more. And whereas formerly demons used to deceive men's fancy, occupying springs or rivers, trees or stones, and thus imposed upon the simple by their juggleries; now, after the divine visitation of the Word, their deception has ceased. For by the Sign of the Cross, though a man but use it, he drives out their deceits. And while formerly men held to be gods the Zeus and Cronos and Apollo and the heroes mentioned in the poets, and went astray in honouring them; now that the Saviour has appeared among men, those others have been exposed as mortal men, and Christ alone has been recognised among men as the true God, the Word of God.[74]

Moreover, our adversary the devil, envying us the possession of such great blessings, goes about seeking to snatch away the seed of the word which is sown within us. Wherefore as if by His prophetic warnings He would seal up His instructions in our hearts as His own peculiar treasure, the Lord said, 'Take heed that no man deceive you: for many shall come in My name, saying, I am he; and the time draws near; and they shall deceive many: go ye not therefore after them' (Luke 21:8). This is a great gift which the Word has bestowed upon us, that we should not be deceived by appearances, but that, howsoever these things are concealed, we should all the more distinguish them by the grace of the Spirit. For whereas the inventor of wickedness and great spirit of evil, the devil, is utterly hateful, and as soon as he shows himself is rejected of all men—as a serpent, as a dragon, as a lion seeking whom he may seize upon and devour—therefore he conceals and covers what he really is, and craftily personates that Name which all men desire, so that deceiving by a false appearance, he may thenceforth fix fast in his own chains those whom he has led astray. And as if one that desired to kidnap the children of others during the absence of their parents, should personate their appearance, and so putting a cheat on the affections of the offspring, should carry them far away and destroy them; in like manner this evil and wily spirit the devil, having no confidence in himself, and knowing the love which men bear to the truth, personates its appearance, and so spreads his own poison among those that follow after him. Thus he deceived Eve, not speaking his own, but artfully adopting the words of God, and perverting their meaning. Thus he suggested evil to the wife of Job, persuading her to feign affection for her husband, while he taught her to blaspheme God. Thus does the crafty spirit mock men by false displays, deluding and drawing each into his own pit of wickedness. When of old he deceived the first man Adam, thinking that through him he should have all men subject unto him, he exulted with great boldness and said, "My hand has found as a nest the riches of the people; and as one gathers eggs that are left, have I gathered all the earth; and there is none that shall escape me or speak against me" [Isaiah 10:14]. But when the Lord came upon earth, and the enemy made trial of His human Economy, being unable to deceive the flesh which He had taken upon Him, from that time forth he, who promised himself the occupation of the whole world, is for His sake mocked even by children: that proud one is mocked as a sparrow. For now the infant child lays his hand upon the hole of the asp, and laughs at him that deceived

Eve; and all that rightly believe in the Lord tread under foot him that said, "I will ascend above the heights of the clouds: I will be like the Most High" (Isaiah 14:14). Thus he suffers and is dishonored; and although he still ventures with shameless confidence to disguise himself, yet now, wretched spirit, he is detected the rather by them that bear the Sign on their foreheads; yea, more, he is rejected of them, and is humbled, and put to shame. For even if, now that he is a creeping serpent, he shall transform himself into an angel of light, yet his deception will not profit him; for we have been taught that "though an angel from heaven preach unto us any other gospel than that we have received, he is anathema" (Galatians 1:8–9). And although, again, he conceal his natural falsehood, and pretend to speak truth with his lips; yet are we "not ignorant of his devices" (2 Corinthians 2:11), but are able to answer him in the words spoken by the Spirit against him; "But unto the ungodly, said God, why do you preach My laws?" [Psalm 49:16] and, "Praise is not seemly in the mouth of a sinner" [Sirach 15:9]. For even though he speak the truth, the deceiver is not worthy of credit. And whereas Scripture showed this, when relating his wicked artifices against Eve in Paradise, so the Lord also reproved him—first in the mount, when He laid open "the folds of his breast-plate" [Job 41:13], and showed who the crafty spirit was, and proved that it was not one of the saints, but Satan that was tempting Him. For He said,"'Get behind Me Satan; for it is written, You shall worship the Lord your God, and Him only shall you serve" (Matt 4:10). And again, when He put a curb in the mouths of the demons that cried after Him from the tombs. For although what they said was true, and they lied not then, saying, "You are the Son of God" and "the Holy One of God" (Matt 8:29; Mark 1:24); yet He would not that the truth should proceed from an unclean mouth, and especially from such as them, lest under pretense thereof they should mingle with it their own malicious devices, and sow these also while men slept. Therefore He suffered them not to speak such words, neither would He have us to suffer such, but has charged us by His own mouth, saying, "Beware of false prophets, which come to you in sheep's clothing, but inwardly they are ravening wolves" (Matt 7:15); and by the mouth of His Holy Apostles, "Believe not every spirit" (1 John 4:1).[75]

It is clear that the thoughts here expressed are identical with the teachings of St Anthony the Great. In this instruction, the idea that created spirits have ethereal bodies without a doubt belongs not only to Anthony, but Athanasius as well. Otherwise, Athanasius would have had no scruples in rejecting it. The materiality of the created spirits is made further clear in the vivid descriptions of the temptations that Anthony the Great suffered at the hands of the demons. Since these temptations are readily available in any collection of *Lives of Saints*, we will not include them here. Many other monks have suffered similar temptations.

St Epiphanius of Cyprus, who died on a ship on the way from Constantinople to Cyprus, had this to say to his disciples in his final conversation with his disciples:

> My children! If you love me, keep my commandments, and the love of God will abide with you. You know through what kinds of sorrows I passed in my life! These sorrows I considered not sorrowful, but I remained joyful always because I hoped in God, and God never abandoned me, but Himself protected me against all the snares of the enemy. "All things work together for good to those who love God" (Romans 8:28). Once, my beloved children, when I was in a deserted place and offered Christ prayer to be delivered from all the snares of the enemy, a host of demons attacked me. They dashed me against the ground and, taking my legs, dragged me on the earth. Some of them beat me. This they did for ten days. After this, I never saw any more demons in their proper form until the end of my days; whoever, they poured out their hatred of me through other people.[76]

The ancient Fathers, as we saw from the citations from Cyril of Jerusalem, agreed with the Scriptures and common parlance in calling spirits by names such as air, wind, or everything that does not have a solid body. In order to give my beloved brothers the most exact understanding of the Fathers' opinion concerning spirits, here is a teaching from Athanasius the Great concerning the souls and bodies of human beings:

> It is well known that the body takes it composition from the elements; it is by the elements that is also destroyed. For this reason, the bodies of men, as well as other animals, died quickly, being made of the

four elements, that is, earth, light, water, and air. These elements
themselves are not free from corruption, and so neither are the bodies,
which are all made of earth. On the contrary, simple essences preserve
themselves easily and remain unbroken to the end. These include the
sun, the human soul, light, the luminaries, air, water, fire, spirits, in
a word, everything that is simple ... As for the human soul, it has five
passions that belong to the soul. They are anger, sorrow, fear, busyness, envy. Whoever has acquired sobriety of mind can control these
passions. The soul itself, in its essence, is like a flame of fire. As flames
boil everything that is put into a put, so also the fiery soul destroys the
food that is placed into the stomach. Even though is called *psyche* (ψυχή;
soul), it is called thus not because it was *psychra* (ψύχρα), that is, cold, as
some of the simple-minded think. The soul has the power and activity
of the soul because it dries up wetness by the power of its warmth. The
sun, being fiery and hot, dries up swampy places and whatever might be
filled with water it dries through evaporation. That the soul is by its very
nature warm we can be assured by those who are about to die, because
in that hour, when the soul departs from the body, all the members
are filled with cold, no less than when it is freezing outside. While the
soul eats in abundance, so long also the body remains in its power and
energy. When it ceases to be nourished, then the body itself becomes
food for the warmth of the body. A metal vessel or a pot in a hot oven
that has no water in it cannot stand the power of the fire, becoming
completely at one with the fire and destroyed in the process. So also the
vessel of the body, if it is subject to a lack of nourishment, begins to fall
apart because it is offered as food for the fiery soul. If you desire learn
how the soul remains inside the body, ask a person this question: "Tell
me, does the soul abide in the entire body or in some part of the body?"
If he answers, "In the entire body," then answer him, "Then why, when
a hand or a foot is cut off, the soul is not also damaged, but the person continues to live without dying?" If he answers, "In a single place,"
then answer him, "Then how do all the other members of the body survive? Because everything that is deprived of soul is dead, and I do not
know what you would like to say. But I will tell you in what place, and
for what reason, and how the soul abides. It positively abides in three

places of the body. As the ray of a sun enters the house always in a single place, yet illumines the entire house, so the soul, living in three parts of the body, illumines the entire house of the body. It lives in the heart, in the upper part of the head and in the vital organs. For this reason, in the house when the heart or head are struck, or when blood flows in great abundance from the vital organs the soul immediately leaves the body, and the body becomes dead. The soul, truly abiding in these three parts of the body, pours out its strength into the rest of the body."[77]

The opinion expressed here by St Athanasius the Great, one of the most educated people of his time, is worthy of especial attention, especially in our time, when the rationalism of Descartes has begun to lose its hold on people, remaining the opinion only of those who have not studied the latest discoveries of science concerning the nature of matter. This passage makes very clear what it was that the ancients called "simple." They called that which was not divisible into constituent parts "simple," essences that could not be broken down in any known way. Water, air, spirit, the soul—these are called simple in the same sense. Then came chemistry and confused our understanding of matter, having shown complexity in those things that were formerly considered simple, showing materiality in those objects that used to be called immaterial, and having achieved precise mathematical knowledge about everything material, at least outside the eternal realm. In this way, science has come to agreement with the Scriptures and the Holy Fathers, who separate the essence of God with an endless distance from all created natures both in nature and in activity. All foolish ideas, all the fantastical idiocies of the philosophers who do now know the positive sciences are rejected and are destroyed by the positive sciences.[78]

Athanasius admits, based only on personal experience, the presence of the soul in three major areas of their body; in all the members he admits the activity of the soul, though he does not admit its presence there. Our most recent studies have confirmed the presence of the soul in all parts of the body. For example, all people who have lost limbs continue to feel the presence of those limbs and feel the ability to use them. Some believe that this is simply the work of nervous tissue. But this is not true. The nerves only act within the body; they cannot act outside the body. These phantom sensations are the clearly sensible members of the soul that remain even after the physical member has been severed.

St John Chrysostom said, "Do you wish to see the angels and the martyrs? Open the eyes of faith and look at this spectacle. For if the entire air is filled with angels, how much more so the church? That the entire aerial region is filled with angels is clear from the words of the apostle, who tell women to cover their heads: 'For this reason the woman ought to have a symbol of authority on her head, because of the angels' (1 Corinthians 11:10). And also, in Genesis: 'the Angel who has redeemed me from all evil' (Gen 48:16). And those who were in the home with the apostle, who told the girl Rhoda, 'It is his angel' (Acts 12:15). And again, 'Jacob went on his way, and the angels of God met him' (Gen 32:1 NKJV). But why is the host of angels here on earth? As the king commands that his armies be placed in all cities to prevent war and unexpected attacks, so God places the armies of his angels against the cruel and fierce demons, the enemies of the world, who constantly battle in this aerial region against the angels, because they have preserved this world for our sake. And so that you may know that angels are angels of this world, hear what the deacon constantly says in prayer, 'An angel of peace, [a faithful guide, a guardian of our souls and bodies, let us ask of the Lord[79]].'"[80]

Rejecting the opinion of those who believe angels are capable of coupling with human women, call angels bodiless, incapable of bearing children, using as proof the words of the Lord: "For in the resurrection they neither marry nor are given in marriage, but are like angels of God in heaven" (Matt 22:30).[81] Chrysostom also says that every person has his own guardian angel; he proves this using the words of the Christians in Jerusalem: "It is his angel" (Acts 12:15).[82]

In his fifty-third homily on the Gospel of Matthew, Chrysostom writes the following:

> The prisoner sorrows the most when he is brought before the judge; he shakes the most as he approaches the place of torture, when he must give answer. Similar to this, many speak of terrible visions that they see at this time (before death), vision that the dying are not able to bear, so powerful that they make the deathbed itself shake, as they look at

those who approach with eyes transformed by fear, when the soul is disturbed, not wanting to leave the body, not able to hold the gaze of the angels that approach. If we shake when we look at frightening people, then what sort of terror will we feel when we see the angels and the fierce powers of evil, when the soul separates form the body weeping bitterly?

And why do I speak of that blessed essence of God? A man cannot even look upon the essence of an angel without fear and trembling. To convince you that this is true, I shall present to you the blessed Daniel, God's friend, a man who, because of his wisdom and justice, approached God with confidence, a man well approved for his many other virtuous actions. I shall show this blessed Daniel utterly weakened, broken up, and distraught because he was in the presence of an angel. And let no one thing he experienced this because of his sins or a bad conscience. His soul's confidence in God had already been proved. Clearly, then, the blame for his condition belonged to the weakness of his nature.

So this man, Daniel, fasted for three weeks, "and ate no desirable bread." Neither wine nor meat entered his mouth; nor did he anoint himself with oil. It was then that he saw the vision since his soul had been made more fit to receive such an apparition because, by his fasting, it had become lighter and more spiritual. And what did Daniel say? "I lifted my eyes and looked, and behold, there was a man clothed in linen [that is, a priestly garment] and his waist was girded with gold of Uphaz. His body was like beryl, and his face like the appearance of lightening. His eyes were like lamps of fire, his arms and legs like the appearance of shining brass. The sound of his words was like the voice of a multitude. I, Daniel, alone saw the vision, for the men with me saw did not see the vision; but a great astonishment fell upon them, and they fled in fear. So I was left alone and saw this great vision, but no strength remained in me; for my splendor was turned into corruption, and I retained no strength" [Daniel 10:5–8].

What does he mean when he says: "My splendor was turned into corruption?" He was a handsome young man. But fear of the angel's presence affected him like a man on his deathbed. It spread a pallor all over his face, it destroyed the freshness of his youth, and drained all the color from the surface of his skin. This is why he said: "My glory was turned into corruption." When a charioteer becomes frightened and lets go of the reins, all his horses tumble down and the whole chariot is overturned. Then same thing generally happens in the case of the soul when it is gripped by some terror or anguish. When the soul is frightened to distraction and lets the reins fall loose from its own faculties and powers of operation, which are rooted in each body's organs of sense perception, it deprives the limbs of their control. Then, because they have been deprived of the power which controls them, these limbs are buffeted on every side and become useless. This is what Daniel experienced at that moment.

What then, did the angel do? He raised Daniel to his feet and said: "O Daniel, man of desires, understand the words I speak to you and stand upright for now I am sent to you" [Daniel 10:10]. And Daniel stood up all atremble. The angel began to speak to him and said: "From the first day you set your heart to understand and to afflict yourself before your God, your words were heard, and I came because of your words" [Daniel 10:12].

Again Daniel fell to the ground, just as happens to those who fall into a faint. Such people, once aroused, come back to their senses and see us clearly when we are holding them and sprinkling cold water on their faces. But often enough, as we hold them in our arms, they faint away again. And this is what happened to the prophet. His soul was frightened, he could not endure to look upon the presence of his fellow servants, nor could he bear the brightness of that light. So he became troubled and confused, as if his soul was hurrying to burst form some chain binding it to the flesh. But the angel still held him fast.

Let those Anomœans listen who, out of curiosity, are investigating into the essence of the Lord of angels. Daniel, to whom the eyes of the lions showed reverence, Daniel, who had more than human power in his human body, could not endure the presence of his fellow servant but lay on the ground before the angel and could not breathe. For he said: "How can your servant, my lord, speak with the lord of this? As for m, no strength now remains in me, nor is any breath left in me" [Daniel 10:12].[83]

In his interpretation of Psalm 41, Chrysostom writes, "How many demons are in the air? How many enemy forces? If only God would allow them to show us their frightening and abhorrent aspect, then would we not immediately go mad? Would we not immediately perish?"[84]

In his thirty-fourth homily on Matthew, Chrysostom says that the demons wander about tombs. In his homily on St Babylas, Chrysostom says:

> The martyr then was moved, but the demon not even then enjoyed freedom from fear, but straightway learned that it is possible to move the bones of a martyr, but not to escape his hands. For as soon as the coffin was drawn into the city, a thunderbolt came from above upon the head of his image and burnt it all up. And yet, if not before, then at least there was likelihood that the impious emperor would be angry, and that he would send forth his anger against the testimony of the martyr. But not even then did he dare, so great fear possessed him. But although he saw that the burning was intolerable, and knew the cause accurately; he kept quiet. And this is not only wonderful that he did not destroy the testimony, but that he not even dared to put the roof on to the temple again. For he knew, he knew, that the stroke was divinely sent, and he feared lest by forming any further plan, he should call down that fire upon his own head. On this account he endured to see the shrine of Apollo brought to so great desolation; For there was no other cause, on account of which he did not rectify that which had happened, but fear alone. For which reason he unwillingly kept quiet, and knowing this left as much reproach to the demon, as distinction to the martyr. For the walls are now standing, instead of trophies, uttering a voice clearer than a trumpet. To those in Daphne, to those in the city, to those who arrive from far off, to those who are with us, to those men which shall be hereafter, they declare everything by their appearance, the wrestling, the struggle, the victory of the martyr.[85]

St Andrew of Cæsarea writes "that there can be no doubt that there is a great multitude of demons; all the saints say that the air is filled with them."[86] "That serpent (the devil) is red in color, which expresses his blood-thirsty nature or his fiery angelic nature, though he was cast out of the angelic host."[87]

St Gregory the Great speaks much about life after death and about spirits. We will choose only several passages. In his homily on the parable of the ten virgins, he describes the following event:

> I will tell you, very dear brothers, a story that will be very edifying for you to ponder, if your charity will listen to it carefully. There was, in the province of Valerie, a nobleman named Chrysaorius, whom the people, in his countrymen's words, called Chryserius. He was a very fortunate man, but also full of vices and resources: swollen with pride, delivered to the pleasures of the flesh and burned with a flame of avarice which excited him to increase his income. The Lord, having decided to put an end to so many bad deeds, struck him with a bodily disease, as I learned from a religious of his relatives who still lives. Having reached the end of his life, just as he was about to leave his body, he opened his eyes and saw hideous and very dark spirits stand in front of him and press him hard to drag him to the hellish prisons. He began to tremble, to turn pale, and to sweat profusely; he implored a respite with loud cries, and frightened, he loudly called out his son Maxime, whom I knew as a monk when I was. He said: "Maxime, come quickly! I've never hurt you, take me under your protection."
>
> Maxime, deeply moved, approached immediately, while the family was gathering, lamenting loudly. They could not see the evil spirits with which Chrysaorius was so hard to attack, but they guessed the presence of these spirits by the confusion, the pallor, and the trembling of the one they carried away. The terror of their terrible appearance made him turn sideways on his bed. Lying on the left side, he could not bear their sight; he turned to the wall, they were still there. Deeply in a hurry, desperate to escape them, he began to beg loudly: "Take respite at least until morning!" Respite at least until morning! But while he was shouting, in the very midst of his screams, he was torn out of his envelope of flesh. It is obvious that if he saw these demons, it was not for his profit, but for ours, because God, in his immense patience, still awaits us. For Chrysaorius, in fact, it was useless to see these horrible spirits before his death, nor to ask for respite, since he did not obtain it.[88]

In another place, "When the day of death forced Stephen to leave his body, then many gathered to show their own souls the death of such a holy soul. And when they all stood before him, then some saw, with their physical eyes, the angels approaching, but they could not say anything. Others saw nothing at all. However, all were possessed with such terror that no one could remain to witness the moment of death."[89]

"For days will come upon you when your enemies will build an embankment around you" (Luke 19:43). Are there any greater enemies of the human soul than the evil spirits who come to besiege it as it goes out? of her body, after having excited her by deceptive delights when she lived in the love of the flesh? They surround her with trenches, putting the faults she has committed under the eyes of her soul, and endeavoring to drag her into their common damnation, so that she is surprised at her last moments, while seeing by what enemies she is surrounded on all sides, yet she cannot find a way to escape, because she can no longer do the good she refused to do when she could.

It is still about these spirits that we can understand the rest of the text: They will "surround you and close you in on every side" (Luke 19:43). The evil spirits tighten the soul on all sides when they come to remind him of the faults that she has committed not only in deeds, but also in word and even in thought: the soul who here has taken at ease in sin in many ways is thus, in his last moments, squeezed by all the sides during the punishment.

The text continues: They will "level you, and your children within you, to the ground" (Luke 19:44). The soul is defeated on the ground by the thought of its faults when its flesh, which it believed to be all its life, is threatened to return soon to dust. His children fall into death when the evil designs to which the soul now gives birth vanish in the chastisement upon which his life comes to an end, as it is written, "In that day all his thoughts shall perish" (Psalm 146:4). These hardened designs can also be signified by stones. Indeed, the text goes on to say, "They will not leave in you one stone upon another" (Luke 19:44). When a perverse soul adds another to a perverse thought, which is even more so, what does it do, if not to put a stone on a stone? But once the city is destroyed, it does not leave stone on stone, because when the soul is led to its punishment, all the construction of his thoughts is dispersed.

The cause of this punishment is given later: "Because you did know the time of your visitation" (Luke 19:44). Almighty God is accustomed to visit every sinful soul in many ways. He visits her relentlessly by her commandments, sometimes by a trial, sometimes even by a miracle, so that she hears the truths she did not know, and—if still she remains full of pride and contempt—that she returns to God in the pain of compunction, or else, overcome by the benefits, that she blushes for the evil she has committed.

But because this soul has not recognized the time when it was visited, it is delivered at the end of its life to enemies whom it will be obliged, by a judgment of eternal damnation, to share forever society. Scripture says it elsewhere: "When you go with your adversary to the magistrate, make every effort along the way to settle with him, lest he drag you to the judge, the judge deliver you to the officer, and the officer throw you into prison" (Luke 12:58). Our adversary on the way is the word of God, which opposes our carnal desires in the present life. To free oneself from it is to submit humbly to one's commandments. In case of refusal, the adversary will deliver to the judge, and the judge to the exactor, that is to say that the sinner will be convinced of his fault in the court of the Judge by his contempt for the word of the Lord. The Judge gives it to the Executioner, because it allows the evil spirit to lead that soul to chastisement, so that this spirit forces it to follow to the torment the one who has voluntarily agreed with him to sin. The Executioner throws the sinner into prison, since the evil spirit sends him violently to hell, waiting for the day of judgment, from which they will be tortured together in the flames of hell.

It is necessary to consider what terror will accompany the hour of our death, what a trembling of mind, what a memory of all our bad actions! It will be well forgotten, then, happiness passed! But what fear, what apprehension before the Judge! What pleasure can we put in the present goods, when all must pass in one and the same instant, without the punishment that threatens us, when what we love is destined to disappear completely, to make room for suffering? who will never go away? The evil spirits seek in the dying soul what they have accomplished there; they remind him of the faults they have inspired him in order to draw him into their torment.

But why are we speaking here only of sinful souls, while the evil spirits also go to meet the dying elect to find, if they can, something that would belong to them? Now there has never been more than one man who can say boldly before his Passion: "I will no longer talk much with you, for the ruler of this world is coming, and he has nothing in Me" (John 14:30). Indeed, the prince of this world, seeing that Christ was a mortal man, imagined that he could find in him something that belonged to him. But it was without sin that he came out of this world of corruption, the one who had come without sin in the world.

Peter himself did not dare to boast that the prince of this world had nothing in him, and yet he deserved to hear: "And I will give you the keys of the kingdom of heaven, and whatever you bind on earth will be bound in heaven, and whatever you loose on earth will be loosed in heaven" (Matt 16:19). Paul did not dare to boast of it, but he did reach the mysteries of the third heaven before he died (see 2 Corinthians 12:2). John, too, did not have the audacity, although he rested on the breast of the Redeemer, at the Last Supper, as the most beloved disciple (see John 21:20). Since the prophet says, "For behold, I was conceived in wickedness, and in sins did my mother bear me" (Psalm 50:7 LXX), which could be without fault in the world after being born with fault? The same prophet says on this subject: "Before Thee shall no man living be justified" (Psalm 143:2). And Solomon declares: "For there is not a righteous man on earth who does good and does not sin" (Ecclesiastes 7:20). In the same sense, John says, "If we say that we have no sin, we deceive ourselves, and the truth is not in us" (1 John 1:8). And James says, "For we all stumble in many things" (James 3:2).

It is true that in all those who were conceived in the pleasure of the flesh, the prince of this world found something that belonged to him, either in their actions, in their words, or in their thoughts. But if he could not then lead them, or take them before, it is because Christ, who, without his having it, paid for us the debt of death, delivered them from their debts; thus, our debts no longer hold us back from the power of our enemy, since the Mediator between God and men, Jesus Christ made man (see 1 Timothy 2:5), has acquitted himself for us in all gratuitousness debt he had not contracted. For whoever delivered his body for death to us without his death delivered our soul from the death due to him. He says, "For the ruler of this world is coming, and he has nothing in Me" (John 14:30).

So we must take care to meditate every day in tears with what fury and under what terrifying aspect the prince of this world will come, the day of our death, to claim what in us belongs to him, since he dared to address even to our God when he died in his flesh, to seek in him something [which belonged to him], without being able to find anything.

What can we say or do—unhappy men we are!—we who have committed innumerable mistakes? What shall we declare to the enemy when he seeks and finds in us many things belonging to him, if not the only truth which is for us an assured refuge and a solid hope, namely, that we become one with in whom the prince of this world sought something which belonged to him without being able to find anything, since he alone is "free among the dead" (Psalm 87:6 LXX)? And we are henceforth delivered from the servitude of sin by a true freedom, since we are united with him who is truly free. It is certain—we cannot deny it, and we even admit it in all loyalty—that the prince of this world has in us many things which belong to him; he cannot, however, take possession of us at our death, since we have become the members of him in whom he has nothing.[90]

I will tell you a fact that my brother priest, Speciosus, who is here, has known well. At the time when I entered the monastery, an old woman named Redempta, who wore the monastic habit, lived in our town near the church of Blessed Mary, still Virgin. She had been a disciple of this Herundo, a very virtuous woman who, it is said, had led the hermit life on the mountains of Préneste.

Redempta had two disciples, religious like her: one named Romula, and another still alive, whom I know by sight, but whose name escapes me. These three women led in one dwelling a life rich in virtues, but poor in earthly goods. This Romula of which I spoke was ahead of the great merits of her life, her companion whom I mentioned. She had an admirable patience, a great obedience; she knew how to impose silence on her mouth and was very zealous in indulging in continual prayer.

But those whom men already judge perfect still often have some defects in the eyes of the heavenly Artisan. Is it not the same when we, laymen in this field, see still unfinished statues and admire them as already perfect, while the artist, he, examines and retouches them again, without the praise heard the stop working on them to improve them? That is why this Romula I mentioned was struck by the disease that doctors call a Greek name "paralysis". For many years she had to stay in bed, having lost the use of almost all her limbs. But these trials could not arouse impatience in her. What was wrong with her limbs was all for the benefit of her virtues, for she was all the more zealous in prayer that she could do nothing else.

One night she called this Redempta, of which I spoke, and which showed the same attention for her two disciples as if they had been her daughters: "Mother, come! Mother, come!" Redempta immediately rose, as did the other disciple. It is thanks to their double testimony that these facts were known to many other people, and that I myself learned them from that time.

In the middle of the night, as the two women surrounded the patient's bed, a celestial light suddenly filled the entire cell. His splendor sprang up with such brilliancy that their hearts were seized with an unspeakable terror; their whole body, as they later said, became stiff, and they remained frozen in stupor. They began to hear a noise like that of a great multitude coming in; the door of the cell was shaken as if it were jostled by the crowd that was entering. They perceived, as they said, the multitude of people who penetrated, but they saw nothing, because of their terror and excessive light. Fear made them lower their eyes, and the intensity of the light dazzled them. This was immediately accompanied by a wonderful perfume, whose sweetness comforted their souls terrified by the radiance of light. But as the brightness was of a brightness impossible to bear, Romula, in a very soft voice, began to reassure Redempta, her spiritual mistress, who trembled beside her: "Do not be afraid, my mother, I do not die right now."

And as she repeated these words, the light that had invaded the room gradually faded, but the good smell that followed. The next day and two days passed without the smell of the spilled perfume disappearing.

On the fourth night, Romula called her mistress again. When she came, she asked him for the viaticum, which she received. Now, as Redempta and her other disciple were still near the sick man's bed, suddenly there appeared on the square in front of the cell door two chanting choruses. According to what they said afterwards, they recognized the voices of men and women: the men sang the psalms, and the women answered them. And while these celestial funerals were being celebrated in front of the cell, the holy soul was delivered from the bonds of the flesh. It was conducted to Heaven, and as the chanting choruses rose, the psalmody became less and less distinct, until its whisper faded into the distance at the same time as the sweet scent.[91]

Even if an angelic spirit is limited, the supreme Spirit of God is not limited. This is why angels can be simultaneously in mission and before him: wherever they are sent, when they go there, it is still within God that they run.[92]

These citations from the Holy Fathers show us definitely the following teachings: 1) The teachings of the Fathers are Scriptural; 2) The teaching concerning spirits in *Orthodox Dogmatic Theology* is identical with the Scriptures and the Fathers; 3) When Western writers have ascribed to the Fathers an incorrect teaching about the complete immateriality of spirits, equal to the immateriality and spirituality of God, they are mistaken.

Western writers have said that the Fathers of the Church were influenced by pagan philosophy and the science of their time. This is fair, but only refers to some fathers and with reference to only a very few subjects. This was noted even by some fathers at the time, and a proper warning was administered.[93] In our times, whoever studies the Fathers as they should be studied, but also has a worldly education, will see that in some things the fathers paid homage to contemporary scientific trends as well as to generally accepted principles of that time. The same cannot be said about the writers of the holy Scriptures. These writers were inspired by the Holy Spirit alone.

Also, someone like St Anthony the Great was illiterate; having purified himself with pious ascetic labor, he become the abode of God and could then give a teaching concerning the spirits in a way that God Himself revealed to Him. St Athanasius the Great, a great scholar of his time, though he was also a man of grace, preferred to transmit Anthony's teaching concerning the spirits, instead of writing his own work based on his own studies and spiritual experiences, since perhaps his level of grace was not as great as that of St Anthony, for he had cares in the world, proper to an archbishop.[94]

St Anthony the Great's teaching concerning the spirits is simple, natural, and vivid. Moreover, he instructs in such detail and completeness that no scholar would be able to manage, no matter how educated he may be. All knowledge concerning the nature of matter must be confirmed by experience. Reasoning alone cannot lead to exact and correct conclusions. Very often ideas that seem on the surface to be unerring end up being revealed as incorrect when verified by experience. Any reasoning that is not confirmed by experience, no matter how seemingly correct, no matter how well-written, is only a postulate or hypothesis, not the truth. This is the conclusion of science, founded on the history of the natural sciences. It is based on many countless experiences. There is no canceling this basic law, nor is there any voice that can speak against it. Any voice that does only proves its foolishness or willfulness and will be judged false by the court of history.

And so, how scientific is Descartes's teaching concerning the immateriality of spirits? This teaching is not a positively proven scientific fact. It is a hypothesis, a postulate subject to the scientific process. For this reason, science, until it can find exact knowledge concerning a subject, may prefer one hypothesis or another, but it does not call it a law of nature. Science will reject a hypothesis as soon as facts begin to prove the falseness of the hypothesis. For example, Benjamin Franklin had a hypothesis concerning the generation of electricity. When subsequent science found positive facts that contradicted Franklin's hypothesis, then the hypothesis became an archival curiosity. Simmer, using newly available facts, developed another hypothesis concerning the generation of electricity. But later work of scientists proved his hypothesis was false as well. However, the formulation of these hypotheses in no way is rejected as harming the further progress of science. A well-formulated hypothesis may become a scientific law if it becomes proven by scientific fact.

What is Descartes's hypothesis concerning spirits? It is the invention of the mind, the recreation of thoughts that were limited by the general scientific knowledge of that time. Now, Descartes's postulate is completely rejected on a scientific level. Scientific acts prove it to be false, as does the teaching of the Orthodox Church, as does even the experience of such phenomena as magic, magnetism, and spiritism, though they be hostile to the Church. Descartes sees the world of the created spirits and the world of matter as complete opposites. Science, however, does not see in dualistic terms, but in terms of graduality and affinity. The fact that a limited object is not subject to our physical senses or our cognition does not mean that automatically has qualities that belong to objects without limitation. Any limitation may be expressed with a number. Even if this number is so great that it is beyond the understanding or activity of man, it remains a number, having the characteristics of other numbers, and remaining distinct from the infinite by an infinite difference.

The teaching concerning spirits that we offer here is only given by the revelation of God, by the faith of Christianity. There are no other means of acquiring this knowledge; all other means lead to false conclusions. This teaching does not have the quality of systematic treatises that are often prepared by the wise of this world, who live by the ways of this world. It is demonstrated in the Scriptures, just as so many other teachings are. It is also clearly laid out in the writings of the Holy Fathers. But only attentive reading and study of both can lead one to this true teaching. This means that the student of the subject must not only lead a pious life, but an ascetic, concentrated life, a life of solitude. The Church cries out to its wise ones: "You have acquired action, O God-inspired one, and the ascent of vision."[95] Only those who reject the world and dedicate themselves completely to God's service can acquire experiential knowledge of the fallen spirits in the thoughts, images, and sensations that those enemies offer, as St Macarius the Great said.[96] Only with the cooperation of internal experience can one come to understand those passages of Scriptures and the Fathers that speak of the invisible warfare. An increase of experience gives more and more knowledge, and the teachings of the Scriptures and the Fathers become increasingly clearer.

St Isaac the Syrian, citing Basil the Great and Gregory the Theologian, mentioned that they first educated themselves in the worldly sciences, taking care to supplement such knowledge by a virtuous life, and only later did they go into the desert to be with their inner man. He later says that the desert is beneficial for those who are strong because they can reach the level of open warfare with the spirits of evil.[97] St John Cassian, having described the pious life of the ancient monks who lived in coenobitic monasteries, says that their holy way of life gave rise to an even more exalted life—the life of a hermit, the kind of life that even in the early church few were able to attempt. These chosen ones John Cassian calls the "flowers of monasticism." They, "not being content with the victory they could acquire among other people, a victory that allowed them to defeat the invisible snares of the enemy, chose to enter open warfare with the demons, and for this reason they did not fear even to depart to the remote places of the deep desert."[98]

For such chosen ones of God, the internal invisible warfare became unbearably fierce, leading them to an incredible victory when the warfare became visible. This only occurred by a special dispensation of God.[99] The Fathers, raised to such a labor, were given special gifts of the Holy Spirit, coming to an exalted spiritual level of illumination, receiving entry into the invisible world through the visible eyes of the world. God's hand opened that world for them. Such men included Anthony and Macarius, the desert-dwellers of Egypt, whom the Church glorifies and Spirit-bearing and calls them both "great." Having abundant experiences and grace-filled knowledge of the spirits, they could speak of them in much clearer ways than other Fathers, whom the grace of God also illumined, who were given other spiritual gifts appropriate to their manner of life and work.

Among the few Fathers who wrote of the spirits with especial clarity is John Cassian. He summarizes a teaching given to him by a monk of Egyptian Scetis, Abba Serenius, who reached a high level of spiritual maturity. Serenius had a vision of spirits in both experience and grace, which is why his teaching is unusually clear and simple.[100] This teaching is identical to the one that we have already seen in the other Fathers and in the textbook of *Orthodox Dogmatics Theology*. When in the fifth century the Conferences of John Cassian appeared, some of the Western thinkers attacked his writings; however, the seventh and eighth, which treats the subject of spirits, was never attacked for any reason. It was only after a widespread acceptance of Descartes's dualism in the West that voices appeared, attacking Cassian's teaching concerning spirits. But no convincing rebuttal was offered; none is possible, and so rebuttals are replaced with *ad hominem* attacks.

At the Seventh Ecumenical Council, a passage was read from the writings of John, the bishop of Thessalonica, in which it is written that the angels have their appropriate form and materiality. It was in this natural form that they appeared to the saints. The Council, based on this passage from the Fathers, universally justified and allowed the depiction of angels on icons. The Fathers of the Council not only never expressed any doubt concerning the teaching of St John, but they did not even comment on it at all. It should be noted that the Seventh Council is accepted in both East and West.

Since our knowledge of spirits is limited, and received only from the experiential knowledge of saints that cannot be well expressed in words (since spiritual experiences go beyond the realm of physical senses), we should be very careful not to give free rein to our imagination when it comes to depictions of the spiritual world, which cannot be expressed adequately using the means of the physical world.[101] The imaginative faculty is especially developed in passionate people. It acts in them to pervert all that is holy into a semblance of its passionate self. This becomes especially clear when we look at a painting on which holy faces and famous sacred events are depicted by passionate painters. These artists exercised their imaginative faculty to express holiness and virtue in all its forms; however, since they were filled with sin, they expressed only sinfulness. Subtle sensuality breathes through images in which the genius-artists wanted to express chastity and divine love, qualities that they have no idea about. Desiring to depict the state of exalted spiritual inspiration in prophets and apostles, such artists instead give them the look of possessed pagan priests or actors from a bloody stage play. The works of such artists only arouse the passions of passionate audiences; however, in people blessed by the spirit of the Gospel, these "works of genius" seem tainted with blasphemy and the stain of sin, and they only give rise to sorrow and revulsion.

The imagination of passionate people who live debauched lives can have no understanding of truth, no sympathy with sanctity; instead, such an imagination can only create false depictions. Their imagination will also delude them, hiding the falsehood, which would be evidently only to those pure in mind, heart, and body. Any action of a person in whom the sinful imagination runs rampant is supported by the works of the fallen spirits, who find it natural to wallow in filth and sin, finding in sin their only pleasure and nourishment. Since all who begin a life of virtuous asceticism, in spite of their good intentions, are still in the power of their passions, still feel a strong sympathy with sin, being bound to it, the Holy Fathers strictly forbid the use of the imagination, commanding to preserve the mind completely without images, without any impression of material things.

One should not imagine heaven, nor Eden, nor the throne of God, nor the brilliance of the glory of God, nor angels, nor martyrs, nor holy men, nor the Mother of God, nor Christ Himself. The fallen spirits try to arouse in us the effects of sinful imagination, and sometimes they themselves appear in various false and seductive phantasms. For this reason, a state of reverie or dreaminess is forbidden, no matter how good it might seem. Not only that, but we are also commanded not to put our trust in any appearance from the invisible world. The appearances of bright angels, departed holy people, or even Christ Himself are assumed by demons to delude and destroy not only the beginner, but those who have advanced spiritually. The only thing we may imagine is the fires of hell, the eternal darkness, the horrifying prison and other horrors of the life after death, and even so, we are to do this only when carnal sensations arise in us. In other words, this active use of the imagination is only allowed in the hour of need, and after it passes, the weapon should be sheathed. If it is used without need, it can bring harm to the mind, making it prone to dreaminess and self-delusion.

In the first centuries of Christianity, there was an especial need to distract the newly converted from idol worship and from imagining angels and even God in crude physical form. Idols were simultaneously images of demons and of demonic passions. Having become used to worshiping these images, a practice that exercised all the emotions of the soul and body and filled the mind with imaginative images, such beginners were under the impression of these images. St Dionysius the Areopagite decided to help lead his contemporaries from such crude practices. He warned them in his wonderful and profoundly spiritual work "The Celestial Hierarchy":

> It is necessary then, as I think, first to set forth what we think is the purpose of every Hierarchy, and what benefit each one confers upon its followers; and next to celebrate the Heavenly Hierarchies according to their revelation in the Oracles; then following these Oracles, to say in what sacred forms the holy writings of the Oracles depict the celestial orders, and to what sort of simplicity we must be carried through the representations; in order that we also may not, like the vulgar, irreverently think that the heavenly and Godlike minds are certain many-footed [16] and many-faced creatures, or moulded to the brutishness of oxen, or the savage form of lions, and fashioned like the hooked beaks of eagles, or the feathery down of birds, and should imagine that there are certain wheels of fire above the heaven, or material thrones upon which the Godhead may recline, or certain many-coloured horses, and spear-bearing leaders of the host, and whatever else was transmitted by the Oracles to us under multifarious symbols of sacred imagery. And indeed, the Word of God artlessly makes use of poetic representations of sacred things, respecting the shapeless minds, out of regard to our intelligence, so to speak, consulting a mode of education proper and natural to it, and moulding the inspired writings for it.[102]

Further, he adds, "perhaps he will also think that the super-heavenly places are filled with certain herds of lions, and troops of horses, and bellowing songs of praise, and flocks of birds, and other living creatures, and material and less honourable things."[103]

Having expressed himself thus about the Heavenly Powers, St Dionysius speaks of God in the following way:

> No doubt, the mystical traditions of the revealing Oracles sometimes extol the august Blessedness of the super-essential Godhead, as Word, and Mind, and Essence, manifesting its God-becoming expression and wisdom, both as really being Origin, and true Cause of the origin of

things being, and they describe It as light, and call it life. While such sacred descriptions are more reverent and seem in a certain way to be superior to the material images, they yet, even thus, in reality fall short of the supremely Divine similitude. For It is above every essence and life. No light, indeed, expresses its character, and every description and mind incomparably fall short of Its similitude.[104]

As compared with every super-essential pre-eminence, the Divine Being was seated incomparably above every visible and invisible power, yea, even that It is exalted above all, as the Reality of all things, as Absolute—not even like to the first of created Beings; further also, that It is source and essentiating Cause, and unalterable Fixity of the undissolved continuance of all things, from, Which is both the being and the well-being of the most exalted Powers themselves.[105]

The Areopagite insists that divine appearances to the saints occurred in a way adapted to human nature.[106]

No one hath seen, nor ever shall see, the "hidden" of Almighty God as it is in itself [68]. Now Divine manifestations were made to the pious as befits revelations of God, that is to say, through certain holy visions analogous to those who see them. Now the all-wise Word of God (*Theologia*) naturally calls Theophany that particular vision which manifests the Divine similitude depicted in itself as in a shaping of the shapeless, from the elevation of the beholders to the Divine Being, since through it a divine illumination comes to the beholders, and the divine persons themselves are religiously initiated into some mystery. But our illustrious fathers were initiated into these Divine visions, through the mediation of the Heavenly Powers. Does not the tradition of the Oracles describe the holy legislation of the Law, given to Moses, as coming straight from God, in order that it may teach us this truth, that it is an outline of a Divine and holy legislation? But the Word of God, in its Wisdom, teaches this also—that it came to us through Angels.[107]

In this work, St Dionysius explains only the mystical vision of the prophets and the spiritual relationship that the angels have amongst each other and with human beings; however, he says nothing about the fallen angels or the physical appearance of angels to simple people, as occurred with Hagar, the slave-concubine of Abraham. Nor does he speak of the capacity of animals to see angels, nor of the angels' habitation in heaven, nor of the fall of the demons from heaven, nor of their torture in the flames of tell, while all of this is spoken of in the Scriptures. Even of the Lord Jesus Christ Dionysius only speak in such terms: "the true Light of the Father, illumining all men who enter the world," not speaking of His incarnation or His human body.

> For it [the Paternal Light of Christ] *never* loses its own unique inwardness, but multiplied and going forth, as becomes its goodness, for an elevating and unifying blending of the objects of its care, remains firmly and solitarily centred within itself in its unmoved sameness; and raises, according to their capacity, those who lawfully aspire to it, and makes them one, after the example of its own unifying Oneness.[108]

It is clear from this book that Dionysius was in that state of vision that he describes in this book; in other works, he speaks more directly about this experience.[109] This state is a state of Christian perfection and is called illumination by the Fathers. St Symeon the New Theologian, citing St Gregory, says, "'The fear of God is the beginning of wisdom' (Proverbs 1:7). For where there is fear, there the commandments are kept, and where the commandments are kept the flesh is purified, together with the cloud that envelops the soul and prevents it from clearly seeing the divine radiance. Where there is this purification there is illumination, and illumination is the fulfillment of the longing of those who desire the greatest of all supernal things or even that which is above all greatness. With these words he showed that illumination by the Spirit is the endless end of every virtue, and that whoever attains it has finished with everything sensory and has begun to experience the knowledge of spiritual realities."[110]

Even the idea of such a state is completely foreign for people who are not consecrated into the mysteries of Christian asceticism! For this reason, the Areopagite wrote his book not for the general use of Christians, but only for those who are already at an advanced level of spiritual maturity. He told Priest Timothy, for whom he wrote this book, to hide this book from carnal people, even if they be pious:

And thou, my son, after the pious rule of our Hierarchical tradition, do thou religiously listen to things religiously uttered, becoming inspired through instruction in inspired things; and when thou hast enfolded the Divine things in the secret recesses of thy mind, guard them closely from the profane multitude as being uniform, for it is not lawful, as the Oracles say, to cast to swine the unsullied and bright and beautifying comeliness of the intelligible pearls.[111]

Anyone who has read this work on the Heavenly Hierarchies must admit that the work is difficult to understand and even strange to read in some places, especially for people who do not know spiritual vision.

Western writers have said that "all human beings have always been able to distinguish living matter from dead matter, incapable of movement. This difference is as old as the world, present wherever man is. All were as assured of the lifelessness of matter as they were sure of the presence of the spirit wherever they saw movement."[112] This assertion is foolish. The movement of matter and the presence of movement within solid matter (the organic life of plants, for example) are witness only of the presence of life, but not the presence of *spirit*. No one at any time has ever said that insects, fish, birds, or any other animals have spiritual lives. They have life, and sometimes that life is called "soul." But the question of the spirit cannot be derived from the reality of living movement.

Man's understanding of the spiritual came from different reasons. It appeared in him, first of all, through self-examination. Man senses inside himself the presence of an essence that is completely distinct from the body. He sees a much more developed kind of life in this essence than in his body. The body has its sensations; but the essence living in the body has separate sensation, and in addition to them, has a reasoning capacity, which in the proper sense is a sensation. This essence that lives inside a person is usually called the soul. Despite the different qualities of the spirit and body, they are intimately connected. The thoughts of the soul give immediate rise to appropriate sensations; these sensations of the soul are further reflected in the sensations of the body. The opposite is also true: the sensations of the body act upon the soul, giving rise to their respective sensations, from these sensations them come corresponding thoughts. This connection of the soul with the body proves that in spite of the significant difference between the soul and the body, they have something in common. If they did not have this affinity, there could not be any connection. If there is affinity, the soul must have a certain accompanying degree of materiality.

When a person lives, the process of life continues through constant breathing. Breath is the essential sign of life. When a person dies, the final process of dying is concluded with a strong exhalation or several repeated strong breaths. During this forced exhalation, the soul leaves the body. After the soul leaves the body, breath ceases; before death, breathing was a sign of the presence of the soul within the body. After its passage from the body, the soul is invisible. For this reason, it would be completely natural to call the essence abiding within man's body both a soul and a spirit. It would be just as natural to consider the soul, or the spirit, an invisible essence, without body or materiality, as distinct from everything that we see in the material reality that is subject to our senses. It would be just as natural to consider the soul to have its corresponding degree of materiality, which is indicated by the length and fullness of the final breath. The admission that the soul continues to live after its separation from the body naturally comes from the sensation and the self-knowledge of immortality found in every human being. In spite of the obvious knowledge that every human being will die, every person still feels and internally considers himself to be immortal, and people often live as though they were immortal. This is an inner sensation and knowledge of the presence of the soul.

All people who do not descend deep into inner contemplation of the nature of the soul, all who are content with a superficial, generally accepted knowledge, indifferently call the invisible part of our essence (which lives in the body and makes us who we are) both soul and spirit. Just as breathing is the sign of life in an animal, such people call human beings animals by their life, and animates by their soul. All other matter they call lifeless or inanimate. Man is called a reasoning animal to distinguish him from other animals, which are called irrational. Most people, who care for little other than their daily vanities, look at all other things superficially, seeing the only difference between men and animals as their ability to speak. But wise people have understood that man differs from other animals by an internal quality, a special ability of the human soul. This ability they have called the power of the word, that is, the spirit. To this ability belong not only the ability to think, but the ability to sense spiritual realities that are much more exalted, subtle, virtuous than physical sensations. In this sense of the words, soul and spirit are quite different, even if in human society both words are used interchangeably.

Tradition has preserved in all nations an understanding that the invisible world exists, that is, there is a life after death for human souls, as well as a knowledge of the existence of spirits—creatures like the human soul. Most human societies have also preserved an understanding that there is a place in which blessed souls will find rest and evil ones will suffer. Such traditions, which are kept in different forms in different nations, are proof that they belong to all mankind. Converse with the fallen spirits, into which fallen mankind entered, which fallen mankind upheld and developed, has led to a lopsided view of the nature of spirits. Ancient philosophy was often combined with magical practices. The hieromartyr Cyprian, the former magician, witnessed that he saw the devil himself during his incantations. He even became a commander of demons, who would perform his will, since he promised to allow Satan himself lordship over is body after death.[113]

The experience of magic has shown that the spirits are bodiless like the soul, having also the power of the word, having also a degree of materiality, having ability to influence matter and be influenced by it in some cases. The Scripture speaks in several places of the communion between rejected men and rejected spirits (see Num 22, and 1 Kgdms 28). Today this communion continues, by the way, through spiritism and magnetism.

The sciences that examine matter have recently progressed to a great degree. Not least among these advances is the inevitable admission of the incredible limitation of our level knowledge. When science was less advanced, man considered himself more knowledgeable. When man thought that heaven was the expanse of sky about, that heaven and earth joined at their extreme ends, he was greater in his own eyes than he imagines himself to be now, when it has been revealed that there is limitless space beyond the sky, that the earth is a barely perceptible mote compared to this expanse. Modern science tells us that we simply do not know our own bodies, even though that we think we know it well through our sensations. The life of the body is beyond our ken. Anatomy examines cadavers, not bodies. It does not see the life of the body; it does not even see the body, strictly speaking. The body remains the body until the moment that life leaves it. As soon as life leaves, corruption begins. More than that: this abandonment of life is the corruption; the further decomposition is simply a consequence of the primary corruption. The decomposition of matter, according to the laws of chemistry, can only occur when constituent parts are removed from it. Here is a suggestion from science about the materiality of the soul, for the separation of something immaterial from matter would not have had any effect on the material object. But the soul is invisible. And what of it? So are gases.

No sooner has the life left the body than it is no longer a body. It is a corpse. The senses and qualities of the body may be described, but not determined. Hypotheses can never be facts, no matter how well imagined. A misuse of science can lead to brilliant postulates that satisfy the curiosity of the ignorant and close their mouths. But to lead a person into delusion through science is unscrupulous. Science, when leading to exact and measurable facts, must lead a person to the most correct relationships with the surrounding world.

Chemistry has definitively shown that all limited objects have their own degree of materiality. Mathematics has just as definitively shown that everything limited is subject to space. Based on these findings, only God can be confessed to be completely immaterial, independent of time and space, limitless in all senses, subject to no change, no outside influence, limitless by His essence and His qualities, endlessly differing from all creatures both in essence and in characteristics. For this same reason, the created spirits, being created being, are limited beings. They by necessity must have their degree of materiality, must be subject to space. That which is limited in essence must have limitations in characteristics as well. To ascribe unlimited essence or quality to a limited being is nonsense.

Chemistry rejects the childish determination of matter's qualities based on our senses alone. Matter must be determined by its own criteria. It can stretch far beyond our senses, which are extremely limited in scope. The existence of something material that has no effect on our senses or that has an effect that we do not understand or notice is impossible according to science. The existence of spirits in the form taught by *Orthodox Dogmatic Theology* in no way contradicts the findings of chemistry and mathematics; it completely accords and agrees with them in their findings. Let us note: these sciences, having separated God from His creation by an endless difference, open the door, as it were, to faith, explaining the necessity for Revelation. They cannot reject faith because of their own inherent admission of God's omnipotence and the independence of His actions from the judgments of man.

Merely human sources of knowledge of the spirits do not give humanity the necessary understanding, because they are limited or false (due to the fall). Fallen man only communed with demons; he knows nothing of communion with holy spirits. And the unique characteristic of the fallen spirits is mindless and frenzied hatred of God, as well as pride and falseness.[114] Because of their pride and their enmity against God, the fallen spirits strove to make fallen man give them the worship due only to God; by their falseness they sued all possible means of delusion to achieve this goal. The demons did not only inspire those who forgot the true God to worship them as gods; to this day, they seek to delude those to whom they appear, including the holy ascetics, and to fool them into false worship.

As St Anthony said, "When they appear, they try to increase the terror (in the one that sees them), to cast them into a profound pit of iniquity, having forced man to worship them."[115] For this reason, the Christian that desires to acquire an unerring understanding concerning the spirits must leave aside all ideas suggested by human traditions, scholarship, magic, magnetism, spiritism, and other similar things, for they can only impart false knowledge, in which man, not renewed by divine grace, will never be able to distinguish truth from falsehood.

The only way to acquire this sure knowledge of the spirits is through Christianity, studied in the Holy Scriptures and the writings of the Fathers of the Orthodox Church, lived in a pious, ascetic life according to the moral traditions of the Orthodox Church. For the beginning, merely theoretical knowledge of the spirits is enough, offered in *Orthodox Dogmatic Theology*. The invisible warfare with the spirits in the thoughts, imagination, and senses is the realm of ascetics, monks, those who labor correctly in monasteries. They acquire a moral, so to speak, understanding of the falling spirits. This state is called spiritual vision by the ascetic writers, because through this state, the ascetic can see the invisible snares of the invisible enemies with the eyes of his mind and sense them with his heart.

This is how St Ignatius the God-bearer described this state of moral knowledge of the fallen spirits "The false spirit preaches himself, speaks of himself, is satisfied with himself, glorifies himself, filled with pride, false words, delusions, cunning ... From his activity, deliver us, O Jesus Christ!" St Ignatius also says: "O thou spirit more wicked through thy malevolence than all other wicked spirits, to utter such words against the Lord? Through thine appetite was thou overcome, and through thy vainglory wast thou brought to dishonour: through avarice and ambition dost thou [now] draw on [others] to ungodliness. Thou, O Belial, dragon, apostate, crooked serpent, rebel against God, outcast from Christ, alien from the Holy Spirit, exile from the ranks of the angels, reviler of the laws of God, enemy of all that is lawful ... "[116]

Such knowledge of the spirits, such vision of them is the kind of knowledge that we truly need. It can be fully acquired through a monastic life. It is a gift of God that crowns one's own forceful labor to come to see the immaterial faces of the demons in the mirror of the Holy Scriptures, the writings of the Holy Fathers, and in his own activity. This is true "discerning of spirits" (1 Cor 12:10), a gift of the Holy Spirit. With this gift is given victory over sinful thoughts, images, and sensations. Whoever is still defeated by these can be assured that he has not yet acquired the gift but deludes himself and is captured by the invisible enemy. Through spiritual vision of spirits, they are seen in their actions: to see the essence of spirits is given only to a select few, by a special providence of God. To willfully tear aside that curtain and veil put down by God Himself, to force oneself willfully into the world of the spirits will lead to terrifying calamities.

In conclusion, let us say that Divine Revelation explained to us the nature of created spirits, our souls, our bodies to the degree to which this knowledge is needed for our salvation. As God's creatures, our soul, spirit, body, even nature itself, remain a mystery to us, their secrets only partially revealed. Through pious contemplation of God's creation, let us glorify our Creator, and in wonder at His omnipotence and wisdom, let us offer a humble and true confession together with David, "Marvelous are

Thy works, O Lord! ... Thy knowledge is too wonderful for me; it is too hard; I cannot attain unto it" (Ps 138:6, 14).

Having examined the opinions of Western writers[117] on the nature of spirits, heaven, and hell, it is evident that the Western teaching is not definitive. In spite of this fact, Abbe Bergier is led, almost by force, to admit that the Lord Himself said that Eden is found in heaven. He is also forced to report, though he will not accept this thought, that hell is found inside the earth.

We have already shown that the teaching of the Orthodox Church very clearly demonstrates that Eden is in heaven and hell is within the earth, showing by this teaching how high man has been exalted by God, as well as the horrors of the sufferings that await those who disdain the gifts of God. This teaching is triumphantly proclaimed in the hymnography of the Church; it is preached by the Fathers of the Orthodox Church. Many quotes are offered in the Homily on Death from liturgical books and the works of the Holy Fathers. They should decide this question once and for all. That being said, more quotes still could be found to support this position.

The Western writers have a hard time explaining the relationship of the spirits to heaven and hell, especially since they will inhabit both places with the resurrected bodies of dead human beings. Evidently, this difficulty comes from a teaching, widespread in the West, concerning the complete immateriality of created spirits. Abbe Bergier, when describing Eden, tries to avoid this difficulty by quoting St Paul, who taught that the resurrected and glorified bodies would commune with the essence of spirits. In his writings of hell, Bergier tries to explain the suffering of immaterial spirits by a material flame by ascribing it to God's omnipotence, and he tries to hide the Western incorrect teaching of the immateriality of spirits by insisting on the complete immateriality of God, which the Orthodox Church never denied.

In summary, we have the following picture. The Western writer is subject to constant vacillation and self-contradiction. He quotes the Fathers of the Eastern Church spuriously, then cites other Fathers that actually contradict his assertions. He simultaneously justifies the Fathers and says they were in error. He rejects the ethereal or gaseous nature of created spirits, but he does admit that they need to assume a subtle body if they want to interact with matter. He tries to hide the teaching of the immateriality of created spirits by stressing the completely immateriality of God. But by doing so, he places the infinite, unlimited God in the same row as His creation, which is clearly blasphemy. Thus, the Western teaching on spirits, being carefully examined, actually contradicts itself. Let us thank God and glorify Him for the great mercy of being born in the bosom of the Orthodox Church. Amen.

CHAPTER 4

Created Spirits and Human Souls

A letter of Bishop Ignatius to a certain cleric who asked about the reason for his assertions concerning the nature of created spirits and the human soul, and why he called the human soul ethereal.

I thank you profusely for your sincere letter of May 29. I hope to answer you with as much sincerity.

After I began the ascetic life and later entered a monastery, though I had various experiences that are typical of this life, I had very vague ideas about the soul and about spirits, sharing in the general superficial opinion that they must be bodiless and immaterial. I had no need to study this subject further. I entered a monastery in 1827, but I began to study the Scriptures and Fathers much earlier. I can even say from childhood. From 1843, independently of me, there arose a need to study the meaning of the soul and created spirits in more detail. Anthony the Great was right when he said that this knowledge is extremely necessary for ascetics, especially those ascetics who are led in their labors by the hand of God into direct battle against the spirits. In fact, this knowledge is beneficial for everyone; it is better to come to know the world of the spirits before death, rather than come to know it for the first time after death, as happens with so many, to their profound horror and surprise, because their knowledge has been formed by incorrect ideas from the West. Experience shows the truth of the teaching of the Fathers conclusively. That which was dark and mystical becomes very clear and simple.

As for the word "ethereal," chemistry uses this word to describe a form of matter distinct from gases that belong to the earth. It is very subtle, but indeterminate. In fact, it is completely unknown to man. Its existence is admitted as an inevitability because space beyond the atmosphere, as

245

indeed any space at all, cannot exist without matter. In the proper sense, only One is immaterial, uncircumscribed by space—God. The created spirits are bodiless, but only in comparison to us. Their essence, like the essence of the soul, remains indeterminate to us, because it is by nature indeterminate. Science admits the impossibility of determining even the nature of our bodies, as well as all bodies that have the organic power of life. Descartes' dream of the independence of spirits from space and time is a completely idiocy. Everything that is limited, by necessity, must depend on matter.

Bishop Ignatius

June 7, 1865

St. Nicholas Babayki Monastery

AFTERWORD

"My Weakness"

A speech given at the Holy Synod by the abbot of St Sergius Hermitage
at his installation as Bishop of the Caucasus & the Black Sea, October
25, 1857

Your Holiness!

In these holy and frightening moments, I cannot help but remember
the words spoken by the Lord to His disciple: "when you were younger,
you girded yourself and walked where you wished; but when you are old,
you will stretch out your hands, and another will gird you and carry you
where you do not wish" (John 21:18).

In the days of my youth, I was attracted by deserted places. "Lo, I ran
away far off, and dwelt in the wilderness. I waited for God, Who saveth
me from faintheartedness," which reveals to man how little grace he has,
"and from [the] tempest" of my passions, which is raised by the delusive
and evanescent pleasures of the world (Psalm 54:8–9). I liked monasticism for itself! But I never thought of serving the Church in any order of
priesthood. To be the lord and master of my own heart and to offer my
thoughts and sensations as sacrifices to God, sanctified by the Spirit—this
was the summit that attracted my gaze.

I did not long enjoy freedom in my youth; I was soon girded and bound
by the incomprehensible providence of God. His almighty right hand, in
contrast to my own desire, seized me from the depths of the woods and
deserted places and put me into the monastery of St Sergius, on the shores
of the sea, on the shore of the sea of life, that great and wide sea. It was
difficult to know the paths of the Lord! Only the Spirit of God knows
the depths of God (see 1 Corinthians 2:10). The God-illumined teachers of
monasticism insist that profound solitude is dangerous for the beginning
monk, for it can lead to dreaminess and spiritual delusion. Young monks

need the medicine and school of human society. Through many interactions with his neighbors, the monk reveals his passion, which hid from him in the secret places of his heart, and which can only be healed with the strong medicine of the teaching of Christ.[1]

Looking deeply at the sicknesses of my soul, I admitted that I needed this strong medicine. But how can I possibly explain to myself this calling that you, holy Fathers, have called me to? What have you found in me, or what can I offer you, other than my many weaknesses? The rank of bishop is terrifying to me, since I know my weakness. I fear that instead of instruction, I will bring temptation to my brothers and instead prepare a more terrible judgment for myself at the judgement seat of Christ. I would have considered it better for my salvation and more according to my strength to live the remainder of my days as I did at the beginning, in the silence of the desert, in contemplation of my own sins.

And again, I am afraid! I fear my own will, I fear that if I follow it instead of God, I will call upon myself unforeseen calamities.[2] "I am shut up, and I cannot get out" (Psalm 88:8 NKJV). In my confusion, I reject myself, and I place both my temporary and eternal fate into the hands of my God. Bound by your choosing and the command of the Most August Anointed One of God, with submission and trembling I lower my head under the yoke that can destroy an unworthy one.

Do not cease to strengthen me with your instructions! Do not reject me when, according to the command of the Holy Spirit, I will come to you for words of wisdom, for words of salvation. The Holy Spirit commanded, "Ask your father, and he will tell you; your elders, and they will tell you" (Deuteronomy 32:7). As you stretch forth your hands to invest me with the great rank of the episcopacy, stretch them out in prayer for me to God, Who reveals His power in the weakness of man. As for me, in this terrible hour, I seek the consolation of my conscience, and I find it in unconditional faithfulness to the will of God, in the knowledge and confession, before you, of my many weaknesses.

A Short Biography of Bishop Ignatius (Brianchaninov)

The future Saint Ignatius was born on April 15/28, 1807, in the village of Pokrovskoye in the Vologda region of Russia. His given name at birth was Dimitry Alexandrovitch Brianchaninov. Of noble birth, his father was a wealthy provincial landowner. In due course the young Dimitry was sent to study at the Pioneer Military Academy in St Petersburg to be educated as a military officer.

Even before entering the Academy Dimitry had aspired to the monastic life, but his family did not support these plans. Nevertheless, as a student he was able to find some time to devote to prayer and the inner life and to find other students with similar aspirations. Remaining obedient to his parents he remained diligent in his studies, winning the praise of his teacher and coming to the attention of the Grand Duke Nicholas Pavlovich, the future Tsar Nicholas I.

After graduating from the Academy he took up his first commission in the army but soon became seriously ill. This made it possible for him to request an honorable discharge and having made a full recovery to at last embrace the monastic life. He was duly tonsured as a monk in 1831 and given the name Ignatius. His spiritual father was the revered Elder Leonid of Optina. Shortly after his tonsure he was ordained as a priest.

Meanwhile, his absence from the army had come to the attention of Tsar Nicholas. As soon as he was able to locate Fr Ignatius in his small monastery near Vologda he ordered him back to the capital. So, at the age of only twenty-six Fr Ignatius was made an Archimandrite and appointed as head of the St Sergius monastery in St Petersburg. He served faithfully in that capacity for the next twenty-four years.

In 1857 he was ordained to the episcopacy, serving as bishop of Stavropol and the Caucasus. This period of his life lasted for only four years, after which he withdrew into seclusion at the Nicolo-Babaevsky monastery in the Kostroma region of Russia. Here he was able to devote the remaining six years of his life to spiritual writing and correspondence with his numerous spiritual children. He composed five volumes of Ascetical Works, the fifth of which, The Arena, has been translated into English.

Bishop Ignatius reposed on April 30/May 13, 1867. The Russian Orthodox Church canonized him at their local council in 1988 and his relics now reside at the Tolga monastery in the Yaroslavl region of Russia.

Notes

All references to source material in the original text were to the classic Russian-language editions. The author followed a Russian cultural practice where one is not necessarily expected to provide all background detail and source material. Unless otherwise indicated, the quotations and their citations have been translated from the original text.

Chapter 1

1. St Ignatius notes here: I have also on occasion heard denials of the existence of the soul. Those who reason thus claim that within us is found an incomprehensible life force (as yet undeciphered by science) that, as with all animals, is active only during the life of the body and dies together with it; and that we are in no wise higher than the other animals, but only count ourselves higher than them due to our pride. That logic belongs to those of an overwhelmingly fleshly existence. "My Spirit shall not strive with man forever, for he is indeed flesh" (Gen 6:3). As the saying goes "It's not the eyes that see, but the person; not the ear that hears, but the soul."

2. St Mark the Ascetic, *On the Spiritual Law.* Chapter 32. Philokalia, Part 1.

3. "Those who rejected the world, though they did not know their letters, were often the wisest, for they were illumined by God's light, more so than those who know the entire Scripture but seek glory in this world. For the Scriptures were given from God for our salvation and for the glorification of the name of God; for this reason we must read it, and study it, and learn from it. But when we read it for our own glorification, then not only will it not be for our benefit, but it will be damaging to us."—St Tikhon of Zadonsk, Bishop of Voronezh, volume 15, letter 32.

4. *Apophthegmata Patrum*—[*The Sayings of the Desert Fathers*] the memorable sayings of Isaac the Great, a priest of Kelli. Kelli is the name of the desert neighboring Mount Nitria. [Mount Nitira is one of the earliest Christian monastic sites in Egypt. St Igtnatius actually quotes St Isaac the Theban, hermit of Egypt and not Isaac the Armenian know today as St Isaac the Great.—Ed].

5. *Apophtegmata Patrum*—(*The Sayings of the Desert Fathers*), *The Sayings of Venerable Pœmen the Great.*

6. St Macarius the Great, Homily 7, chapter 31.

7. Ibid., Homily 4.

8. Ibid., Homily 6, chapter 13.

9. Homily 74 [St Isaac the Syrian].

10. [This form of delusion was especially frequent in the nineteenth century, due to the preponderance of various Spiritist and occult movements in Russia.—NK].

11. Second discourse on the parable of the rich man and Lazarus, Chapter 2. [St John Chrysostom] [www.tertullian.org/fathers/chrysostom_four_discourses_02_discourse2.htm].

12. Chapter 3. [St John Chrysostom] [Translated by George Prevost and revised by M.B. Riddle. *From Nicene and Post-Nicene Fathers*, First Series, Vol. 10. Edited by Philip Schaff (Buffalo, NY: Christian Literature Publishing Co., 1888. Revised and edited for New Advent by Kevin Knight, 2001, www.newadvent.org/fathers/200128.htm].

13. From the life of St Pachomius.

14. *The Lives of the Saints*, September 7, the Feast of St John of Novgorod.

15. St Isaac the Syrian, Homily 1.

16. St John of Damascus, *Complete Exposition of the Orthodox Faith*, book 3, chapter 1.

17. St John Cassian, Conversation 8, chapter 12.

18. St Isaac the Syrian, Homily 36.

19. That is, Carthage. Cf. the life of Martyr Artemius, October 20.

20. *Lives of the Saints*, September 22. [St Peter the Tax-Collector].

21. *Lives of the Saints*, October 24.

22. St Isaac the Syrian, Homily 65.

23. Homily 8, chapter 6 [St Macarius the Great].

24. *The Ladder*, Homily 3, On dreams [Available in English translation as: *The Ladder of Divine Ascent*, trans. Archimandrite Lazarus (London: Faber and Faber, 1959)].

25. See the life of St Basil the Great, January 1, or the Tale of Theophilus who fell and repented, June 23.

26. [St Ignatius probably means animal magnetism or "mesmerism," a nineteenth-century pseudo-scientific fad.—NK].

27. Note that there are different opinions among the fathers concerning this biblical event. In the life of the Hieromartyr Pionius of Smyrna (March 11) as told by St Dimitry (Demetrius) of Rostov, there is a footnote that mentions the possibility that it was a demon who appeared to Saul, pretending to be the prophet, and the prophecy was simply a guess based on previous prophecies of Samuel's that had come true and based on the actual facts of the coming war. It is also possible that God allowed Samuel himself to appear, for the righteous of the Old Testament, before the coming of Christ, went to hades after death with all other

human beings, being in the power of the devil, though their state after death was not as grievous as that of sinners.

28. See the life of St Macarius Zeltovodsky, June 15.

29. Homily 41 [St Isaac the Syrian].

30. See Gen 14:18.

31. *The Prologue* from February 23.

32. St Isaac the Syrian, homily 2.

33. St Macarius the Great. Homily 4, chapters 6 and 7.

34. *Sancti Antonii magni opera*, PG 40:960.

35. *The Life of St Anthony.*

36. Lausaic HIstory, chapter 28.

37. "Piety towards Christ" is understood to mean strict orthodoxy, combined with a strict life according to the Gospel commandments.

38. Revised from: www.newadvent.org/fathers/2811.htm (chapters 21–43 *of The Life of St Anthony*).

39. This section is apocryphal, in that it is a Greek translation of the Latin text of the life of Anthony by Evagrius. St Dimitry of Rostov used this translation to compose his own life of Anthony. Evagrius acknowledges the limitations of his translation, but this translation was done by an experienced monk who had experiential knowledge of the eremitic life, and so is still valuable.

40. Homily 55 [St Isaac the Syrian] I did find this text already translated ("The Ascetical Homilies of Saint Isaac the Syrian" from Holy Transfiguration Monastery, 1984 and 2011—text available online here: https://www.you-books.com/book/Unknown/66C7Cfb6Ebb577452472E2554266D199) Interestingly, it does not appear to be Homily 55, but under the header "An Epistle to Abba Symeon of Caesarea" Triads are a type of hymn composed of verses three words in length. The Syriac reads here madrashe.—Ed

41. *The Lives of the Saints* by St Demetrius of Rostov, February 14 and January 31.

42. *The Lives of the Saints*, September 1.

43. St Macarius the Great, Homily 26, chapter 3.

44. Chapter 73 of the second volume of the Philokalia in the Russian translation.

45. This is what happened to St Isaac of the Kiev Caves, who worshiped the devil that appeared to him in the form of Christ and suffered greatly as a result.

46. *The Prologue*, April 22 [In English this can be found in chapter VI "On Humility" from the *Wisdom of the Desert Fathers*.—Ed].

47. The last of the greatly beneficial chapters of St Gregory of Sinai [Volume 1 in the Russian translation of *The Philokalia*—NK].

48. Manuscript.

49. *The Lives of the Saints*, May 15.

50. Homily 7, chapter 7 [St Macarius the Great].

51. *The Ladder*, Step 27. St Nilus of Sora, Homily 11.

52. St Nilus of Sora. Homily 11. Other teachers of Christian monasticism say the same.

53. St Tikhon of Voronezh writes much on spiritual blindness in his letters. Vol. 14 & 15.

54. The Russian version of *The Philokalia*, part 3. [In English *The Philokalia*, Volume 1–4, trans. G. E. H. Palmer, Philip Sherrard, Kallistos Ware (London: Faber and Faber)].

55. St Isaac the Syrian, introduction to Homily 59.

56. St John Kolobos, *Apophtegmata Patrum* [Also known as St John the Dwarf—Ed].

57. Ibid.

58. As quoted by Saint-Patriarch of Constantinople, Saints Kallistos and Ignatius Xanthopoulos in their Homily *On Stillness and Prayer*, chapter 68.

59. *The Ladder*. Step 4, chapter 35. This is the universal teaching of the Fathers of the Church.

60. St Hesychius, Homily on Sobriety, chapter 43.

61. Homily 38 [St Isaac the Syrian].

62. [St Macarius the Great] Homily 4, chapter 13.

63. [From the third sticheron on the Praises (Lauds) of Pentecost—Ed.]

64. Concerning spiritual sensations, see Homily 8 of St Macarius the Great and Homily 1 of St Symeon the New Theologian.

65. St John Cassian. Conference 2, chapter 10. On Discretion. [www.newadvent.org/fathers/350802.htm].

66. *Apophthegmata Patrum (Sayings of the Desert Fathers)*.

67. Abba Dorotheus, Instruction concerning not abandoning one's own reason.

68. Russian version of the *Philokalia*, part 1, chapter 33.

69. We find this thought in the life of St Paisius Velichkovsky, a very experienced leader of monks, who died at the end of the eighteenth century.

70. The Life of John Kolobos, *Apophthegmata Patrum (Sayings of the Desert Fathers)*.

Chapter 2

1. [This appears to be a reference to the 1848 "Encyclical of the Eastern Patriarchs"; however, no such passage is found in that document—NK].

2. [St Macarius the Great] Homily 22 [https://stromata.co/fifty-spiritual-homilies-homily-22].

3. Homily 7 [St Macarius the Great].

4. Homily 4, chapter 9; Homily 5, chapter 6 [St Macarius the Great].

5. Homily 7, chapters 6–7 [St Macarius the Great].

6. Homily 6, chapter 8. When describing the supernatural action of divine grace during prayer, St Macarius said, "In that hour, together with the words

of prayer leaving the mouth, his soul also leaves." Evidently, this happened to Macarius himself.

7. In the nineteenth century, according to St Ignatius, two monks were found worthy of seeing their own souls leave the body during prayer: a Siberian hermit named Basiliscus, who died in 1825, and Schema-monk Ignatius of the St Nicephorus Hermitage, who died in 1852. The latter personally described this experience to St Ignatius (Brianchaninov), who had the honor to live together and be friends with some of the schema-monk's disciples.—NK.

8. It is well known that spiritual men and spiritual writings express the thought of the Spirit in great detail, often using the language of contemporary human society, since that would be best understandable to all. What they did not care about is whether or not such language corresponded with accepted human science. As Joshua said, "Sun, stand still!" (Josh 10:12), and the day lengthened beyond what was normal. The power of God responded to the spiritual word of Faith, though it came from a weak body. Pointless are the recriminations of human erudition that criticize the material exactness of a word that expresses a supernatural reality! Having delved deep into the writings of the Fathers, we will find that the word "spirit," by their own contemporary understanding (which we have only lost recently) always indicated gases and vapors, and most often air itself or wind or human breath. See especially St Gregory of Sinai in his first chapter of the fifteen chapters on stillness and the two forms of prayer (Russian version of *The Philokalia,* book 1).

9. See the previous homily for more detailed information about spiritual vision of spirits.

10. See the commentary of Blessed Theophylact of Bulgaria on chapter 3, verse 8 of the Gospel of John. St Gregory of Sinai also says, "The Lord said that the spirit goes where it will, using an example of the movement of physical wind" (chapter 3 of the fifteen chapters).

11. The angel is "incorporeal and immaterial" compared to humans. "For all that is compared with God Who alone is incomparable, we find to be dense and material. For in reality only the Deity is immaterial and incorporeal." (St John of Damascus *Exact Exposition of the Orthodox Faith, book 2, chapter 3.*) "In this way, then, God brought into existence mental essence, by which I mean, angels and all the heavenly orders. For these clearly have a mental and incorporeal nature: incorporeal I mean in comparison with the denseness of matter. For the Deity alone in reality is immaterial and incorporeal" (ibid., chapter 13). "Neither the wise by their wisdom nor the prudent by their prudence were able to comprehend the subtilty of the soul, or to speak of it as it is, but only those to whom through the Holy Ghost that comprehension is revealed, and the exact knowledge concerning the soul is declared. Consider here, and discern, and understand, how. Listen. He is God; the soul is not God. He is the Lord; it is a servant. He is Creator; it is a creature. He is the Maker; it the thing made. There is nothing common to

His nature, and to that of the soul" (St Macarius the Great, Homily 49, chapter 4 [https://stromata.co/fifty-spiritual-homilies-homily-49]). "For though we maintain that some spiritual natures exist, such as angels, archangels and the other powers, and indeed our own souls and the thin air, yet we ought certainly not to consider them incorporeal. For they have in their own fashion a body in which they exist, though it is much finer than our bodies are, in accordance with the apostle's words when he says: And there are bodies celestial, and bodies terrestrial: and again: It is sown a natural body, it is raised a spiritual body; (1 Corinthians 15:40, 44) from which it is clearly gathered that there is nothing incorporeal but God alone" (St John Cassian, Conference 7, chapter 13 [https://www.newadvent.org/fathers/350807.htm]).

12. St Gregory of Sinai, chapter 123: "These demons were once celestial intelligences; but, having fallen from their original state of immateriality and refinement, each of them has acquired a certain material grossness, assuming a bodily form corresponding to the kind of action allotted to it. For like human beings they have lost the delights of the angels and have been deprived of divine bliss, and so they too, like us, now find pleasure in earthly things, becoming to a certain extent material because of the disposition to material passions which they have acquired. We should not be surprised at this, for our own soul, created intellectual and spiritual in the image of God, has become bestial, insensate and virtually mindless through losing the knowledge of God and finding pleasure in material things. Inner disposition changes outward nature, and acts of moral choice alter the way that nature functions" ([https://orthodoxchurchfathers.com/fathers/philokalia/st-gregory-of-sinai-on-commandments-and-doctrines-warnings-and-promises-on-thoug.html] Accessed 5 September 2022—ED).

13. It is entirely obvious that the closest facets of an object appear larger to the eyes, while more distant parts appear smaller. The entire science of descriptive geometry is built on this fact.

14. [St Macarius the Great] Homily 16, chapter 8 [https://orthochristian.com/78118.html].

15. From a manuscript of the Neamţ Monastery that includes the life of St Gregory of Sinai written in Slavonic. Also found in the Russian version of the *Philokalia Part 1*.

16. The Life of St Basil the New, March 26.

17. [St Symeon of the Holy Mountain] May 24, as well as a manuscript life of St Euphrosyne.

18. Part one of the Russian version of the *Philokalia* [https://www.orth-transfiguration.org/resources/library/writings-of-the-saints/st-gregory-sinai-1282-1360/ Accessed 7 September 2022—Ed].

19. The Life of St Symeon of the Holy Mountain, May 24.

20. The Life of St Andrew the Fool for Christ, October 2.

21. *Eternal Mysteries beyond the Grave*; Archimandrite Panteleimon (Jordanville, NY: Holy Trinity Publications, 2012), p. 106.

22. St Peter of Damascus. "On the first reason" Book one, part three of the Russian version of the *Philokalia.*

23. https://classicalchristianity.com/category/bysaint/standrewfool

24. Adapted from *The Soul After Death* by Fr Seraphim Rose (St Herman of Alaska Brotherhood: Platina, California, 2009), pp. 137–139—NK.

25. After the resurrection, the body will be spiritual as well. See St Macarius the Great, Homily 6, chapter 13.

26. Hell or Tartarus is a Greek word that means an extremely deep place. Gehenna is a Hebrew word, actually a proper name of a deep ditch found near Jerusalem.

27. The Holy Church believes this sentence to refer primarily to the soul of a person, who for his transgression of the divine command is doomed to be buried in both body and soul. This sentence is heaviest of all for the soul, which, after its separation from the body, preserves its ability to think and feel, and so it alone of man's two constituent parts can sense the action of the sentence. The body, after separating from the soul, lies completely insensate. St Athanasius the Great, in his homily on Pascha, said, "Human nature, united to the divine in the person of Christ made the abyss tremble. Hell cried out groaning to the Harrower: Why are you perverting the law that you uttered justly over mankind: dust you are, and to dust you shall return"? (Opera omnia sancti Athanasii, Tom 4, Pag. 1,079).

28. Exact Exposition, book 3, chapter 29.

29. The NKJV differs here, having "seaweed" instead of mountains. The Greek text clearly has "crevices of the mountains" (σχισμὰς ὀρέων)—NK.

30. Exegetical Homily 14, chapters 17 and 20 [St Cyril of Jerusalem].

31. https://www.holycross.org/blogs/sermons-homilies/sermon-of-st-epiphanius-of-cyprus-for-holy-saturday (Translated from the critical Greek text in André Vaillant, "L'homélie d'Epiphane sur l'ensevelissement du Christ," *Radovi Staroslavenskog Instituta*, 3 [1958].)

32. *The Lenten Triodion*, trans. Mother Mary and Kallistos Ware (London: Faber and Faber, 1977), p. 622.

33. The complete text as translated by Mother Mary and Archimandrite Kallistos Ware may be found in *The Lenten Triodion* (London: Faber and Faber, 1977), pp. 623–644.

34. Step 7 of *The Ladder*, "On Joy-producing Sorrow." [Available in English translation as: *The Ladder of Divine Ascent*, trans. Archimandrite Lazarus (London: Faber and Faber, 1959).]

35. St Athanasius the Great references hell's place within the earth, as does St Basil the Great (*On Isaiah, chapter 5:14*) St Cyril of Alexandria, as we will see, considered hell to be within the earth, as do other fathers. The Russian hierarch Dimitri

of Rostov said, "At the dread judgment, Christ our God will say to the sinners: go forth from Me into the eternal flames. At that moment, the earth will part under the feet of the sinners, just as it did under the feet of Korah, Dathan, and Abiram before Moses, and then all sinners will fall into hell. The earth will then come back together. The sinners will be in hell within the earth, locked for the eternal ages like in a metal box" (Part 2, second teaching for the Entry of the Lord into Jerusalem).

36. St John Chrysostom says, "Do you ask where Gehenna is found? I believe it is outside this entire world. As the prisons and mining tunnels of a king are far from his palace, so Gehenna will be outside this world. Let us not try to find where it is, but rather let us seek the means of escaping it! (Homily 31 on Romans). Such an opinion in no way contradicts the idea that hell is within the earth, but rather confirms it. What better way to hide hell from the gaze of the cosmos than to bury it in the bosom of earth? Chapter 16 of the Gospel of Luke verse 22 reads thus in certain Greek manuscripts: "the rich man also died, and they buried him in hell." Even the version accepted by the Greco-Russian Church, "the rich man also died and was buried," has the meaning that the rich man was taken down to hell in his soul. This is how Theophylact interprets these words. Chrysostom, though he did not approve of curiosity concerning the place of hell, not only does not forbid such thoughts about hell that lead to the fear of God and the cessation of evil actions, but he even advises that one constantly submerge one's mind in such thoughts, having before one's eyes the fires of Gehenna that await the iniquitous (Homily 1 on Repentance to Dimitri). After Chrysostom, the Church expressed itself precisely concerning the place of hell in its hymnography for the universal hearing and edification of the people. Other revelations from God given to the saints confirm this.

37. Taxiotis had lived a sinful life. When plague hit Carthage, where he lived, Taxiotis remembered himself and repented in his sins. He moved away from the city. However, in the country, he fell into adultery with the wife of the landowner with whom he settled. Soon, he was bitten by a snake and died before he had time to repent of his sin. He was buried in a monastery nearby. Six hours after his burial, he resurrected, and barely managed to come back to himself after four days. Then, he told everything that had occurred with him after death to Tarasius, the bishop of Carthage. See the *Lives of the Saints* for March 28.

38. St Cyril lived in the fifth century and chaired the third ecumenical council. This teaching can be found in full in the *Sequential Psalter*. Patriarch Theophilus, the uncle and predecessor of St Cyril, also has a similar teaching.

39. *Eternal Mysteries beyond the Grave*; Archimandrite Panteleimon (Jordanville, NY: Holy Trinity Publications, 2012), pp. 93–96.

40. See the *Lives of the Saints* for August 15.

41. The Skete Paterikon.

42. Commentary on Matt 22:14 [Blessed Theophylact of Bulgaria].

43. The Skete Paterikon.

44. Patrologia, Vitae Patrum, Lib. VI, cap 13.

45. The Skete Paterikon.

46. *The Prologue*, October 17.

47. Step 6 of *The Ladder*, according to the Slavonic translation found in the Niamet Monastery.

48. Ibid., Step 5.

49. The Skete Patericon.

50. A Prayer at Vespers of Pentecost.

51. Homily 1, chapter 2 [St Macarius the Great according to the 1833 Russian edition.—NK].

52. To the Most Reverend Nun Xenia, chapter 9, 10 [https://orthodoxchurch-fathers.com/fathers/philokalia/st-gregory-palamas-to-the-most-reverend-nun-xenia.html].

53. This is the opinion of St Pœmen the Great (Skete Paterikon). It is shared by many other holy Father, including St Tikhon of Zadonsk. It is safe to say that this is the official position of the Church, because it is based on the words of the Saviour. Having healed the paralytic at the sheep's pool in Bethesda, the Lord said to him, "See you have been made well. Sin no more, lest a worse thing come upon you" (John 5:14). To the woman found in adultery, the Lord said, "Neither do I condemn you; go and sin no more" (John 8:11).

54. According to the interpretation of this Gospel passage by St Gregory Palamas in the aforementioned letter to Nun Xenia, Blessed Theophylact of Bulgaria, and others.

55. Homily 7, chapter 1 [St Macarius the Great].

56. Gregory Palamas to Nun Xenia, chapters 11–16 [https://orthodoxchurch-fathers.com/fathers/philokalia/st-gregory-palamas-to-the-most-reverend-nun-xenia.html].

57. These postulates concerning the eternality of the sufferings in hell are taken from well-known mathematical theories concerning infinity. We often turn to this theory to describe how creatures relate to their Creator, especially since this relationship is ineffable and beyond explanation. No other science than mathematics is capable of such explanations. Only mathematics, proving the inapproachability of infinity, places all numbers (that is, all creatures) in proper reference to it. Infinity is comprised of numbers, and all its constituent parts are made of numbers, but the person who is not well versed in the mysteries of mathematic in no way can understand the idea that all numbers, no matter how different they may be compared to each other, are equal to each other when compared with infinity. The reason for this equality is simple and clear: it is found in the endless, consequently the constantly equal, difference between infinity and any number taken individually. Thanks to the inarguable conclusions of mathematics, it becomes

evident that the very idea of numbers is relative, not essential. This limitation, which makes up the natural essence of organic, reasoning creatures, in no way can belong to the essence of an infinite being. Infinity, which contains within itself all numbers, at the same time also remains above any individual number because of its quality of perfection, having no limitation or even the ability to be subjected to limitation. Because of this, infinity, encompassing all impressions, remains above all impression, otherwise it would be subject to change, which is a quality natural to numbers, but unnatural to infinity. If, however, a number does not have essential meaning, then it is completely natural for the world to be created from nothing through the action of the infinite, which alone has essential meaning. It is natural for the infinite to be beyond the knowledge of man. These are the irrefutable truths that mathematics has given to the human mind. Even zero, which expresses the idea of that which does not exist, turns into a number when infinity acts upon it. Natural science also comes to aid mathematics in this, and indeed math is to science as the soul is to the body. Without math, they cannot exist; they are built and are held together by mathematics, like flesh on a skeleton. In all of nature, the strictest mathematical valuation exists. What do natural sciences reveal to us? This: that the nature of matter, in the midst of which we exist, that which we see and sense in various ways with our hearing, taste, and smell, that this matter is not only not understood or conceived by us, but it is actually inconceivable … Technically speaking, there are no beings in nature: there are only phenomena. The same law applies to numbers. There is no number that will not change by addition or subtraction. There is no number that could avoid being turned into zero. Every number, thus, is a phenomenon. Only infinity constantly remains unchanging; it does not change either by addition or subtraction. Only infinity contains within itself all of life; it alone is, technical speaking, being. If this is so, then the creation of the world by God is a mathematical necessity and truth. It is also true that the created world, as the word of an infinite mind, cannot be conceived, judged, or verified by man's limited mind. The first truth reveals to man the necessity of the divine word; the second truth shows human reason that it has neither the right nor the ability to reject the words concerning creation that we read in Genesis. This is again proved by science. From the heavens, the apostle John thunders to us, "In the beginning was the Word, and the Word was with God, and the Word was God." Mathematics answers from earth, "Truth, all-holy Truth! It cannot be otherwise. This is the nature of infinity; only it can exist in itself and with itself. It is life and the source of life. Its actions on numbers, no matter how great they may be, do not have nor cannot have any influence on the manner of infinity's existence, which is separated from all creatures by an endless difference, abiding among creatures while remaining completely independent of them. There is similarity between being and being." Again the Theologian thunders, "All things were made through Him, and without Him nothing was made that was made."

And again mathematics answer, "Truth, all-holy Truth! Phenomena, like numbers, must have their source, a source that does not run out, and this source is infinity, it is God!" "No one has seen God at any time," continues the heavenly herald, and again in answer mathematics offers this confession: "Truth, all-holy Truth! By the endless difference between infinity and any number, there is no possibility for any limited being, no matter how exalted, to see God neither with physical vision nor with the mind!" God abides in unseeable light in all senses, says the apostle. God declared concerning Himself in the Gospel, "I am life." This life is so almighty that it gave life to all creation, which exists with the existence taken from the source of life, a source that returns life to those creatures that lose their life in death. Eternal life cannot fail to be anything but almighty. In agreement with positive science, the Church confesses that the souls of men and angels are eternal not by nature, but by God's grace. What a true statement: it was made at a time when math remained silent about the subject. It is necessary to assimilate these understandings of the endless difference between infinity and numbers, in essence and in qualities, and whenever we discourse concerning God, to constantly keep in mind this difference, to bring it to the foreground, lest we get lost in ideas that supersede our ability to understand, which will lead to incorrect ideas by necessity. Without this, we will be forced to claim that our nonsense is truth, to our destruction and to the destruction of mankind. Dreamers became atheists, while those who studied math deeply always admitted the existence not only of God, but of Christianity, though they did not know Christianity as they should. I speak of Newton and others. It is desirable that an Orthodox Christian, having studied the positive sciences, should then come to study deeply the asceticism of the Orthodox Church, and to then give humanity a true philosophy established on those precise understandings, not only self-willed hypotheses. Plato even forbade his students to study philosophy before they studied mathematics first! This is the correct way of things. Without a preliminary study of mathematics, with the other sciences that build from it, and without active and grace-filled study of Christianity, it is impossible in our time to build a correct philosophical system.. Many who believe themselves to be philosopher but who do not know mathematics and natural science find in the works of the Materialists various self-willed dreams and hypotheses, but cannot discern these from actual knowledge taken from science. They cannot give a satisfactory answer to the most idiotic nonsenses of some dreamer, very often becoming enamored of this nonsense to their own delusion, even considering it to be the truth. Only logic alone can survive without mathematics; but logic in essence is connected intimately with mathematics, and it can take from the latter especial exactness and positivity. What is a syllogism? It is an algebraic equation. What are proportions and progressions? They are logical sequences of concepts.

58. *The Lives of the Saints*, January 17.

59. Abba Dorotheus, Instruction on the Fear of Future Punishments.

60. Letter six of the Athonite. More recently, a certain eldress of the Goritsy [name of village] Convent, near the city of Kyrillov in the Novgorod governorate [today in the Vologda Oblast], saw the tortures of hell in her dream, and in proof of the truth of her vision, the hellish stench remained in her nostrils for seven days, not allowing her to eat anything during that time. St Dimitri of Rostov also reminds his readers that hell is filled with fires that never go out.

61. Step 6 of *The Ladder*.

62. The Paterikon of the Kiev Caves Lavra. St Athanasius is commemorated on December 2.

63. The Skete Paterikon.

64. Ibid.

65. Ibid.

66. The Life of St Paisius Velichkovsky.

67. The Skete Paterikon.

68. The woman was subject to demonic temptation because she had abstained from Holy Communion for six weeks. In the early Church, when the grace of God flowed with much greater abundance, even such small sins that in our time might seem insignificant were followed by severe punishments of God (see Acts 5).

69. Cassiani collation VIII. This is also evident in the writings of many other Holy Fathers.

70. Homily 4, chapter 3 [Macarius the Great]. The fact that the power of Satan over the fallen angels and mankind, over the world and the age, does not properly belong to him, but was acquired from those who gave it to him willingly, is something that he himself admitted to the Savior, when he showed him "all the kingdoms of the world in a moment of time," and when he said, "all this authority I will give You, and their glory; for this has been delivered to me, and I give it to whomever I wish" (Luke 4:5–6).

71. St John Cassian believes that Satan was one of the cherubim before his fall. Other fathers agree that he was among the highest-ranked angels.

72. "Death was struck with dismay on beholding a new visitant descend into Hades, not bound by the chains of that place. Why, O porters of Hades, were you scared at sight of Him? What was the unwonted fear that possessed you? Death fled, and his flight betrayed his cowardice. The holy prophets ran unto Him, and Moses the Lawgiver, and Abraham, and Isaac, and Jacob; David also, and Samuel, and Isaiah, and John the Baptist, who bore witness when he asked, *'Are You He that should come, or look we for another'* Matt 11:3? All the Just were ransomed, whom death had swallowed; for it behooved the King whom they had proclaimed, to become the redeemer of His noble heralds. Then each of the Just said, *'O death, where is your victory? O grave, where is your sting?'* For the Conqueror has redeemed us." Cyril of Jerusalem, 14 Catechetical Lecture, chapter 19. [Translated by Edwin Hamilton Gifford. *From Nicene and Post-Nicene Fathers,*

Second Series, Vol. 7. Edited by Philip Schaff and Henry Wace (Buffalo, NY: Christian Literature Publishing Co., 1894.) Revised and edited for New Advent by Kevin Knight. http://www.newadvent.org/fathers/310114.htm].

73. When the Lord Jesus Christ descended into hell, the princes of hell were afraid and cried out, "Open the sorrowful gates, for the King of glory, Christ, enters." When the Lord harrowed hell and having freed from its prisons the souls of the righteous, ascended into heaven, then the heavenly powers, wondering at this new miracles, cried out, "open the gates!" One of them cried out, "Who is this King of glory?" The others answered, "It is the Lord of hosts, Who ascends in the flesh, God the Word, He Who sits on the throne of glory, the Son of the Father, Who abides with the Father before eternity, Who descended to earth, Who assumed humanity and took it up with Him to the heavens. The King of glory!" This interpretation of the third kathisma of the Psalter was taken from an edition of the Kiev Caves Lavra with commentaries on the margins.

74. St John of the Ladder tells of a certain Stephen, living in Sinai, who loved the desert and silence, and who remained for many years in the ascetic life of fasting and tears, who had many other spiritual qualities, including active repentance. This man, one day before his death, went into a trance-like state, looking to the right and to the left side of his bed, and, torn apart by invisible creatures, said aloud, "Yes, that's exactly right, but I fasted this number of years for that sin. Then, "No, you lie, I never did that." Then, "Yes, that is so, yes; however, I wept and gave myself as a servant to my brothers. And again, "No, you slander me." As for other accusations, he answered, "Yes, that is so, I do not know what to say to you, but God is merciful." This invisible testing appeared terrifying to the monks witnessing it; most frightening was that the demons kept accusing him of sins he had never committed. Alas! Even this silent ascetic said concerning some of his sins, "I do not know how to answer you," and this was a man who had lived forty years as a monk, and had the gift of tears. Where did the words of Ezekiel hide then: "I shall judge you, O house of Israel, each one according to his way" (Ezek 18:30). For truly he did not come to see anything of the sort: the more glory to the One Who Knows All. And some even have told, bearing witness to the Lord, that Stephan fed leopards in the desert with his own hands. But his death was accompanied by such testing! And we remain in the dark concerning how this testing ended ... (*The Ladder*, step 7). "Deliver me not over to the souls of them that afflict me, for false witnesses are risen up against me, and iniquity hath lied to itself" (Ps 26:12)—this is how the Holy Spirit inspired man to speak concerning the invisible battles with the invisible enemies.

75. *The Lives of the Saints*, August 15.

76. Chapter 65 [St Athanasius the Great] [Robert T. Meyer Translator, *St. Athanasius: The Life of St. Antony* (Ancient Christian Writers Series) (New Jersey: Paulist Press, 1978), p. 65.

77. St John Chrysostom, the Homily on Patience and Gratitude.

78. Homily 16, chapter 18 [St Macarius the Great].

79. From the rite of the 12 Psalms [*A Psalter for Prayer*, trans. David James (Jordanville, NY: Holy Trinity Publications, 2019), pp. 368–369].

80. St Nephon lived in the second half of the third, first half of the fourth century. December 23 in the *Lives of the Saints*.

81. St Symeon lived in the sixth century. *Lives of the Saints*, July 21.

82. The Prologue from December 19.

83. The Prologue from March 13.

84. Homily 5, chapter 22 [St John of the Ladder].

85. St Isaiah [the Recluse], Homily 1.

86. Answer 145 [Barsanuphius].

87. Homily 1 [Abba Dorotheus].

88. Chapter 25 [St John of Karpathos].

89. "On Watchfulness and Holiness" chapters 149, 161, 4. [St Hesychius].

90. Chapters 60, 75 [St Theognostus].

91. The Prologue, October 27.

92. Collected works of George, Recluse of Zadonsk. Part 1, page 65 (1850 Russian edition).

93. *A Psalter for Prayer*, trans. David James (Jordanville, NY: Holy Trinity Publications, 2019), pp. 100, 251.

94. A *kontakion* (pl. *kontakia*) is a special hymn found after the sixth ode of a canon which gives a more concise summary of the person or event celebrated. The *ekos* (pl. *ekoi*) is a verse which occurs immediately after the kontakion to a saint or feast.

95. St Ignatius quotes from the "Psalter of the Mother of God," a collection of 150 prayers to the Theotokos based on the Psalms which has not yet been translated into English.—ED.

96. Kallistos Ware and Mother Mary Translated, *The Lenten Triodion* (London: Faber and Faber, 1978), p. 440. This is sung in matins in the fifth week of Great Lent.

97. The Oktoechos contains prayers and compositions used in the daily services that change according to the saint or feast being remembered. "Oktoechos" means the "Book of Eight Tones" because the services of the entire week are sung in a specific tone and there are eight in number—ED.

98. Friday, Tone 4, Ode VIII of the Matins Canon—ED.

99. Thursday, Tone 4, Ode VI of the Compline Canon—ED.

100. Wednesday, Tone 4, Ode VIII of Compline Canon—ED.

101. Friday, Tone 3, Ode VI of Matins Canon—ED.

102. Saturday, Tone 2, the Theotokion on Matins Aposticha.

103. *The Great Book of Needs* (St. Tikhon's Seminary Press: South Canaan, PA, 2022) Ode I, troparia 1 and 2 and Ode 7, troparion 2. [Revised text—ED].

104. The Paterikon of the Caves.

105. Orthodox-Dogmatic Theology of Metropolitan Macarius. Volume 5, page 85 of the 1853 Russian edition. "The teaching concerning toll houses is constant, present throughout, and appropriate at all times of the teaching of the Church, especially among the great teachers of the fourth century. This is undoubted proof that it was given to them by the teachers of the preceding centuries and is founded on apostolic tradition" (ibid., p. 86).

106. *Eternal Mysteries beyond the Grave*; Archimandrite Panteleimon (Jordanville, NY: Holy Trinity Publications, 2012), p. 101.

107. St John of the Ladder writes that during his time at a certain monastery near Alexandria, a certain former thief came into the monastery for the sake of repentance. The abbot of the monastery commanded him to publicly confess his sins in front of the entire assembled brotherhood in the church. When the thief concluded this confession with fiery zeal and self-rejection, the abbot immediately put the great schema on him. St John later asked the abbot, "Why did you tonsure him so quickly?" The abbot pointed to the fact that the thief, because of the nature of his confession, was found worthy of total forgiveness of his sins. "And do not disbelieve that fact," added the abbot, "because one of the assembled brothers assured me, saying that he saw a certain terrifying person holding a pen and manuscript in his hands. When the confessor uttered all his sins, that terrifying person crossed out each of the sins, and rightly for the Scriptures say 'I have acknowledged my transgression and my sin have I not hid; I said, Against myself will I confess my transgression unto the Lord, and so Thou forgavest the irreverence of my heart'" (Ps 31:5). It would also not be excessive to mention here a more contemporary event. In the area around Vologda, there is a large village called Kubenskoe that has several parishes in it. One of the parish priests fell ill, and, being on his deathbed, saw his bed surrounded by demons that were preparing to catch his soul and take it into hell. Then three angels appeared. One of them stood at the bedside, and began to argue with the most horrifying demon who held an open book with all the sins of the priest. During this time, another priest came to help his brother in his passage to the next life. Confession began at that moment; the sick man, looking with terrified eyes at the book, confessed his sins with self-rejection, as though casting them from himself. And what did he see? He saw vividly that no sooner had he spoken the sin than the sin disappeared in the book, leaving only an empty space. Thus, through confession he wiped away all his sins from the demonic book, and then, having received healing, lived the rest of his life in profound repentance, telling all his neighbors this vision, which was sealed by his miraculous healing, for their instruction.

108. *Eternal Mysteries beyond the Grave*; Archimandrite Panteleimon (Jordanville, NY: Holy Trinity Publications, 2012), p.102.

109. *Eternal Mysteries beyond the Grave*; Archimandrite Panteleimon (Jordanville, NY: Holy Trinity Publications, 2012), p.104.

110. *The Lives of the Saints*, April 5.

111. The Skete Patericon. Several of Macarius's disciples saw his ascension into heaven, for they were especially holy. This account comes from St Paphnutius, who then became the abbot after Macarius.

112. St Mark the Ascetic. On Paradise and the Spiritual Law.

113. St Macarius the Great, Homily 2: 4.

114. St Macarius the Great Homily 37: 5 and St Mark the Ascetic, homily 6.

115. Quoted in Nilus of Sora.

116. St Hesychius of Jerusalem, Homily on Sobriety, chapter 23.

117. "When the devil sees that someone does not wish to sin, he is not so unskilled in the doing of evil as to begin to suggest to him some kind of obvious sins. He does not say to him, go and commit fornication, or go and steal; for he knows that we do not desire this, and he does not consider it necessary to suggest to us what we do not desire. But he finds in us, as I have said, a single desire, or a single self-justification, and thus under the pretext of something good he does harm to us. Wherefore again it is said, *A bad man does harm, wherever he meets a just man* (Prov. 11:15). The bad man is the devil, and he does harm *wherever he meets a just man,* that is, when he joins with our self-justification; then he becomes stronger, then he does us more harm, then he is more effective. For when we keep to our own will and follow our justification, then in doing what seems to be a good work, we lay snares for ourselves and we do not even know how we are perishing" Abba Dorotheus, Fifth Instruction [https://orthochristian.com/60650.html].

118. Homily 4:23 [St Macarius the Great].

119. We see this very clearly in the life of St Anthony the Great, St John the Longsuffering of the Kiev Caves and many others.

120. St Hesychius of Jerusalem, chapter 23.

121. Homily 21:5 of St Macarius the Great.

122. The Prologue, August 12.

123. Homily 53 [St Isaac the Syrian].

124. This is the interpretation of St Macarius the Great, Homily 2, chapter 3.

125. In the *Apophthegmata Patrum* (*Sayings of the Desert Fathers),* we find the following words of St. John Kolobos: "The gates of God are humility. Our fathers ascended, rejoicing, into the temple of God through much humiliation."

126. The sixteenth letter of the Athonite.

127. St Macarius the Great.

128. Nilus of Sora.

129. St Macarius the Great, Homily 49, chapter 2.

130. Chapter 19 of the Life of St Anthony [https://www.newadvent.org/fathers/2811.htm].

131. Homily 12 [St Isaac the Syrian].

132. Homily 86 [St Isaac the Syrian].

133. Homily 41 [St Isaac the Syrian].

134. Excerpts from Step 6 of *The Ladder* [Translated by Archimandrite Lazarus Moore (New York: Harper & Brothers, 1959) (http://www.prudencetrue.com/images/TheLadderofDivineAscent.pdf)].

135. Answers 229, 623 [Barsanuphius the Great].

136. Answers 799, 645 [Barsanuphius the Great].

137. Answers 799, 644 [Barsanuphius the Great].

138. St Philotheus of Sinai, chapter 2 of part 2 of the *Philokalia*.

139. Homily 7 [St Nilus of Sora].

140. Step 8 of *The Ladder*.

141. St Philotheus of Sinai: Forty Texts on Watchfulness: chapter 6 [https://orthodoxchurchfathers.com/fathers/philokalia/philotheos-of-sinai-forty-texts-on-watchfulness.html].

142. Ibid., chapter 13.

143. Ibid., chapter 21.

144. Ibid., chapter 38.

145. Homily on sobriety, chapter 17 [St Hesychius of Jerusalem].

146. Practical and Theological Treatises, chs. 66 and 67 [Symeon the New Theologian].

147. Taken mostly from Homily 7 of St Nilus of Sora. It is worth noting that sudden death only takes those who do not care for their salvation. This is promised by the Lord Himself (see Luke 12:46). According to Barsanuphius the Great, "God will not take the soul of an ascetic who battles his passion until he brings him to the measure of a perfect man" (Answer 265).

Chapter 3

1. [In the original Russian language manuscript, St Ignatius quotes extensively from the work of Abbe Bergier who wrote primarily against the rationalists of the eighteenth century. Those citations are not included in this English-language edition as the St Ignatius's own summary contains the thrust of the argument.—NK]

2. The Exact Exposition of the Orthodox Faith: Book 4, chapter 13 (https://www.orthodox.net/fathers/exactiv.html#BOOK_IV_CHAPTER_XIII).

3. Epistle to Seraphion, Vol. II.

4. Patrologia Graeca Vol. 29. Against Eunomius, Book 5, On the Holy Spirit.

5. The life of St Sylvester, January 2.

6. [Blessed Theophylact's Explanation of the Holy Scriptures: possibly from a pamphlet]. 1850.

7. Homily 49, chapter 4.

8. Chrysostom Vol. I.

9. The Works of St John Chrysostom Vol. 1.

10. Patrologia Graeca Vol. 28.

11. Homily 4, chapter 11 [A.J. Mason, Fifty Spiritual Homilies of St. Macarius the Great the Egyptian (London: SPCK, 1921), p. 26].

12. Chapter 13 [ibid., pp. 27–28].

13. Chapters 9 and 10 [ibid., p. xxi].

14. Chapter 10 [ibid., p. 26].

15. Catechetical Lecture 16 [*Nicene and Post-Nicene Fathers, Second Series*, Vol. 7. Edited by Philip Schaff and Henry Wace (Buffalo, NY: Christian Literature Publishing Co., 1894), pp. 118–119].

16. "On Repentance" [St Cyril of Jerusalem].

17. It used to be asserted that zero multiplied by infinity would result in one. But this is not true. It gives a number, that is, all numbers in general, which, with reference to the infinite, are all equal and are distinguished from the infinite by an infinite different, not being able to produce in it any change evident in nature. This is the greatest idea that science could ever come up with concerning the world.

18. Exact Exposition, Book 2, chapter 3 [St John of Damascus: *Nicene and Post-Nicene Fathers, Second Series, Vol. IX Hilary of Poitiers, John of Damascus*. Edited by Philip Schaff (New York: Cosimo, Inc, 2007), p. 19].

19. Homily 16, chapter 5 [St Macarius the Great].

20. [In Russia of the nineteenth century, there was one officially sanctioned textbook of Dogmatic Theology used in seminaries.—NK]

21. Mankind for a long time did not know of the existence of gases. For this reason, whenever they spoke of gaseous substances, they expressed it generally, without specificity. The existence of gases was only discovered at the end of the eighteenth century.

22. This is evident from the *Lives of the Saints*. The battle at sea created by the demons is mentioned in Ikos 5 of the Akathist to St Nicholas.

23. The Slavonic Bible reads "A spirit" not "the spirit" here, i.e., an angel, not the third Person of the Holy Trinity.

24. Catechetical lecture 17, chapter 5 [St Cyril of Jerusalem].

25. Ekos 8 of the Akathist to the Mother of God ["Book of Akathists: To Our Saviour the Mother of God and Various Saints," Vol 1 (Jordanville, NY: Holy Trinity Monastery, 1994), p. 127].

26. Nature abhors a vacuum.

27. Homily: God is not the author of evil, Vol. 3.

28. St Cyril of Jerusalem, Catechetical Lecture 14, chapter 19.

29. *The Lives of the Saints*, March 3.

30. [St Ignatius use the word "душевныя тѣла" (soul-bodies). See 1 Cor 15:44–46: "It is sown a natural body, it is raised a spiritual body. There is a natural body,

and there is a spiritual body. And so it is written, 'The first man Adam became a living being.' The last Adam became a life-giving spirit. However, the spiritual is not first, but the natural, and afterward the spiritual." —Ed]

31. *The Lives of the Saints*, October 28.

32. The Patericon of the Kiev Caves Lavra.

33. *The Lives of the Saints*, January 20.

34. The Skete Patericon.

35. *The Lives of the Saints*, November 23.

36. [The order of the Great Schema or Angelic Habit is conferred by the abbot—if the practice of Greater and Lesser Schema is followed—after great struggle having reached a spiritual level and often near the end of a monk's life.—Ed]

37. The Patericon of the Kiev Caves.

38. Ibid.

39. *The Lives of the Saints*, October 2.

40. The Life of St Andrew, the Fool for Christ. [His life can be found in the Great Synaxarion and in the Prologue from Ochrid.] http://full-of-grace-and-truth.blogspot.com/2015/09/st-andrew-fool-for-christs-vision-of-st.html

41. The Prologue, October 6.

42. The Life of St Nephon

43. Patericon of the Caves.

44. See the life of the martyrs Theodore and Basil of the Kiev Caves.

45. *The Lives of the Saints*, September 7.

46. Handwritten life of St Nilus.

47. *The Lives of the Saints*, October 7.

48. *The Lives of the Saints*, July 12.

49. The expansive account of the conversation of Schemamonk Cyriacus, his vision in the altar, his constant abiding in a state of grace while a monk in the Valaam monastery, was written down in his own hand, according to the command of his abbot Nazarius, in the spirit of profound humility, only in fulfillment of his sacred obligation of obedience. The account was published several times.

50. [The Trisagion is a hymn. It translates as "Thrice Holy" and describes God as Holy, Mighty and Immortal. It is common to all Orthodox Christian liturgies and was an exclamation at the Council of Chalcedon in 451.—Ed].

51. The Life of St Niphon, December 23.

52. Homily 86 of St Ephraim the Syrian, the Life of St Arsenios the Great.

53. Chapter 38 [St Basil the Great] [*"On the Spirit: Chapter 16" Nicene and Post-Nicene Fathers, Second Series, Vol. VIII Basil: Letters and Select Works.* Edited by Philip Schaff (New York, NY: Cosimo Classics, 2007), p. 24.]

54. Chapter 54 [*"On the Spirit: Chapter 23" Nicene and Post-Nicene Fathers, Second Series, Vol. VIII Basil: Letters and Select Works.* Edited by Philip Schaff (New York: Cosimo Classics, 2007), pp. 34–35.]

55. [St Basil the Great] [*Saint Basil; Exegetic Homilies*. Trans by Sister Agnes Clare Way (Washington, D.C.; Catholic University Press, 1963), pp. 262–263.]

56. Homily on How God is not the source of evil [St Basil the Great].

57. On the Prophecy of Isaiah [St Basil the Great].

58. [*St.Basil the Great, Commentary on the Prophet Isaiah*, Translated Nikolai A. Lipatov (Hamburg, Germany: Mandelbachtal,/Cambridge Druck und Einband, 2001), pp. 290–291].

59. The Skete Patericon Vol. 29: The Life of St Basil.

60. Oration 45 [St Gregory the Theologian] [*Nicene and Post-Nicene Fathers, Second Series, Vol. VII*. Edited by Philip Schaff (Buffalo, NY: Christian Literature Publishing Co., 1894.) https://www.newadvent.org/fathers/310245.htm].

61. Theological Oration 2. [St Gregory the Theologian] [From the unpublished manuscript of Stephen Reynolds, Gregory of Nazianzus: Five Theological Orations (The Estate of Stephen Reynolds, 2011), pp. 43–44 PDF at: tspace.library.utoronto.ca

62. [St Gregory the Theologian] Oration 38 Vol 2.

63. First Invective against Julian [https://www.tertullian.org/fathers/gregory_nazianzen_2_oration4.htm]

64. [St Cyprian] Vol 1 Oration 24 Chapter 9.

65. *The Philokalia* (in the Russian translation), part 4, chapter 9.

66. Patrologia Graeca, Athanasius Vol. II, The Life of St Antony.

67. "Discourse against the Arians," The Works of St Athanasius Vol IV.

68. On the Holy Trinity, St Athanasius. Vol IV, Chapter 12.

69. St Athanasius, On the Eucharist.

70. Questions to Antiochus, question VII. Tom. IV.

71. Synopsis of the Holy Scriptures [St Athansius].

72. [St Athanasius the Great] ["On the Incarnation of the Word," *Nicene and Post-Nicene Fathers, Second Series, Vol. IV. Anthanasius*. Edited by Philip Schaff (New York: Cosimo Classics, 2007), p. 50.

73. Ibid., p. 61.

74. Ibid., p. 62.

75. [St Athanasius the Great] [St Athanasius the Great] ["Circular to Bishops of Egypt and Libya," *Nicene and Post-Nicene Fathers, Second Series, Vol. IV. Antha-nasius*. Edited by Philip Schaff (New York: Cosimo Classics, 2007), pp. 222–235.] [https://www.newadvent.org/fathers/2812.htm].

76. The Works of St Epiphanius, Vol. I.

77. The Works of St Athanasius the Great Vol. IV.

78. It would be wise for the newest philosophers to remember the words of the father of pagan philosophy, Plato, who would not allow anyone entry to philoso-phy until a person had come to know mathematics well. Natural sciences, in their current form, are a sub-division of the mathematical sciences, belonging in large part to applied mathematics.

79. This is a common petition found in Orthodox Christian divine services: "An angel of peace, a faithful guide, a guardian of our souls and bodies, let us ask of the Lord."

80. The Works of St John Chrysostom Vol. II.

81. Homily 22 on the Book of Genesis [St John Chrysostom].

82. Homily 26 on the Acts of the Apostles [St John Chrysostom].

83. Third Homily on the Incomprehensible Nature of God [St John Chrysostom].

84. The Works of Chrysostom, Vol. I.

85. *Nicene and Post-Nicene Fathers, First Series, Vol. IX. Chrysostom: On the Priesthood, Ascetic Treatises, Select Homilies and Letters, Homilies on the Statues,* Ed Philip Schaff (New York: Cosimo Classics, 2007) [First published 1889], p. 143.

[St Ignatius contains a quote about the demon feasting on the evaporation of blood which is not found in the Homily on St Babylas and not included in this English translation.—NK].

86. Chapter 9 of his interpretation of the Book of Revelation [St Andrew of Cæsarea].

87. Ibid., chapter 12.

88. Homily 12 on the Gospels [St Gregory the Great] [(https://sites.google.com/site/aquinasstudybible/home/matthew-commentary/gregory-the-great-homily-12-on-the-gospels].

89. Homily 35, chapter 3 [St Gregory the Great].

90. Homily 39 on the Gospels, chapters 4, 5, 8, and 9.

91. Homily 40 on the Gospels, chapter 11 [St Gregory the Great] (https://sites.google.com/site/aquinasstudybible/home/luke-commentary/gregory-the-great-homily-40-on-the-gospels).

92. Homily 34 on the Gospels, chapter 13 [St Gregory the Great] (https://sites.google.com/site/aquinasstudybible/home/luke-commentary/gregory-the-great-homily-34-on-the-gospels).

93. See Barsanuphius the Great, Answer 611.

94. St Macarius the Great explains the reason why holy men who preach the word of God to the world cannot dedicate the time necessary to acquire a state of spiritual vision (Homily 8, chapter 4). This same reason was offered by Arsenius the Great, when he asked why he avoided the society of people so much, even of holy men.

95. A general troparion to a martyred priest or bishop.

96. Homily 21 [St Macarius the Great].

97. Homily 55 [St Isaac the Syrian].

98. Conference 17, Chapter 6 [John Cassian].

99. See the life of John the Much-suffering in the Patericon of the Kiev Caves.

100. Conference 7 and 8 [John Cassian].

101. St Isaac the Syrian, Homily 55.

102. Chapter 2, section 1 [Dionysius the Areopagite] [https://www.tertullian. org/fathers/areopagite_13_heavenly_hierarchy.htm#c2].

103. Ibid., section 2.

104. Ibid., chapter 2, section 3.

105. Ibid., chapter 13, section 4.

106. Chapter 1, section 2 [Dionysius the Areopagite].

107. Ibid., chapter 4, section 3.

108. Ibid., chapter 1, section 2.

109. A letter to the apostle Paul concerning Dionysius meeting the Mother of God.

110. "On Faith." [St Symeon the New Theologian] [https://sites.google.com/ site/stsymeon/on-faith].

111. On the Celestial Hierarchies, chapter 2, section 5. [Dionysius the Areopagite]

112. Abbe Bergier's Encyclopedia of the Faith.

113. The Lives of Cyprian and Justina, October 2.

114. See Isa 14:13, 14; John 8:44.

115. Life of St Anthony, chapter 18. We can see a vivid example of this in the life of Venerable Isaac of the Kiev Caves and in the life of St Pachomius the Great.

116. [St Ignatius the God bearer] ["Epistle to the Philippians- (Spurious)" *Saint Ignatius of Antioch (30-107)* Trans by Alexander Roberts and James Donaldson; http://www.logoslibrary.org/ignatius/philippians/11.html]. [St Ignatius the God bearer, Letter to the Ephesians, paragraph 13: "Try to gather together more frequently to celebrate God's Eucharist and to praise him. For when you meet with frequency, Satan's powers are overthrown and his destructiveness is undone by the unanimity of your faith." [https://www.christianstudylibrary.org/article/ frequency-lord's-supper-celebration]

117. [St Ignatius included quoted material from the work of Abbe Bergier against the rationalists of the eighteenth century which are not included in this English-language edition.—NK].

Afterword

1. Homily 55 of Isaac the Syrian. Answer 2, 108, 311, 342 and others of Barsanuphius the Great, Homily 4, chapters 35, 36, 74 of St John of the Ladder. St Nilus of Sora, homily 11.

2. Abba Dorotheus. Instruction 5.

Subject Index

Scripture Index

10:20, p. 31
12:4–5, p. 103
12:20, p. 87
12:32–46, p. 141
12:46, p. 267 n.147
12:47, p. 119
12:47–48, p. 60
12:49, p. 63
12:58, p. 224
13:10, p. 48
16:11, p. 151
16:19–31, p. 59
16:22, pp. 86, 258 n.36
16:26, p. 102
18:1–8, p. 119
19:43, p. 223
19:44, pp. 223, 224
20:3, p. 170
20:36, p. 179
21:8, p. 213
23:43, pp. 59, 66
24:4, p. 61
24:16, p. 11
24:31, p. 11
24:32, p. 49
24:38–39, p. 62
24:39, p. 185

John
1:18, p. 156
3:8, p. 169
4:24, p. 63
5:24, p. 96
5:25, p. 59
5:26, p. 154
6:46, p. 155
6:63, pp. 99, 160
6:68, p. 99
8:44, p. 25
8:56, p. 30
9:40, p. 43

11:25, p. 133
11:25–26, p. 96
12:6, p. 47
13:2, p. 47
13:27, p. 47
14:6, p. 154
14:21–24, p. 2
14:30, pp. 119, 225, 226
19:30, p. 169
20:12, p. 61
21:18, p. 247
21:20, p. 225

Acts
1:10, p. 61
1:11, p. 181
2:2, p. 174
5, p. 262 n.68
5:3, p. 48
6:15, p. 182
7:55–56, p. 106
8:26, p. 203
8:39–40, p. 174
10:30, p. 181
12:7–11, p. 174
12:15, pp. 62, 218
12:23, p. 177
13:10, p. 15
16:17, p. 7

Romans
5:5, p. 53
7:10, p. 99
8:13, p. 98
8:35, p. 32
11:33–34, p. 54
11:36, p. 54
16:18, p. 49

1 Corinthians
2:9–10, pp. 67, 70